Mother's Madness
a daughter's report
surviving abuse
at the crossroads of race, class, and lunacy
by
Janis A. Pryor

MOTHER'S MADNESS: A Daughter's Report
Copyright 2024 – Janis A. Pryor
All rights reserved.
Printed in the United States of America

No part of this book may be used or reproduced, stored in a retrieval system, or transmitted in any form or by any means, electronic, mechanical, photocopying, recording, or otherwise, without the prior written permission of the author except in the case of brief quotations embodied in critical articles or reviews.

Print ISBN – 978-1-949802-40-5
Published by Black Pawn Press

FIRST EDITION

Dedicated to my grandparents;
William and Josephine Lawrence,
two extraordinary people
who loved and protected me,
and to
the Gaynor Family
Arthur and Evelyn,
and their three children;
Alison, Chris, and Jennifer,
whose emotional generosity and affection
saved my sanity.

"Not enough is known about the lives of black girls."
bell hooks
Author, Scholar, Poet
1952-2021

CONTENTS

Dedication	3
Part One – This is Who I Am	**11**
Chapter One – March, 1996	13
Chapter Two – An Unusual Story	19
More Words About Who People Think I Am	25
An en caul birth...	28
Chapter Three – Two Leos, One Virgo	29
Chapter Four – But First, A Word About My Father, Harry	34
More Words About Harry	39
Chapter Five – Uncle George	41
Same Questions, Different Man	44
Chapter Six – The Dining Room	47
Chapter Seven – Family and Friends	52
A Word About Skin Color	61
Chapter Eight – William Augusta Lawrence, Papa, My Grandfather	63
Chapter Nine – I Want Mama	75
Chapter Ten – Where is Gulfport?	88
Chapter Eleven – So Many White People	94
Chapter Twelve – Abour Drora	98
Part Two – Meeting Tina	**107**
Chapter Thirteen – Welcome to New York	109
Chapter Fourteen – School	120
Chapter Fifteen – Payback, Psychics, Junior High	129

Chapter Sixteen – Meanwhile	139
Chapter Seventeen – One Dance	143
A Caveat on Precariousness	145
Chapter Eighteen – What Does Tina Do?	146
Chapter Nineteen – Preparing for War	150
Chapter Twenty – Some Things Tina Told Me (and Terry)	153
Part Three – Conflict	**165**
Chapter Twenty-One – Blood and Rage	167
Chapter Twenty-Two – It's On	175
Chapter Twenty-Three – Bloodletting	178
Chapter Twenty-Four – What Tina Taught Me	184
Chapter Twenty-Five – Moving	190
A Word About Rio…as in Brazil… and Tina	197
Chapter Twenty-Six – Enter Dr. Gaynor	198
Chapter Twenty-Seven – Vermont	208
Chapter Twenty-Eight – The Day the Earth Stopped	213
Another Caveat – High School	216
Chapter Twenty-Nine – I Went to Bennington	218
Chapter Thirty – The Taconic to Routes 9 and 7	225
A Caveat – Tina's Reflection on Suicide	234
Part Four – Saved	**237**
Chapter Thirty-One – Stream of Consciousness	239
Some Words About Suicide, My Constant Companion	243
A Word About Braunwyne	247
Chapter Thirty- Two – A Sidebar About Depression	251
Chapter Thirty-Three – An Embarrassment of Riches	255

Chapter Thirty-Four – It's Late September, and I Really Should Be Back In School	259
Many Words About a Quick Trip to Europe	262
Chapter Thirty-Five – The "Short" Story About the Seventies	264
Chapter Thirty-Six – The Seventies – Part Two	273
Chapter Thirty-Seven – Tina!	279
Chapter Thirty-Eight – My Grandfather Left	283
Chapter Thirty-Nine – 1980	285
Chapter Forty – They Die	286
A Caveat – Tina's Shenanigans	294
Chapter Forty-One – 1986 and 1989	295
Chapter Forty-Two – No Good Deed Goes Unpunished	304
Chapter Forty-Three – Mama Dies	310
Chapter Forty-Four – Tina's Revenge	315
Chapter Forty-Five – Lawyers, Money, and Books	317
An Addendum – Tina's Reflections in 1997	324
Chapter Forty-Six – He Died… Finally	326
Chapter Forty-Seven – Up the Mass. Pike	333
Chapter Forty-Eight – "Traditionally Conflicting Constituencies"	340
Chapter Forty-Nine – Reality	345
Chapter Fifty – What Peggy Told Me	348
Chapter Fifty-One – Reality 2.0	354
Chapter Fifty-Two – The End Was Coming	359
Chapter Fifty-Three – Not Yet	367

A Caveat – Signs and Omens	372
Chapter Fifty-Four – Stepping Towards Death	377
A Word About Tina's Imaginary Family	383
Chapter Fifty-Five – Please Allow Me to Introduce Myself	388
A Word About Tina's Bedroom	393
Chapter Fifty-Six – Countdown	398
Chapter Fifty-Seven – Tick Tock	405
Chapter Fifty-Eight – Roughly 24 Hours	408
Chapter Fifty-Nine – Soon	411
Chapter Sixty – 4:46 AM	414
A Few Words About the Funeral	417
A Reflection	421
This is the End of My Report	424
To Be of Use	427
Teach Your Children	428
Acknowledgments	429
About the Author	431

PART ONE:

This Is Who I Am

Chapter One

March, 1996

When I opened the front door of the condo I had been renting for years on Bond Street, in Cambridge, Massachusetts my two American cocker-spaniels, Prince and Murphy, were waiting, paws crossed, tails wagging, with the tacit but urgent message, "Let's go!"

As I tore up the stairs, past my office and into the bedroom, I saw the light flashing on my answering machine. I ignored it. After putting on a pair of jeans and the first sweatshirt I could find, I was ready for our walk.

The light on the answering machine was still flashing and something said, "You better get that." Meaningful clutter was piled everywhere on my desk and the bookshelves above it. Every object and momenta held a piece of my public life. But that light was still flashing.

"Gimme a minute," I said to Prince and Murphy. "We're going. Hold on!" I pressed the button and heard the following message.

"Miss Pryor, this is Detective DeGatano from the Bronx Office of the District Attorney. Could you call me as soon as you get this message?" With all the calm of a cool summer breeze, he left his phone number.

It was 5:45 PM. Maybe he was gone. "Dear God," I thought to myself, "They've finally got me on those parking tickets I never paid." The fact that I had lived in Cambridge, Massachusetts for twenty plus years, and not New York City meant nothing to me. Had to be the parking tickets. "Damn it!"

I called and heard, "DeGatano."

"Hi, this is Janis Pryor returning your call."

"Oh! Miss Pryor, thank you so much for calling back. I'm calling to inform you that your mother, Leontine Pryor, has forged your signature on some insurance documents."

"What?!" I realized I had shouted.

"Don't worry. We checked your signature card from Bank of Boston. It's definitely a forgery." He also told me that she had placed my name on her school payroll.

I explained that I was *not* an employee at her school. The only time I ever worked there was during a non-resident work term as part of my curriculum at Bennington decades ago. He told me he wasn't interested in that. This is more recent. I heard myself say, "I don't live in New York anymore. Haven't lived there since the early seventies."

I was stunned. I was enraged. This was insane. She wasn't that stupid! "*Detective, what are you talking about?! What is going on?*"

"You know, everyone we've talked to has had the same shocked reaction," he said.

"Everyone?" I thought. "Detective, what do you mean everyone? *What are we talking about?*" How widespread is this I wondered?

He rattled off a list of charges encompassing a range of criminal activities including unfair labor practices, abuse of power, and misappropriation of funds spanning twenty years! Ultimately, she was charged with close to two hundred counts of wrongdoing. I was thankful my grandparents were dead. This might've crushed their souls. As I listened to the detective, I realized my career in politics was now compromised. What politician would want to employ someone involved in or associated with a scandal of this size? You can't be a bigger story than your boss. Something like this only worked for Billy Bulger, State Senate President for the Massachusetts' Legislature, whose brother was Whitey Bulger, notorious crime boss, and on the FBI's most wanted list. The Bulgers were also white Irish Catholics. I wasn't!

My resume already had the names of the Massachusetts' Legislative Black Caucus, Senator Edward Brooke, Senator Edward Kennedy, Senator John Kerry, Reverend Jesse Jackson, Institute of Politics at Harvard, Wheelock College, and all three network affiliates of Boston, along with numerous local and state politicians. My titles ran the gamut from Legislative Aide, Special Aide, Advance, Special Events, Assistant Field Director, Associate Producer, Editorial Director, Coordinating Producer, Producer, political consultant, speech writer. I had now gone from an asset,

to a liability. Forget working in the White House! Maybe I was overreacting. But I doubted it. At no time did I ever forget how my bosses saw me. Nobody hired me because I was cute. Nor did I ever forget I had to be twice as good to get half as much because I wasn't white.

I realized the detective was asking me about Tina. For years I had managed to keep her at arm's length. For a while I made sure she didn't have my phone number. But now, she had jeopardized my livelihood and well-being again. I saw all of it vanish into the horizon of lost possibilities.

"Why would your mother do this?" the detective asked.

"She's not well," I said. "She has some problems."

"I heard about the cancer…"

"That's not what I'm talking about. She has a personality disorder. All you have to do is keep asking her questions. You'll see." I could feel DeGatano tighten up. Maybe he thought I was trying to lay the groundwork for an insanity plea on her behalf. As he continued to talk, I realized I should probably get a lawyer, a good one, fast.

"So, Miss Pryor, is this the best number to reach you?"

I refocused and said, "Yes." He said something about arranging a conference call the Assistant District Attorney and appearing before a Grand Jury. The minute we ended our conversation, I looked at Prince and Murphy and pleaded with them to just hold on. In a minute! I called Tina.

A girlish, thin voice answered. It was almost flirtatious. "Hello."

"Tina, what have you done? I just got off the phone with Detective DeGatano from the Bronx Office of the District Attorney. You forged my name on some insurance documents and had me on the payroll! *What is going on?*"

She was silent for a moment and then said with perverse confidence, "Well, daughters can't testify against their mothers."

"What?! There is no law that says that! I'm going to have to get a lawyer. Do you understand?" I asked. "Listen to me, you better get one too, a criminal attorney!"

"Oh, this will blow over," she said. "Why you always have to run and get some lawyer, I don't know. It'll blow over."

"This will not blow over. Forgery may be a federal offense, Tina."

There was a pause and then she stated, "I'm your mother. I should be able to sign your name to anything I want."

It was the tone of her voice that scared the hell out of me. This superior, arrogant, delusional tone. But way in the back of my mind, I knew. Her act was finally falling apart. This was the beginning of the end. I had no idea, however, of the scope and magnitude of the finale that awaited.

Prince, Murphy and I headed outside. We hurried down the brick path that connected this cluster of free-standing condos to the sidewalk. My brains felt like they were flying around my skull like lettuce in a salad spinner. I knew Tina was crazy the first time I met her. As a child of five or six years old, I remember standing next to my grandmother, whom I called Mama. She wanted me to believe Tina was my mother. I was skeptical. Mama and I had to come north so I could start school. Until then I had no memory of my mother. Tina would tell me over and over, after I arrived in New York, that she would come visit me down home. There were some photos. I didn't care. I never saw her in any of those photos with me. All I knew, as I looked at her, was she had "too many people" inside her. Something was wrong and I was afraid. Even at that young age, I looked in her eyes and knew she rarely told the truth. I could see it and *I could feel it.*

Prince, Murphy, and I darted across the street to the grounds of the Harvard Smithsonian Observatory. Quite a few people from the neighborhood walked their dogs there. Dog Group was a big part of my life. It helped stabilize me. As I headed up the hill and circled around to the rear parking lot, I asked myself, "Who the hell is this woman?" I knew Tina was
crazy but it was hard to believe she was this stupid. How many times had I heard Mama and Papa warn her that she couldn't "act like these white folks in big jobs. They're always watching you, waiting for you to make a mistake. They don't want you to have nothin' anyway. If you have anything, they'll do everything they can to take it away from you." I understood that. I saw it every day in one form or another. How come Tina didn't know this? We were raised by the same people. Maybe it was because, as the saying goes, she was "light, bright and

damned near white", a "high-yellow" African-American woman, a blessing and a curse in this country. Maybe that's why she thought the rules didn't apply to her. I think she was poisoned by the Kool-Aid of colorism. What the hell happened? Was the world about to find out what I had known the minute I met her as a child? Sooner or later it all catches up.

> "Women have died a thousand deaths before they are twenty years old. They've gone in this direction or that, and have been cut off.
> They have hopes and dreams that have been cut off also.
> Anyone who says otherwise is still asleep."
>
> "…tears carry creative power."
>
> Clarissa Pinkola Estes, Ph.D., *Women Who Run With Wolves*

Chapter Two

An Unusual Story

I've been told my life has been unusual. I've been told I'm unusual! So, this has to be told in an unusual way. *My life has been a loop, not a straight line.* My story winds back on itself too often creating conflicting multicultural layers of meaning. All time is now, has been, and continues to be an erratic, quantum, reality for me. The past is always present and the future sparkles in front of me like a distant star going in and out of focus at the same time, or a stone skipping in the water creating endless ripple effects.

I give you fair warning. This is complex and far from a traditional western memoir or recounting with a beginning, middle, and end fulfilling traditional expectations. This is *a report* and contains what some might define as essays, analysis, narrative poetry, commentary. I had to let go of writing according to the "rules." Not everything fits into a genre already established. I ask for your patience and your attention.

This *report* lands at the intersectionality of race, class, and lunacy, with the universality of the human condition in the second half of the twentieth century framing everything and everyone. Writers are instructed to "show, don't tell." That rule will be broken from time to time because If you're white, you may not understand what you're being shown because *you don't have to*. If you're black, or Native American, some of us wish we *didn't know* what this looks like while trying to survive every day. For us, the human condition hurts and that hurt often forces us to rely on a different sense of continuity and sequence. The past sits on one side trying to finish us off. The future, on the other side seducing us with promises we can't trust because those promises were not meant for us. They were lies, like those found in the Declaration of Independence that say, "*All men are created equal...*" And then they throw in "*life, liberty and the pursuit of happiness.*" None of that applied to red and black people who were forced to make the Founding Fathers secure in their ability to become rich, stay rich, and keep the power that comes with *wealth* accrued from generation to generation, for "as long as the rivers run and the grass is green." This is language found in very old trust documents, preceded by, "This trust shall last in perpetuity..." Imagine the wealth needed for someone to declare that it shall last forever!

It was always about money and power. Tina knew that. I often wonder how many people keep reading the Declaration of Independence and give thought to the following sentence(s). "*That whenever any Form of Government becomes destructive of these ends, it is the Right of the People to alter or abolish it, and to institute new Government, laying its foundation on such principles and organizing its powers in such form, as to them shall seem most likely to affect their Safety and Happiness.*" Black and red lives are inexplicably entangled with the politics and sociology of this country, not to mention the stewardship of the land. Tina couldn't avoid it. None of us could.

Clarity comes through more than one lens for us just like comfort and salvation came through *music, the Lord, and the Great Spirit*. It's the reflection of the multilayered reality that shapes our lives as people of color in this country. Our lives haven't been blessed with simplicity no matter what it looks like through white eyes. This story embodies that thorny, complex reality.

I started writing this book for the second time in 1996, three years before my mother, Leontine Lawrence Pryor, also known as Tina, died. (I've had several people ask why I call my mother Tina. *I call her Tina because that was her name.* She was a person who entered my life. I had someone taking care of me, Mama, my grandmother and someone protecting me, Papa, my grandfather, and they both loved me.)

That draft was finished in 2002. The next draft was finished years later. The very first draft was written in the late eighties. That's why there are details and conversations that might otherwise be lost or submerged in generalities. I had a lot to work with including conversations and notes I took from talking with our relatives and Tina.

Now, in 2024, with mortality closing in and time softening a few jagged edges of this experience, I felt I could face the darkness of my life, and not succumb to what doctors euphemistically describe as "a major depressive episode" that often leads me to the threshold of suicide where I have to make a decision, live or die, sometimes on a weekly basis. I need a lot of energy and faith to constantly choose living over dying. Too often I land in between and that's worse than dying.

Tina's story and my story were intertwined in a deadly battle about control that started at my birth. Minutes after I was born somebody, probably my grandmother who was present, told Tina I was born with a veil covering my face. How much that motivated Tina to give me to her parents remains a mystery. I left Manhattan at seven weeks of age in the safe hands of my maternal grandmother, Josephine Adams Lawrence, down to the Gulf Coast. Gulfport, Mississippi became home and I still regard it as home.

I was born in Harkness Pavilion, in New York City at Columbia Presbyterian Hospital, or as I was fond of saying, "I was born on a small island cuddled by the Atlantic, Manhattan."

Mother's Madness

I kept Tina in labor for most of the night. That gave me great satisfaction! How did I know this? She told me.

And she constantly stated, "You were born with a damned veil* over your face," in an accusatory voice! "Put a damned rag around your head and tell fortunes." As a child, I didn't know what she was talking about.

She bragged about where I was born constantly and never let *me* forget that I was born in "the exclusive wing of Harkness Pavilion where the white women had their babies." I always wanted to ask, "So did the white women give their children to their parents because they didn't figure out that they had to care for them once they were born?"

Nobody down home (in Gulfport or any southern Black community) thought this situation was unusual. Many black babies and young children were often taken care of by their grandparents or some other relative who was usually back in "the old country," the South.

I always had a hard time sorting that out. Intellectually, I knew. *Black women had to work.* There was no staying home, being bored, caring for children while yearning to get out of the house to do something "meaningful." A two-income household was a necessity for the majority of Black families during those times and still is for many. So, when children came along... There weren't many safe or affordable options outside of your immediate family back then. No fancy nursery schools for black babies and toddlers. All I knew and felt was she didn't want me but I had Mama and Papa, my grandparents.

Being born with a veil (or caul) terrified Tina, so combat began. She won many battles. But I won the war in 1999. The price for victory was high and I've come to the conclusion that the price was too high. Through the grace of God and good therapists, I survived. Money helped because shrinks are expensive and unlike many Black families, we had money. But the fact was, even with therapy, I was emotionally crippled for life, burdened with the daily task of appearing normal. It's hard work.

Had it not been for Mama and Papa, Josephine and William Lawrence, and the presence, emotional generosity, and shelter of the Gaynor family, Dr. Arthur Gaynor and his wife, Dr. Evelyn Gaynor, and their three children, Alison, Chris and Jennifer, I would've been institutionalized or dead. They became my family of choice. Thankfully, the Gaynors lived three blocks from us in Riverdale, New York. Riverdale is in the northwest corner of the Bronx much in the same way Beverly Hills is a part of Los Angeles!

I thrive on information and understanding. I want to know why people do what they do. One lesson learned from my family, Black people can't afford to feel or show feelings… too much, to succumb to emotional pain, and certainly you can't let it show the same way many white people do, especially white women who often have a vested interest in appearing dainty, delicate, and helpless within a patriarchal society. It's a dangerous generalization. But it's also deeply rooted in an ugly truth. Maybe Black women could be dainty, delicate, and helpless in some other country, but we would never survive in the United States of white America exhibiting those qualities. Black fragility was an absurd and risky indulgence. Some of us might think it was a sure sign of insanity!

Slave owners and the colonists didn't care how we felt, nor how much pain we experienced. Remember enslaved Africans were considered three-fifths human. And Native Americans were looked upon as savages. Native Americans play an important role in my family. We have the blood of three races, Native American, African, and white European. If you have a highly developed visual vocabulary, you can see it in our color, our facial structure, and all of the different hair types, from straight to curly to kinky and everything in between. But, as far as white people are concerned, we are Black. It didn't matter how we self-identified. Terms like biracial or mixed race didn't exist when I was growing up. You were white or not white.

First lesson learned, show no vulnerability or weakness because it would be used against us. During slavery we could be beaten or killed for being "emotional." White folks didn't care. They took our children and sold them or sent them to schools where they tried to beat the Indian out of us one way or another… hoping to brainwash us into being white. That didn't work. We're still here but the admonition of, "don't you dare cry…" quietly floated in the air I breathed. Crying wasn't allowed in my house. It was frowned upon at best and I was made to feel ashamed if tears ever left my eyes.

So where do the tears go?

More Words About Who People *Think* I Am

I don't want people to hate me, but I don't spend a lot of time worrying about it either. It drives people crazy! It drove Tina nuts. How does one live a meaningful life without making some enemies or pissing somebody off?

I'm not a perfect person. If you cross me or mess with me, I will find a way to throw you in the trunk of a car, lock it, destroy the key and help people look for you. (I may repeat this line, just for fun.) Or I will wait for just the right time before retaliating. *I am extremely patient.*

A colleague said, "People tend to underestimate you. They don't understand until they cross you. You have a strategic anger."

I am fascinated by how some people perceive me. I often wonder who they see when they look at me, because it's not the person I see! What follows is a compilation of impressions people have of me.

First of all, I'm "too different." I hear this from several people of varying colors and ethnicities, including Tina! She couldn't abide what she called my "defiance". White people in particular are quick to say, "It's your sense of style, artsy but sophisticated!" While teaching at Wheelock College, I had a white student tell me, "You're too smart." She was *deeply perplexed* and enraged.

Many Black acquaintances are uncomfortable with my preference for wearing blue jeans and pants. My short hair is some kind of cloaked message about my sexuality. The truth is, I have cheap streaks! I'm not spending hundreds of dollars every month on my hair. I can spend that money on other things like books or pastels... or shoes!

Another Black male friend I've known for decades said, "Well, among other things, you've been everywhere! You're always going somewhere different where nobody else is going at the time!"

A white South African friend said, "Oh my dear! You're not like everybody else here. You are so European... Really you are. Americans are so... well, you know. You're like an avatar dear, really." I had to look it up and this is what I found. "As part spirit, the Avatar possesses an innate connection to the Spirit World and is at their strongest in that realm, due to being surrounded by spiritual energy. The Avatar uses that connection to the Spirit World *to be the bridge between the two worlds in order to keep peace between them and ensure harmony.*" Or among the Hindu, "...an Avatar is an incarnation or representation, of a god. Avatars usually take the form of humans or animals." I was stunned.

People come back to my appearance. Another friend said, "Your short Afro and the silver gray that's taking over... Your eyes and what you do with them. They're intriguing, that fixed gaze you emote, or the eye rolls! There are some unusually beautiful women... not in the traditional Vogue magazine sense... You are one of the unusually beautiful women." (I think this was his way of saying, Janis, you're strange looking!) "And your behavior enhances your beauty. Your crankiness, it's a part of your charm. You use that to lure people... The way you dress. You don't have a lot of clothes, *but what you have is high quality*, and the way you carry yourself with a certain confidence that can be mistaken for regality but stops short of arrogance. For a

Black woman, you grew up very well off and that sets you apart from most Black people. You are part of an unorganized club."

This unorganized club was shocking according to a friend's roommate who was appalled and probably offended I didn't grow up dirt poor the way she had or poorer. Her response when my friend tried to explain my reality? "Oh, so she's one of those high-class niggers…" That roommate is white, works at Home Depot, doesn't know much and has no desire to learn. So much for sisterhood. Comments like this keep me grounded about the ugliness of racism. But there were other comments from so-called friends that ignite a seething rage. I designed a brochure with comments from former students at Wheelock College and the Institute of Politics at Harvard. I showed it to one of these "friends." She read it. Looked at me and said, "I don't believe any of this." Money and intelligence only go so far if you're Black.

"You have an integrated intelligence, a relational intelligence. *You have a powerful ability to think, and that's the goal of a college education, not the accumulation of facts or knowledge.*"

"You're not an open person. You've been hurt, so you tend to keep yourself closed, although you do it in a very sophisticated way."

"Your life has a controlled quality. You make sure everything is in the right place, but you're not obsessive. You believe everything has a place, even though you can be messy, your messes have places. *The concept of place is important to you.* Those little bronze pigs you have are always on the far, left edge of the coffee table."

A college friend said, "Pryor'll give you a mile…in inches!" She was right. I watch people for a variety of reasons. This ability is a gift from Tina. *I watched her.*

Mother's Madness

"Janis, you really don't know how you come across to some people. What you dare to think and actually do… You need to know this", said an old friend I met through work.

An astrologer said, 'The Virgo in you is embarrassed by the Leo in you!"

I guess most of this is flattering. But some people don't have enough to do! I wonder how this book will impact their perceptions. Who they see is not who I find when I look in the mirror. And Tina? How did she perceive me?

You. Little. Red. Bitch.

*"An en caul birth is when the baby comes out still inside an intact amniotic sac (caul). This might make it look like your newborn is completely gift-wrapped in a soft, Jello-like bubble. An en caul birth is also called a 'veiled birth.'
This rare thing of beauty happens in less than 1 in 80,000 births."

"Caul bearer children are strange and stand out as quiet with an unnerving presence. Natural leaders, but supportive followers… They have difficulty connecting with money… They are sensitives, visionaries and healers, writers, poets, artists. Have frequent nose bleeds. They will tell you that they see ghosts…They will blurt out precognitions…They have strong connections to animals and nature. They are essential links to the here and the hereafter. They will make you feel as if, in complete silence, they know your deepest darkest secrets…"
caulbearersunited.webs.com/traitsofacaulbearer

Chapter Three

Two Leos, One Virgo

My mother was born on August 7th. My grandmother was born on August 16th and I was born on August 23rd. We were astrologically doomed! The three of us were quite different. If we were starving and had no food, my mother would steal. My grandmother would beg. I would starve.

Too often Tina reminded me of a twisted, miserable character you'd find in the original television series, Twilight Zone, or some painful Scandinavian film directed by Ingmar Bergman, maybe a movie about the mob directed by Martin Scorsese! One of Tina's idols was John Gotti, a crime boss in New York City, known for being well dressed and somewhat flamboyant. Tina thought he was extremely handsome. During the 1980s, he was always in the news. His clothing was exquisite. Tina gushed over him.

When she wasn't admiring Gotti, she was fixated on her skin. It can't be emphasized enough how pleased and proud Tina was of her skin color. She used her skin color as a disguise, slipping into places where she didn't belong and hearing things that weren't meant for Black people to hear. High yellow, light skinned, "damned near white," all of that applied to Tina and she never let you forget it. But she wasn't quite light enough.

Mama? She could kill if she had to. She was a quiet storm that never erupted, a container of grief, hope, rage, and dignity. Josephine Adams Lawrence, sweet and proper on the outside, deadly and determined on the inside. She was hard working and highly respected. After she died, I kept her cosmetic luggage case that had her initials embossed. Eventually I looked through it. Wrapped in a handkerchief, I found a pair of brass knuckles. "Oh my God," I muttered. And then it dawned on me. We went back and forth every year on the train. We had a Pullman bedroom on the Crescent Limited in car SR23. Mama always had me pull the shades down when we stopped at a station anywhere south of Baltimore. Once the train left, the shades went back up. Why? What if one white person or a group of white people saw us and decided we didn't belong? We shouldn't ride in "that fancy Pullman car"! What if they rushed on board, kicked down the door, intent on hurting or killing us? She would push me into the small bathroom and then fight them off, or die trying, praying they never saw me. I watched Mama so I could learn what it meant to be prepared, to be quiet, and not call attention to yourself.

I avoided Tina like spoiled food. Even as a child, I'd seen enough to know. I'm not sure where Tina was born. New Orleans? Gulfport? Houston, pronounced as Hauston, Mississippi? I finally located it on a map in northern Mississippi once I understood the linguistic adaptation. Wherever Tina was born she was ashamed of it. My grandmother was born in Alabama, grew up in Pollard, I believe. (Pollard is located in south-central Escambia County in the extreme south-central part of the state, on the Alabama-Florida state line just northeast of the Conecuh River.) Mama wasn't a liar. You could believe what she said. She had no reason to lie and it was against her morals. God didn't want you to lie. Mama told me that all the time, pounded the value of telling the truth in my head along with the Ten Commandments. All of this was reinforced in Sunday School. Jesus Christ didn't lie. He didn't steal. End of conversation.

Tina? She was smart. She graduated from Spelman College and did graduate work at Columbia University where she received her Masters' Degree. Her area of concentration? Early childhood development and education. Tina lied all the time and asked me to lie on at least two occasions. I knew better and told Tina, "I'm not doing that!" The first time she told me to lie I was in elementary school. The second time I was in high school. The problem with lying is there's always a trap door somewhere. It opens when you least expect it, and you fall into a puddle of facts that drowns you and exposes the lie. You look like a stupid fool. I wasn't interested in that.

Mama was still working when she brought me down home. For a while, Mama and Papa hired someone they trusted, Miss Gibson, to take care of me while they worked. One of my first memories was Miss Gibson (who was rather rotund) lying on the living room floor by the front door while I crawled all over her! I remember looking up and seeing Mama walk in. I gazed at her black shoes. I could feel Mama's chagrin! She tried not to laugh.

It was decided Mama should stay home to take care of me. Somehow, my grandfather would make it work and he did. He always did. He made sure we never had anything to worry about for as long as he lived. As I grew older, I began to understand all that he did and the regard Black and white people had for him. It was unusual. Among other things, he was a graduate of Tuskegee University. He was a master carpenter. He owned property and had several "rent houses." If he were white, they would've called him a residential developer! At one point, he was a cook for a café and worked part-time for the only grocery store, Saumas, near us during my early years, that was owned by a Greek couple. I could see the store from our front porch. (A few years later, Rial's Grocery opened next door. It

Mother's Madness

was owned by Mr. and Mrs. Rials, who were Black, but their store wasn't as big or well stocked as Saumas. The meat was always a little suspect. They did carry Borden's milk and that was what mattered to me.)

Papa also worked at Keesler Field, the Air Force base in Biloxi. We had a big backyard and Papa always had a garden: corn, sugar cane, collards. Mama told me how Papa and she ran a cab service for Black folks early in their marriage. I don't know when they rested.

All that was important to me was Papa. He was my world, and he's all I cared about. He let me go with him just about everywhere. I watched him build houses, collect rent, buy food, cook food, and interact with white folks without getting killed while they paid him for his work.

We didn't live in a shotgun house. We lived in a three-bedroom home, with a living room, dining room, kitchen, bathroom, front screened in porch. (Mosquitoes were active realities on the coast!) It was ten blocks north of the beach, also known as, "the Redneck Riviera." Beautiful beaches with white sand and palm trees that we weren't allowed on.

My grandfather built our house. After Hurricane Katrina, it was the only house left standing intact on our block. It was the same house my mother and her brother, George, called home. Tina and her brother, Uncle George, were raised in remarkable conditions for anyone growing up Black on the Gulf Coast of Mississippi. Ever since Reconstruction, Papa's family owned land. There was talk about leasing gravel rights, selling lumber, and there was some oil. One of my grandfather's earliest memories as a child was "riding to town on a donkey to pay the property taxes..." Some of that land is still in his family. There's a missing chapter in Papa's story. How were they able to keep that land? How much land, if any, was on the reservation? Was there a white family or a powerful white man protecting the Lawrences, and if so, why? Did it have something to do with his maternal grandfather who was said to be a white Episcopal missionary? So many questions hang in the air like fog. There's something or someone we, or I, don't know about.

Uncle George died when he was twenty-one from tuberculosis. He was almost finished with college. Yet he was described on his death certificate as a "common laborer" not a college student. My grandmother had photos of him on her dresser. I don't think she ever recovered from losing him. There was a strong resemblance between him and me and that made Mama hold me as tightly as possible in every sense of the word. She considered me God's gift to her after having lost her son, a son that she adored. How did I know? She told me. And then there was that winter morning when I was three years old.

Chapter Four

But First, A Word About My Father, Harry

This is just about the time when people start asking, "What about your father?"

I respond with, "What about him?" The truth is both simple and complex, contradictory and perfectly aligned. This is what I know.

My father, Harry Pryor, and my mother, Leontine Lawrence, were married in New Jersey. She was 26. Tina notified Mama and Papa via telegram. Mama told me she screamed when she read it. When she received a photo of him from Tina, Mama told me she cried. Mama never cried.

J.W., Tina's cousin, told me, "Harry was too crude for Uncle Lawrence. You know, Uncle Lawrence was a Southern gentleman. He would tip his hat to the ladies... I don't think Uncle Lawrence ever forgave Tina for marrying Harry. As far as Uncle Lawrence was concerned, there were only two things Tina did right. One, she had you, and I can't remember what the second one was!"

Since Tina and Harry had no money, they spent their honeymoon in Gulfport with Mama and Papa. How they got enough money to go home remains a mystery. Maybe Papa paid their way home.

This is where things get stranger. My father and I *never* had a real conversation. Although every now and then he'd say, "Hey."

And yes, all three generations eventually lived in New York City under the same roof when Mama and I came north so I could go to school.

The first house Mama and Papa owned in New York was a four-story brownstone with a garage and a backyard, next to a Jewish synagogue in Manhattan. It was in a neighborhood Harry wasn't familiar with.

Harry was a binge alcoholic and violent. You never knew what to expect on the weekends.

When drunk, he stumbled. I would lie awake on Friday and Saturday nights, listening for the front door to open, listening for his footsteps to tell me *how drunk* he was and *how dangerous* the night would be. He was a little over six feet. When drunk he would open Tina's dresser drawers, throw them on the floor and begin to rip her nylons in two over his knee. It's a sound I never forgot. To this day, I'm ambivalent about falling asleep. Things that go "bump" in the night have a deeper meaning for me.

He sorta worked.

He was born in Newport News, VA.

His mother died when he was a child.

He had a sister who was institutionalized in Massachusetts. I didn't find that out until I was in my forties!

He had a brother (that I never met) who still lived in Virginia. I don't know his name. I wouldn't recognize him if you showed me his photo. This brother had a habit of locking his children in a closet as a disciplinary measure.

Harry had another brother who never recovered from shell shock as a result of World War II. I don't know what happened to him. I don't know his name either.

Harry fought in the Korean War. He was a Master Sergeant and earned the Bronze Star. I found it among his things after Tina died. I discovered that "the Bronze Star is the fourth highest ranking award a member of the arms services can receive for a heroic and meritorious deed *performed in combat*. The Bronze Star or Medal is a signal of their sacrifice, bravery, and honor while serving their country." I wondered if that's where he learned to kill or, did he already know.

I never called Harry anything but Harry. I often tried not to call him anything.

He was brown skinned, a bit like gingerbread. I have his smile and I suspect his sense of humor. Tina married him because he was handsome and promised to take her places. They never went anywhere that I knew about.

I was terrified of him. Why? Because he tried to kill us on more than one occasion. He had a fondness for weaponizing cast iron skillets and putting a knife to your throat. There are no sharp knives in my house, or cast iron skillets that I use in the presence of others.

He loved fine clothes and fine cars and one or two other women.

He owned a mink coat. When he wore it, he looked massive and a little ridiculous. My grandparents thought he was crazy. They wondered where he got the money to buy this coat and what was he putting aside for my college education. It was something they didn't dwell on.

Harry had some shady associates, one of whom was portrayed in the movie, *American Gangster*, starring Denzel Washington and Russell Crowe. I had heard Harry and Tina mention, Frank Lucas and Bumpy Johnson on more than one occasion. I had no clue who these men were until I saw the movie. I tried to remember why their names were familiar to me, and when I did, I heard myself say while watching the movie, "Oh my God." My hand silenced my mouth.

Harry spent a lot of time in parts of Harlem especially on the weekends. Playing the Numbers was a weekend activity he boasted about. It was some form of sketchy gambling and it wasn't legal. That's all I know.

He hated Mama and he wasn't wild about Papa either. He treated me like I was invisible, so I guess I didn't exist.

There was no getting rid of him. One summer when I was down home, I wrote Tina telling her how afraid I was of him. During the weekly call Mama and I made to Tina she told me, "Don't you ever write me another letter like that! Ever!" I was nine and remember being terrified by the tone of her voice. It was vile, coated with deep animosity.

Harry beat Tina from time to time and threatened to push her out a fifth story window once. I learned to call the police at an early age. I also learned to barricade my bedroom door with a chair under the doorknob. (Television was a great teacher.) Being "spoiled" I had a phone in my bedroom. It allowed me to call the police on more than one occasion.

If we were lucky, he'd go storming out of the house Saturday after his murder attempts were thwarted and vanish until late Sunday. What I found strange as a child, was after these incidents, no one ever talked about them. It was as if nothing had happened. The house was weighted down by silence. Tina's eyes darted about the mornings after his assaults. She wouldn't look anyone in the eye. Her mouth was always tensely fixed with the lower lip pulled back and down. Mama was miserably quiet and I was beginning to think I was going crazy. And Harry? He was just "fine".

Tina refused to divorce Harry but she did take him to court for child support. I found the whole thing confusing and yes, she told me of her efforts. She let Harry lie on the floor unconscious for roughly an hour towards the end of his life. He wasn't drunk. Eventually, she called an ambulance. He lived.

If I asked questions about Harry and his murderous impulses, Tina usually told me, "This is none of your business." Her favorite response that she could never quite deliver with strong conviction, but with amazing arrogance was, "Other families have fights. Why don't you grow up?" I guess I was supposed to believe that other fathers tried to kill their families. That alarmed me. What was real? What was true? Is this normal? Was the world make believe like on television, until the front door closed, and then murderous fathers let loose? I had to know. So, I asked her, and Tina said, *"Stay outta my life! You're just a child!"* More confusion to contend with. Was I to "grow up" or be "just a child"? Her comments made me believe she was crazy and hated me, and the only one that counted was Harry, who tried to kill all of us.

At the brownstone, Harry, Papa and I often ate dinner in complete silence while Mama and Tina watched us.

Harry died in the early nineties. From what? Tina never said. Our cousin, Terry, told me. It was a diabetic coma. I didn't go to the funeral. Tina was horrified. She said, "What will people think? Please don't do this to me." I responded, "You married him. You lived with him. You bury him. I won't be there. I don't care what people say."

A few weeks or maybe it was months after Harry died, Tina told me, "Harry was going to leave you fifty thousand dollars in his will. But he said you were a bad daughter and didn't deserve anything."

Now you know what I know.

But this wasn't enough for one of my oldest friends. She wanted to know more. What was his impact on me?

More Words About Harry

"So, what was his impact on you?" my friend asked. I had to control myself when I heard this question, because my first impulse was to scream and ask, "What the fuck do you think it was given what you've read?!" But assumptions are dangerous things. So, for the sake of truth and clarity, let me list his impact on me.

- I live with a constant sense of terror.
- I've been diagnosed with PTSD.
- Harry, combined with growing up during segregation in the deepest, darkest part of the South, have made me hypervigilant. I put Harry and the Klan in the same column.
- For years I'd jump at the slightest noise.
- I never sit with my back to a door, opened or closed.
- I walk in a room and immediately locate the exits.
- I try not to sit in the middle of a row of chairs. It's harder to get out if something should happen.
- I'm afraid to go to sleep.
- I can smell danger miles away!
- I can sense when someone has anger issues within ten minutes of meeting them.
- I believe no one will protect me from anything!
- My life is not worth very much.
- I love locked doors.
- I repeat, there are no sharp knives of any kind in my house.

- Being held at gunpoint in a foreign country was nothing compared to living under the same roof with him.
- I hate math. He excelled at math.
- Any man who reminds me of Harry I want nothing to do with. Therefore, I avoid men who drink, smell of liquor, and slur their words.
- Any man who shows the slightest tendency towards violence I want nothing to do with.
- Any man who tries to hide those tendencies, shame on him because somehow, some way, I'll find out. Adult children of alcoholics have a sixth sense about this. We're like heat seeking missiles. Too often we know someone has a drinking problem before they do.

I spotted Tina's alcoholism when I was in grade school. First beer, next scotch, and then liquid rage splashed over ice cubes of bitterness.

Had it not been for Papa and Dr. Gaynor I would never trust any man. Nor would I have known how to recognize a good man, flaws and all.

Harry came through in a psychic reading and said, "Tell her I'm sorry."

Too late. I'm not that good.

Chapter Five

Uncle George

It's still so clear in my mind. That morning was verification for my grandparents. It was a turning point in my very young life.

I was three years old. It was cold, cold for Gulfport! I remember that it was late fall. Aside from the linen and my pajamas, a pillow and my stuffed animal, Elsie the Cow, there was a very heavy blanket along with a quilt that weighed me down. I still equate warmth with heaviness, heavy coats, heavy blankets, heavy sweaters.

It was early, but not that early. I opened my eyes and propped myself up on my elbows. The shades were drawn. There was a yellowish light shining across the foot of the bed. Seated there, glowing in this yellow light, was Uncle George! He looked exactly the way he looked in the photos! He was familiar and I could feel him smiling at me. I wasn't afraid. I was excited, and awestruck. There was something remarkable and almost magical going on. The rest of the bedroom seemed to disappear. The only thing I knew at that moment was Uncle George had come to see me. I knew he had died a long time ago. For some reason that didn't bother me.

The longer he sat there the more aware I became that he was telling me something. It was almost as if he was planting a thought in my head to be remembered at a later date. When he finished "talking" to me, I could feel the warmth of his presence, or maybe it was the comfort of his presence. Then he began to fade from sight.

I looked around the room, popped out of bed, and ran to the kitchen. Mama was fixing breakfast and Papa was reading the paper. It was a sunny day, and the kitchen door was open wide enough that I could see the big pecan tree and the side of the garage.

"Mama, Mama! I saw Uncle George." I was very small, even for a three-year old, so I struggled to climb up on my kitchen chair at my place setting. My chair had two phone books and a pillow I sat on. I scanned the table looking for the cereal box and orange juice. I only drank Borden's milk and I wondered if Mama made biscuits. Papa was finishing his eggs. I loved our kitchen. Papa had bought this great stove that had something called a deep well. It also had a grill, four burners, and two ovens!

"You did," Mama said referring to Uncle George.

Papa continued to read the paper.

"I did. He was in this yellow white light and he told me something," I stated. "Can I have some cereal please?"

Papa put the paper down and asked, "Pumpkin, what did he tell you?"

"I can't remember," I said.

Mama paused and said, "Um-hmm." She opened the cereal box and poured some in my bowl while saying, "I'll pour the milk, baby."

"Okay," I said. My hands were still too small to manage a carton of milk.

"You'll remember when it's time", Papa said. "Jo, get the baby some bacon."

And I did remember, fifty plus years later at Trinity Church Boston during a leadership meeting. It took my breath away. I had questions. I still have questions.

At the time, I didn't appreciate how critical my grandparents' reaction was and what that experience signified and verified about what I was and how I'd be regarded in the cultures I had been born into, but I would.

I ate my breakfast. Mama and Papa talked. I looked out the side window and watched the sunlight talk to the green leaves on the trees. Our fig tree stood patiently like a lady in waiting. Aunt Emma, one of my grandfather's sisters, who lived in the middle of our block in a shotgun house, would preserve those figs, and pears, both in sugar, homemade syrup, and cloves. I preferred the pears. Both were excellent accompaniments to biscuits.

Same Questions, Different Man

After reading about Uncle George, another friend asked how did that (seeing a dead man seated at the foot of your bed) impact your life? I thought that was one of the dumbest questions I'd ever heard, and I love questions. I was annoyed. And then I started thinking about it.

It wasn't *seeing Uncle George. It was realizing there were other places or dimensions* that existed, the same way some people experience NDEs*. I grew up among people where seeing the dead and being born with a caul or veil covering your face was highly regarded. Having been born that way my immediate family was simply waiting for verification or a sign. Uncle George was both. Others would follow. During my early years, I didn't think this was a big deal.

As I got older, straddling two radically different parts of this country, not to mention two, sometimes three conflicting cultures, it slowly settled in that seeing the dead and seeing into other realms was something I shouldn't talk about. And I shouldn't talk about any accompanying psychic skills that blossomed within me as I grew older, much less my interactions with non-human, intelligent life. People tend to freak out or dismiss things they don't understand or perceive as threatening. Being called "crazy" or being disdained was not something I enjoyed much less welcomed. The impact?

My belief system is complicated.

I can't stand deliberate ignorance, those who refuse to learn because they're afraid it will force them to think differently.

I have contempt for people who dismiss and denigrate what they don't understand because *they can't comprehend it*. These are people who often say, "That's impossible."

I expend a lot of energy keeping all of who I am a secret. I walk in many different worlds on earth, many of them cradled in a web of what my late friend and neighbor, Dr. John Mack, would call "extraordinary experiences."

I have to find other ways of justifying the things I know through these abilities. It's hard for some people to accept there are different ways of knowing.

I can always sense someone's true intent.

Sometimes it doesn't matter what I know. Sometimes I can't help people, and that drives me crazy.

I spend a great deal of time thinking about how to explain "this" when someone *genuinely wants to know* and very few know…until now.

I often feel like Cassandra.**

Sometimes I wonder, "Why me?" Then I ask, "Why not me?"

"This" is not only seeing those who have passed over but being able to see what's going on in different dimensions, adjusting to flashes of information and pictures, like pop-up ads on computers, that may or may not make immediate sense.

I have an experiential understanding of the power of meditation and prayer.

I have to manage being clairaudient and clairvoyant during my daily life without driving off the road and/or reacting among people.

I try to stay away from crowds. Parties are out. I pick up too much random information about people and it drains me. The older I've become, the intensity of all this has grown.

There are ranges of side effects I have to manage.

It drives me crazy how little we know about the human brain and its relationship to intelligence and anything that lies outside of the five senses.

I spend time trying to draw or paint what and who I've seen in some of these other dimensions much in the same way Dr. Eben Alexander is trying to re-create the music and sounds he heard during his NDE when he was in a coma for seven days.

I surprise myself when what I "see" turns out to be true and can be verified.

Why see a psychic with all these "abilities"? This phrase comes to mind. "A lawyer who defends himself has a fool for a client."

What I saw in the first quarter of 2022 frightened me.

I make sure no one person knows everything about me and that included Tina. She knew enough and what she knew terrified her.

*NDE – Near Death Experiences
**Cassandra – Cassandra or Kassandra, was a Trojan priestess of Apollo in Greek mythology cursed to utter true prophecies, but never to be believed. In modern usage her name is employed as a rhetorical device to indicate someone whose accurate prophecies are not believed.
*** "There is more to this life that you live than we can see." Pg. 16, *Universal Human*, by Gary Zukav.

Chapter Six

The Dining Room

Houses hold energy of events that took place there. How do I know? Because I can feel the energy. Something allows that information to make itself known to me. Everybody has that ability to one degree or another. I'm one of those people who walks in a room and feels everything that's been experienced there; tears, fear, joy, rage, sadness, terror, anger, love, betrayal. It's a useful skill but you have to be careful. It can overwhelm you. I can "read" a room or a house the same way I can read a book. Imagine what I went through standing in the hallway leading to the Oval Office in the White House. You know the expression, if these walls could talk? White House walls scream.

Walls soak up events like dry sponges swelling from water. Nothing wrong with that unless the water exceeds the capacity of the sponge or it exceeds your capacity to hold it and the information it carries. This is why I stay away from old houses. It's why I built a house and why I'm working to build another. All I would have to worry about is the land and not the experiences of previous tenants seeping from the walls.

Mama and I often went to visit her brother, Uncle Jim. He lived a cab ride away. We'd take the "colored cab" run by Mr. Ivory who also owned Ivory's Pool Room and Café at the south end of our block. Aside from shooting pool in the back room, you could buy ice cream cones, soda and chili hot dogs in the café section. I loved banana ice cream and Cream Soda.

I'd get in the cab, worried about the destination. The worry was always present. It didn't matter how old I was.

"Mrs. Lawrence, where y'all want to go?" the driver would ask.

"I'm going to see my brother over in Soria City." It was pronounced, "Surra."

"Yes ma'am. I'll get y'all there."

And off we went. He knew where Uncle Jim lived. I don't know how, but he did. In twenty minutes or less, we'd pull up to Uncle Jim's house. It didn't matter how sunny it was outside, Uncle Jim's house was always dark. The house scared me. Even the trees looked scary over there. I was perfectly content to sit on the porch for the entire visit. His house was similar to ours but not as big, small dining room, small kitchen. The backyard was always overgrown with sugar cane and banana plants. I made sure I went to the bathroom before I left home.

Uncle Jim was Mama's only living sibling. Their sister had died. I don't know how. Mama's family was small unlike Papa's family with twelve children, who were my great aunts and uncles, and I knew most of them. Three had died before I was born. Uncle Jim had been married "a few times" and buried at least two of his wives and one or two children. Based on what I overheard and could see, Uncle Jim resembled his mother, Rosa Adams. He was dark skinned, slender, and he had the same nose that Mama had! A photo of their father in a round wooden frame hangs on my wall regardless of where I live. It's very formal and so is he! Mr. Adams had a long beard and searing eyes. Friends of mine who've seen his photo think he's white. I know two things about him. One, he had a grocery store. Two, black and white people came from miles around to have him "tell their fortunes and listen to his predictions." They regarded him as a seer.

Sooner or later, Mama would ask me to "go back to the kitchen and get me a glass of water."

"Yes ma'am", I'd say and reluctantly go. I was usually watching the trees and remembering stories I had heard about Uncle Jim's house.

I opened the screen door and walked into the living room. It was small and hazy with all the requisite pieces of furniture and you didn't know if it was night or day. Something kidnapped the light. I would always stand in the doorway for a minute or so deciding if I should run to the kitchen or simply walk very quickly. I'd scan the rooms and my eyes would lock on the dining room, and there they were, two children waiting for me, a boy and a girl. They shouldn't be there, I thought. But they were.

I raced through the living room and the minute I set foot in the dining room, I felt like I had stepped through some kind of brown gauze or net-like film, a veil. The children ran around the dining room table giggling. Yes, sometimes I could hear them. Standing in the corner was someone else. I never knew who, and never told my grandmother the courage it took for me to get her a glass of water! In an instant the children ran around *me*. I could feel the breeze created as they ran. I always freed myself and made it to the kitchen. Got the water and dreaded returning to the front porch. The children were waiting for me in the dining room. I was never able to see their faces, just their form. They wanted someone to play with. Years later I found out that everyone who had died in Uncle Jim's house was "laid out" for the wake in the dining room. Some of those souls got stuck there!

I was always relieved when we went back home.

As a little girl, I slept in the same bed with my grandmother when we were home. After we went to bed, I kept hearing things. One night I sat up in bed, terrified. Shaking Mama, I woke her up.

"What is it, baby?"

"There's somebody in the dining room," I whispered.

"No, baby. There's nobody there."

"Mama, I can hear them. They're moving furniture! And they're whispering."

Mama was awake now. "C'mon, lay back down and go to sleep." She gently pulled me down. I found my stuffed animal, Elsie the Cow, and clutched it. Mama went back to sleep. I didn't. I heard them whisper and move around for another hour. By the time I fell asleep, it was getting light outside. Although I didn't know it then, I was demonstrating clairaudience. I still have this ability.

That night is embedded in my mind because it made me think dying was not quite what most people were led to believe and that my grandfather was right. He didn't want me to be afraid of the dead. When I was four or five, Papa took me to a wake held for someone he and Mama knew. (By then, Black folks had the kind of funeral homes we know today.) There were two funeral homes for us, us being Black people: Lockett's that was across the street at the north end of the block and Hall's, two blocks south from us.

When my Uncle George died, he too had been laid out in our dining room for the wake.

Hall's had the distinction of being the first funeral home for Black people in the area. Mrs. Hall was my Godmother. Our burial site is adjacent to their burial site at the cemetery for Black folks. It's where I will be buried, next to my grandparents, Uncle George, and Great Grandmother Rosa, Mama's mother.

Each summer when Mama and I got home, my first responsibility was to walk the two blocks that separated our houses and let Mrs. Hall know I was home. She was always delighted to see me and always called me baby. "The baby's home," she would say smiling with open arms. She had a wrap-around porch and a second story to her house. She grew calla lilies and introduced me to cushaw, a sweet tasting member of the squash family.

The offices for the funeral home were on the far side of her driveway in a separate building.

I became familiar with death very early in life. It was nothing foreign, nothing that could be avoided. It was an inevitability and not many could see beyond that veil to the other side and know the truth of death, unless you were someone like me. This is a skill that could never be included on a resume.

Chapter Seven

Family and Friends

As an only child, I spent a lot of time alone. My best friends were books, art, and television. Specifically, we met each other at age three. That's when Mama taught me how to read. And then, thanks to Ding Dong School with Miss Frances, Mama helped me create my first work of art; a collage of a bright red duck! Miss Frances came to your house through television. Ding Dong School originated in Chicago. At age three, I had no idea where Chicago was.

The red duck was important to me because it was red. Miss Frances instructed us to cut out various rectangles and squares from the construction paper we had. There were a few triangles also. There was a small jar with white paste and a brush to spread it on your paper. Mama and I patiently cut the red pieces of paper and assembled them to create a red duck. We pasted the pieces in their exact spots on a piece of white construction paper. Mama and I were delighted. Look what we made! Mama and I would make many things together. She watched John Nagy, Learn To Draw, with me. Every now and then she'd encourage me to keep drawing, not to get discouraged. I kept drawing and still draw. I met the world through television.

I wasn't allowed to go outside nor play with anyone except Sandra, who lived next door. We were allowed to talk at the fence that separated our yards, and sometimes ride our bicycles down the street and back. The first time I got on a two-wheeler, I almost knocked over a lady slowly walking in front of me with some of her friends. I can still hear Sandra laughing as I yelled, "Watch out, lady!" I liked Sandra and hoped she liked me. She was bigger than I was, but just about everybody was bigger than I was! My size became a defining characteristic of my identity.

I had these cousins, first cousins once removed. In other words, these were the children of my mother's first cousins, or specifically, the children of my grandfather's nephew, Romeo. He was dark skinned, angular, and thin with high cheekbones, coal black curly hair, maybe five-eight with a mustache and tired, cloudy eyes. He drove a cement truck. Romeo and his wife, Ethel, had five boys, Rommie-Lee (or Larry), Tyrone, Glen, Terry, and Gerald. Rommie-Lee (pronounced Roma-Lee) and Tyrone went into the army and made a career out of military service. Rommie-Lee died on Valentine's Day of 2022, while eating dinner with his wife. Something shattered in me when Terry called with the news. Glen, who was my age, died in his early thirties from a stroke. Gerald almost had a way out through college football, but something happened. Not enough college money probably. He was interested in sociology.

At the north end of our block, Uncle Houston (my grandfather's youngest brother) and his wife, Aunt Ella Floyd, lived with their children, Ronald, Donald, Sonny, Brenda-Anne and Loretta, now known as Laura. (Uncle Houston was Tina's Uncle.) I didn't spend much time with them. Ronald, Sonny, Brenda-Anne and Laura left Gulfport to pursue their education and get good jobs elsewhere. Donald was problematic from an early age. He threw sand in my face once when we were kids. He eventually became a statistic. Donald has been in and out of prison so much, that it became obvious he couldn't adjust to living as a civilian. I was told, the last time he was released from prison, he walked into a casino and stole some money right in front of a security camera. Incarceration appeared to be Donald's preference, but it didn't work out. Donald has been released from prison. He has lupus. Caring for him is something the state of Mississippi wants nothing to do with.

Ronald? He became a minister. As I write this, he's in Texas and serves as a Chaplain for COVID patients. His other siblings have come back home from across the country, and according to Ronald's Facebook page, someone's asked him to return to Gulfport. He's got mixed feelings. Doesn't know what to do. He did take the opportunity to boast about the Lawrence family on Facebook. I smiled when I read it. And in the middle of the block? Aunt Emma, one of Papa's sister, who was a very good cook and Romeo's mother, grandmother to the five boys I grew up with: Rommie-Lee, Tyrone, Glen, Terry and Gerald.

The question, "Who are your people?" was a familiar echo in my ears. It was an inquiry about your origins, your roots, your kin, your standards, not your last name. "Your people" are who you are, who you were, and who you will be. "Your people" tell the community what you stood for unless you did something to shatter the reputation of "your people." We had one answer, "the Lawrences." Would I go back to Gulfport? I never dismiss it as being unreasonable. It's still home. With all the danger and contradictions, it's still the place I felt safest.

Terry occupied a unique place in my life and still does. There's a photo somewhere of me, at age four, sitting on the living room couch, and holding him in my lap shortly after he was born. Mama became his Godmother. She adored Terry and pleaded with his mother, Ethel, to give him to her on more than one occasion. I can still hear Ethel's voice. I think she knew Mama wasn't completely serious, but Ethel wasn't sure!

"Oh, Miss Josephine! I couldn't give you my baby! No ma'am." They would both laugh. But Mama and Papa played a significant role in his life just as they did in mine. The reasons were different. The outcome was different, but the impact was undeniable.

Terry became the closest thing I had to a younger brother. He weaved in and out of my life like tides ebbing and flowing. On several occasions, Terry came north with Mama and me to attend school. Trips north to pursue a better education was almost a ritual among our people and uniquely Southern. Education was highly valued in the South among our people. It was your way out and up. If you had the opportunity and the money, the children of my generation usually headed north. For Terry, it started when he was six or seven at the behest of "Aunt Josephine and Uncle Will." I was ten or eleven and would help him with his homework, especially reading. To this day, Terry will tell you I taught him how to read. That's an exaggeration. There was so much he had to adjust to, including Tina. She was horrified that he had so few clothes. Immediately after he arrived, she took him shopping. Shoes, socks, shirts, pants, coats, whatever he needed. Tina took over! She described his wardrobe as being "defunct".

That first year, Terry got awfully homesick and pleaded with Papa to let him go back home. Every time Terry asked, I became frantic. He was practically my brother. He couldn't just leave. I would miss him so I would plead with Papa to not send him back. It was an emotional see-saw. We eventually balanced out, teetering in the middle with the certainty of going home at the end of the school year.

One night (in New York) I heard Tina laughing as she left Terry in the bathroom. The sound of her laughter always made me uneasy. My stomach tightened and I fought off trepidation.

I asked her, "What are you laughing at?"

"He's scrubbing himself with Ajax!" And then she let out, "Ha! Ha! Ha!" With a cigarette in one hand, she pranced to the kitchen, oddly victorious.

Later that evening, I asked Terry, "What were you doing?"

He looked up at me and said in a very matter of fact voice, somewhat bemused, "I'm trying to scrub off this black..."

He wasn't able to do that. As far as Tina was concerned, Terry and I were the wrong color(s). Terry is dark-skinned, like his parents. I'm kind of tan. Both colors were dangerous markers. Tina had me apply skin-lightening cream every night before bed starting at the age of seven or eight. It didn't do anything but make me mad and confused. She gave detailed instructions on how I should rub the cream in upward motions so your hands resembled wings! Upward motions with skin lightening cream would also help prevent wrinkles. As I did this every evening during the school year, she would chant the following, "The price of beauty is great, baby!"

Terry and I had to rub Jergen's Lotion on our legs so they wouldn't be "ashy" or dry and flakey. Based on Tina's behavior, there was a lot wrong with the way Terry and I looked. We got the message. Every time I look in the mirror, I still hear her criticisms and pointless insistence on using skin
lightening cream. I still see her disgusted expression when she thought I wasn't looking, and I still see that look transform to one of saccharine, phony approval the minute she realized I was looking at her.

I don't know how or when Terry learned his color was permanent and he would stay brown for the rest of his life. Was it in New York and not Gulfport? If it was Gulfport, what happened? Gulfport had enough signs, literally and figuratively, informing you that *"by 9 AM of every day of your life someone will remind you of your race and your place"* as Jesse Jackson once said to me. What happened in New York that made Terry try the Ajax solution? Did somebody say something, or did he simply want to be like "everybody else"? He was outnumbered while attending elementary school in New York. So was I.

I can't remember not knowing I was the "wrong color" in America. That knowledge was (and still is) in the air I breathe. But there were some alarming differences in how that information was acquired based on geography. The bottom line? If you are Black, nowhere in the United States are you safe, much less acceptable unless you were extraordinary, and after four hundred years, you're still not safe regardless. It's 2022.

Tina's audacity around color and face creams and her fixation on appearances were most likely based on *her looks*. Many white people thought she was "foreign", not Black. Black people were not fooled. Most knew the truth. More importantly, Tina knew, and she hated being "almost white." There was no power in being "almost" anything! I think it was the primary source of her rage based on how she talked about white folks. Her favorite descriptive phrase regarding them was, "Dirty, rotten, sons of bitches!" If Mama or Papa were around, it changed to, "Dirty, rotten, sons of so and so!" She referred to aging white women as "cracked ice" because they inevitably had wrinkles.

I found it fascinating following the roll of genetic dice in our family through our looks, a nose, cheekbones, eyes. Sometimes it was nothing specific, but if you turned your head a certain way, or realized the lines in your face were the same as Mama or Papa, or in my case some amalgamation of Mama, Tina, Uncle George, and Great Aunt Elizabeth. From what I saw in old photos, Tina's color reflected her paternal great grandfather, the rumored white Episcopal missionary, more than his Choctaw wife. Nor did Tina resemble her maternal grandfather, the man that my white friends thought was one of them. As for the Choctaw branch of our family, Tina wanted nothing to do with it.

I have a photo of my great-great grandparents. My maternal great-great grandmother was from the Mississippi Band of the Choctaw Nation. According to Tina, "She looks like any other Negro woman to me. We don't have any Indians in this family." The two formal photographs I have of my great great-grandparents speak differently. Mama never talked about any Native American connection. Tina believed there were no slaves in our family either. It was hard knowing what the truth was.

J.W. told me, "Uncle Will and Aunt Josephine had indoor plumbing and electricity long before any Black people in Gulfport. Tina had her own room. George had his own room. Tina and George lived in luxury!" At one point during his childhood, J.W. lived with Mama and Papa. He was Mama's nephew who seemed to know Tina like nobody else. They were both renegades, but I could tell by the look on J.W.'s face when talking about Tina that he paled in comparison to his cousin. "Tina was wild."

Mama used that same phrase to describe her daughter. How wild? The secret I uncovered was Tina originally attended Hampton Institute. She was so out of control, the President wrote Mama and asked her to come and get Tina. She was "too wild." Mama talked with her minister for advice. It was suggested that Mama send Tina to Spelman. That's how she ended up there.

While J.W. talked, I remembered how class distinctions were made in the Black community then. The distinction was made only in part by material things. The critical difference was *the aspiration to rise* regardless of the limitations white people imposed. As bell hooks said in, *where we stand: Class Matters*, "Class involves your behavior, your basic assumptions, how you were taught to behave, what you expect from yourself and from others, your concept of the future, how you think, feel, act, etc." All this is often signified in the black community as, "good home training."

My family, the Lawrences, thought, felt, and acted differently from many other Black people they knew. It set them apart. It set Tina apart. It set me apart. But, as bell hooks writes, "No amount of money could change the color of one's skin."

The public school Terry and I attended in New York was overwhelmingly white with a large percentage of children whose parents were Holocaust survivors. There was a sprinkling of Catholics, and fewer Latino and Asian children. All of us who were not white stood out. I was the only African-American child in any of my classes from the first to the sixth grade. Because there were so few of us, we didn't present a threat or danger to other students or teachers. We were anomalies, not problems.

"All races and religions/they come to our school/we work and play together and live the golden rule/our halls so gayly lighted/our murals on the wall/ the teachers of our lovely school/ we love them one and all!/our dear old alma mater/our dear one seven three/" These were the lyrics of our elementary school song. And yes, I remember.

That perception of "our lovely school" where all races and religions attended with the Golden Rule binding us together, changed when I was in the fourth grade. Walking home from school, a classmate ran by me and said, "Nigger! Nigger! Nigger!" He laughed and kept running. That's when I felt outrage for the first time. This is what Black parents try to prepare their children for, the slimy slur full of hate inevitably thrown at you. *Hear this: nothing prepares you and you will never get over it.* To this day, I know exactly what he looked like. His name is embedded in my soul. I won't reveal it because I had good home training.

My speech-writing "career" started at twelve years old! My speech was chosen to be delivered at our sixth-grade graduation ceremonies. I remember being terrified and wanting to throw up! I focused on the clock that hung in the back of the auditorium. That way everyone in the auditorium would think I was looking at them when I was really blocking them out! If I looked at all those people, I was afraid I'd either collapse or freeze. That would be a fate worse than death. Tina would be so humiliated and I'd be blamed for embarrassing her, for making her look ridiculous.

Outside of the classroom, I had little contact with children my age. There was Terry, my books, my dolls, drawing, painting and television, Mama and Papa and "them", Tina and Harry. Tina vacillated between being malicious and dismissive or indifferent until she wanted to show me off like some small four-legged at a dog show to some of her friends. It didn't work because I refused to be cute and charming. Going home at the end of June was a huge relief. It felt like I was being released from prison.

The best part of the trip home was the train ride. We'd get on that Pullman Car, SR23, settle in from New York City to Gulfport on the Crescent Limited. We'd leave Pennsylvania Train Station around 2:30 in the afternoon and arrive home close to five o'clock the next day. Hallelujah!

A Word About Skin Color

Skin color is an important reality in the United States, especially for the Black community, and for anyone whose skin is not white. Colorism lives. The formula is simple for us. The lighter you are the better off you are. You'll probably have an easier time and won't scare white people as easily as your darker brothers and sisters. (You don't want to be too big and "scary" either especially if you're a Black man. The darker you are the scarier you are, and if you're a woman, the darker you are, the uglier you are.) Of course, the trade-off is your sanity. And if you have straight hair, God has doubly blessed you. I grew up with these beliefs and Tina reminded me on a daily basis in case I had a lapse and stayed in the sun too long, became fat, or God forbid, decided to cut my hair and wear it natural.

This "color thing" drenches our entire being. It impacts how you see yourself, how you carry yourself, and how other people (of all colors) see and/or judge you. Its influence is pervasive and it moves within you like a deadly virus if you're not careful. A dark-skinned person can't act like a light skinned person. They can't pretend to be one. Won't work. It's a matter of authenticity. It shapes how you see the world, how you see yourself, and how you interact with others. This insanity is something white folks created. The power of (skin) color defies description, especially in the United States, but not exclusively. You should see all the color classifications they have in Brazil for their citizens. Tina would've done well in Brazil, maybe that was why she loved Rio.

Tina was very fair, and proud of it. She was one of those Black folks who, as previously said, was "light, bright, and damned near white." No one else in her immediate family was as light as she was with the exceptions of her Uncle Edward, Papa's oldest brother, his youngest brother, Uncle Houston, the middle brother, Uncle Robert, and down the genetic line. Since I first wrote that line, I've found out that quite a few white folks were sprinkled in our family. There was more than one Native American. I always suspected that, but I was still surprised. Everybody else that I knew in the family was copper, butterscotch, tan, bone, and café au lait. Aunt Elizabeth, Aunt Alberta, Aunt Emma, and Aunt Ophelia, my great aunts, Papa's sisters, had some version of "good hair", another blessing.

I've always wondered, how much of Tina's obsession with color had to do with me concentrating on color field painting when I got to Bennington. When I'm asked what was my subject in painting? I say without thinking twice, "color", and I can tell you which artists I bow down to for their command of color and knowing the relationship of one color to another, and how color evokes emotion from the viewer. Color on canvas or paper becomes evocative. Color on human flesh also becomes evocative and sometimes deadly. Trust me. People have died over this color thing.

Tina was possessed by the power of color. This is worth repeating. Make no mistake, you were judged according to your color, not only by Tina, but the rest of the world. It's instantaneous. Judgments are made about you before you open your mouth, by Black and white alike. That judgment could shape the direction of your life. That's not an exaggeration. Color isn't a minor concern for us. *Black women can't afford to be casual about color. We are no one's priority.*

Chapter Eight

William Augusta Lawrence, Papa, my Grandfather

I don't talk about my grandfather because I miss him too much. He was my anchor, my heart, my life. The attachment and adoration were quite simple. I didn't and still don't need to know why. It simply was. Anything that was meaningful and real I learned from him. Did he have faults? He did. Did I care? No. I didn't care then and I don't care now. He could be cantankerous, stubborn and exacting. Did I idealize him? No. I just learned to live with and accept his imperfections. As a result, I try to meet people where they are for who they are.

One day Aunt Emma, Papa's sister, asked me, "Baby, what are you going to do when your granddaddy dies?" Papa and I were sitting on the front porch. I was scrunched in the chair with him. Maybe I was five, maybe six. It didn't take me long to answer. I looked at her and said, "I'll die too."
Aunt Emma didn't know what to say. She smiled and shook her head. I thought it was a stupid question. My life was devoted to Papa. What else was I going to do?!

I was a "difficult" child. Once I overheard someone say I had arrived in this world "already owning myself." I watched and listened to adults very closely. That old adage that children should be seen and not heard lingered in the air. I took advantage of it. I think Papa knew that.
Uncle Houston came to see Papa one evening. We were sitting on the porch, and as usual I was scrunched in the same chair with Papa. Uncle Houston was the short brother, light skinned.

Mother's Madness

He resembled his mother, "Miss Alice". It was the roundish nose. Aunt Elizabeth, Aunt Alberta, Aunt Ophelia and I have that nose. I watched and listened to Uncle Houston talk, and heard myself say, "That's not true. You're lying." Uncle Houston's face froze. He looked at Papa, and said, "Will, you gon' let her say that?!" Papa took a deep breath and asked, "Is it true?" I remember looking back and forth from Uncle Houston to Papa. Uncle Houston hemmed and hawed. Papa said, "If you weren't telling the truth there's nothing I can say." And what did Uncle Houston say? I can't remember. All I knew was he was lying. I had no idea why, but I could feel it. The truth literally feels differently from a lie. I was convinced your heartbeat faster when you lied. That's what lie detectors measure, unless you can sense it the way I do. Some police officers can do that too.

Papa liked to tell stories about how he took care of me when I was an infant. At night, my bassinette was by his side of the bed so he could make sure I was breathing and Mama could get some rest. He drove a standard shift and held me in his left arm when going to pick Mama up from work. There were no infant carriers then, no seat belts either. He had to hold me. I've never forgotten how he would explain to anyone who would listen, "I held her in my left arm and drove with my right." There's a photo of Papa holding me while I held the stuffed animal I slept with, Elsie the cow, of Borden's Milk fame. It's the only photo of me smiling as an infant. Papa's smiling also.

Everything I know about love and devotion, generosity, truth, honor, the sanctity of the earth, the power of the spoken word, the need for personal power, and the wisdom of silence, I learned from him. He gave me his love for animals and proficiency for growing things. Roses gave him great joy. He didn't care about the thorns. If I reached for one, he'd tell me quietly, "There're thorns. Be careful."

We have the same middle name, Augusta.

Everybody knew who he and Mama were. He helped people. Papa was one of the few Black people at home who knew how to "work the system." He fought for people, wrote letters to the government, told people how to handle certain things, and he knew a lot of people.

He was openhanded. Mama thought he was too giving and was always fussing at him for lending people money he'd never see again. But he taught me an important lesson about money, "Never lend more than you can afford to lose. No friendship is worth it."

He lived a long life. He was born in early November of 1890 and died in January of 1980.

He battled serious illnesses. During one of those times, J.W. told me he remembered visiting Papa. He was in bed at home, propped up on some pillows. "Doctors didn't know if Uncle Will was going to make it. He told me he had to get well because he had to live long enough to raise you. And he did."

He catered to my every need, encouraged my talents, spoiled me in unique ways. Papa gave me my first typewriter for my ninth birthday. It was a portable, blue Smith Corona, in a tan case. I would sit on the front porch and write stories! Kids would pass by, whisper to each other, and look at me strangely. I didn't care.

I'm sure I tested Papa's patience! But he never seemed surprised, was never irritable with me. Only once did he threaten to spank me. We were in the front yard. I had a little car with pedals I was driving on the sidewalk and in the yard. I had never seen snow except on television. For some reason, I wanted to experience snow falling from the sky. I ran in the house, found a pair of scissors and a piece of white paper. As soon as I got back in the yard, I cut the paper in small pieces, threw them up in the air, and watched them fall to the ground. I was thrilled and pleased with myself. Papa had been watching and told me I had to clean it up. Looking up at him, I said, "No, they'll melt. Snow melts." After he threatened to get a switch, I picked up the "melting snowflakes." And what stands out after all this time? His stillness, the stillness I imagined in the twenty-third psalm, "He leadeth me beside still waters…"

Papa helped me memorize the twenty-third psalm and the Lord's Prayer. He helped me every night with my prayers. *"Now I lay me down to sleep/If I should die before I wake/ I pray thee Lord my soul to take/ God bless…"* And then there was a litany of names, starting with Mama and Papa, Tina, and Papa insisted I include Harry. I didn't see why I had to include Harry but Papa did.

School forced me to confront grief. Education demanded I leave Papa for roughly nine months of the year. I've never recovered. Mama and I lived this bicoastal existence determined by the school year. I hated it.

Papa was the second oldest in his family. Great-Uncle(s) Houston and Uncle Robert were brick masons, Uncle Edward (the oldest, lived to be close to 100), Great-Uncle Daniel, Great Aunt(s) Emma, Aunt Ophelia, Aunt Elizabeth, and Aunt Alberta. I discovered recently, there were three others who died early in life. These were the children of Eugene and Alice Lawrence, my maternal great-grandparents. *Great grandfather Eugene put all his children through college.* I knew most of my great-aunts and uncles, except for Uncle Daniel and those great aunts who died before I was born.

According to Tina, Uncle Daniel gave George tuberculosis. In the next breadth she wanted me to know that Papa was the most successful. That's all she seemed to care about, Papa's success. The fact that *her grandfather* sent his son, Daniel, to Arizona to seek treatment for tuberculosis, didn't matter one bit to her, much less sending all his children to college! She dismissed the significance of that.

I could talk with Papa about "big" things: heaven, hell, hypocrisy, truth, death. We'd also talk about Kraft Theatre on NBC, and how we often disliked it, and we always discussed the news! I loved the news because he loved the news. He would explain politics, and he told me about the letter he received from FDR commending him for helping people get Social Security! I remember watching the Democratic National Convention with Papa and seeing somebody named Adelaide Stevenson and some young man with a funny accent named John F. Kennedy. I was fascinated.

Papa taught me about the earth and animals and cooking and saving money. He taught me things that had to do with indigenous practices and beliefs. I didn't realize that until I was in my thirties. I started reading about Native Americans and too much of it was familiar to be a coincidence. It was the memory of Aunt Emma's references and stories that verified these lessons from my grandfather and our connection to the Mississippi Band of the Choctaw Nation. And it was finding most of his siblings' names on one of the census records kept at the reservation that's not too far from Jackson, Mississippi.

It was Papa who insisted we always have enough food to feed at least one other person. Often, there was a place at the table set for one more person, just in case. He told me that some people didn't have enough food to eat. Those who were fortunate enough to have should be gracious enough to give. Greed was an unattractive quality. Although we were very fortunate, Papa told me there was no need to flaunt what you had. "To whom much is given," he said, "much is expected." I would have to find my own way to give, to help others, to make things better. Everybody can do something.

Papa embodied the spirit and teachings of his college, Tuskegee, especially when it came to issues around pride and drive. E. Franklin Frazier pointed out in *Black Bourgeoisie* that, "From the head of Tuskegee…the students learned that 'A man never begins to have self-respect until he owns a home.' And that 'art and music to people who live in rented houses and with no bank account are not the most important subjects to which attention can be given. Such education creates wants without a corresponding ability to supply these increased wants.' Papa earned a living that made it possible for his children, Tina and her brother, (Uncle) George, and his granddaughter, me, to indulge in these increased wants of art and music.

In *When and Where I Enter*, by Paula Giddings, she wrote the following, "…after the death of Booker T. Washington in 1915, and the militancy of Blacks after the war, a new means of racial accommodation had to be found. And by 1920 the perceptible presence of a Black middle class provided a vehicle for that accommodation. Now, there was a class of educated Negroes whom Whites could talk to, and who, presumably, could represent the race as a whole." Papa, his brothers and sisters were among that class of "educated Negroes."

Papa's brothers had also gone to Tuskegee. They owned homes and sent their children to school, many of whom went on to college. The Lawrence family has teachers, ministers, master carpenters, brick masons. Privilege is relative and as far as our people were concerned, William Lawrence was a successful moneyed man of his time. He understood the nature of money. He knew how to amass wealth. He translated his earnings and land into the security that this Capitalist country respects. I wouldn't let myself imagine what he would have accomplished had he been white and gone to business school. So, when I go home and somebody asks me, "Who are your people?" Without hesitation I state, "The Lawrences." And that's exactly what Tina says also.

Papa was slender, copper skinned, high cheekbones and quiet eyes, and just under six feet. He had a way of destroying people quietly with words. His tongue could be razor sharp and all his siblings knew not to make him mad, because "Will can preach your funeral!" The way he used words and silence had a shattering effect. People found his calmness unsettling at times.

He could be friendly and gracious and gently straightforward when he had to be especially around white people.

If no other man ever loved me, that would be okay because my grandfather loved me. Papa made me feel safe, protected, cared for and respected.

Papa contracted tuberculosis when I was very young. I remember going to the hospital in Gulfport with Mama to visit him. We couldn't go inside to see him. But he was on the first floor and we could go around to his window and visit. Unlike his son who had tuberculosis, Papa recovered and came home. That led me to believe that people went to the hospital to get well, not to die.

Years later, after Mama and I were in New York so I could go to school, Papa developed some serious stomach problems. The next thing I knew, Tina found him a doctor and Papa had to come to New York to see a surgeon, Dr. John Fletcher Pruden at Columbia Presbyterian Hospital.

I spent significant amounts of time sitting by Papa's bed in Columbia Presbyterian Hospital. The nurses knew me. No one ever said I was too young to be there. And no one dared suggest I leave.

Dr. Pruden died in the late nineties. I read his obituary in the New York Times. While reading it, I remembered he took me to his lab to see where he did all his research. He had to lift me so I could see everything. There were tubes, microscopes, papers, files, and diagrams. I was impressed.

But I was more impressed with his ability to make Papa well. Dr. Pruden performed three operations on Papa over the course of several years: the first to reposition his stomach, the second to remove a growth from the back of Papa's neck, and the third one was ground-breaking. Dr. Pruden used shark cartilage to replace a vein in my grandfather's leg that had deteriorated due to arteriosclerosis. This technique was mentioned in Dr. Pruden's obituary in the New York Times.

Papa liked paying people in cash. The night before he was released from the hospital after his first surgery, Tina was there. Dr. Pruden walked in. I still remember his crisp, starched, white coat. He was tall, graying dark hair, clean shaven and wore shiny black shoes. He sat on the edge of Papa's bed and commented on his extraordinary willpower and recovery. Papa smiled and nodded at Tina. She opened her handbag and gave Papa a white envelope. Dr. Pruden looked puzzled, until Papa said, "I like paying my bills in cash." Papa counted out quite a few hundred-dollar bills. I lost track. He handed the money to Dr. Pruden. Looking back, I think Dr. Pruden was stunned. Cash payment was unusual, and cash payment from a person who wasn't white was some kind of abnormality!

Papa came north two additional times to get me. Mama left me with "those people," Tina and Harry. I experienced a visceral response to abandonment. I was frantic with fear. Who knew what Harry was going to do? Tina was always pretending that nothing happened. Harry could kill me and she would pretend she knew nothing about it. "That couldn't be! Harry wouldn't kill anybody. Janis must be missing. She'll turn up."

Mother's Madness

Papa hit the roof the first time Mama showed up without me, but I know he never made a sound. That wasn't his way. I heard Mama tell her friends down home how upset Papa was that she left me. Papa took a plane for the first time and flew north to get me. It was the nineteen fifties. I remember that everyone was frightened. What if the plane fell out of the sky? Papa would die. What if Harry killed me? Papa would kill Harry and then nothing else would matter for any of us.

It was cold when Papa came to get me. I had to wear a heavy coat, a hat, gloves and knee-length socks. Maybe it was Christmas vacation. I was back home in Gulfport in less than 72 hours after Mama left.

The second time Mama left me was at the end of the school year. That was a grave offense! Tina told Mama I should stay with her for the summer. There was a fight. I overheard some of it. Same drill, Mama left me. Papa came and got me. That time we returned home by train. Car SR 23 to the rescue. But I stopped talking. Papa told me I had to talk. And I did, when we got home.

Eventually Papa came north and stayed. He needed to be closer to his doctors. Now "down home" would be locked up until Mama and I came back after school, and Papa would stay in New York.

The story for public consumption was if Papa got sick, better for him to be in New York with quality health care. His health was of great concern to his brothers and sisters and to us. But that wasn't the primary reason he came north to stay.

Harry was the real reason. He tried to kill me. It was becoming routine and I was convinced he'd succeed one night. But this time, he literally kicked in the front door. Staggering up the stairs, I heard him stumble and fall against the wall every few steps. I ran into Mama's bedroom, and we bolted the doors shut. Mama called Papa (in Gulfport) while I listened to noise created by brute strength, rage, and alcohol. I was petrified. Mama got off the phone and told me to sit next to her. She held my hand, looked at me and said, "I called your daddy. He'll call the police." In minutes they arrived. Harry was yelling, "I'll break your neck." I could hear Tina running downstairs to the front door. The police rushed in and confronted Harry who had to be "calmed down." Someone knocked on Mama's bedroom door and I heard, "Mrs. Lawrence, are you in there? It's the police." Mama unlocked the door. The officer scanned the room and his eyes landed on me. "Sweetheart, it's going to be okay." I knew he was lying. Sometimes the police would take Harry away, but Tina would never press charges. Harry would be back in twenty-four hours. Everything was "fine." Tina got the front door fixed. I ate my breakfast and spent Saturday reading and watching television. I didn't know what Saturday night would bring. This was a normal weekend.

Within a month, Papa arrived to stay. His presence seemed to temper Harry somewhat. But eventually he resumed his pattern of binge drinking on the weekends with threats and attempts to kill us. This would happen at least once a month, often twice. It felt like it happened every weekend, because every weekend I was scared. Nobody would ever press charges. I dreaded the weekends.

Mama and Papa offered to pay for Tina to divorce him. They begged her. She consistently refused. I began to lose respect for her. I held her more responsible for this craziness than anyone else.

Mama and I would go down home for the summer and Papa would stay in New York. It was another reason for me to be terrified. What if Harry killed Papa? Loss and grief haunted me. They became active, ongoing realities in my life. Loss and grief felt like blood relatives.

I always left New York thinking Papa was going to be hurt. Sometimes he came home with us. I really needed the comfort and oxymoronic safety of the Deep South. Things were so clear at home. Nobody was trying to kill me or Mama or Papa, not even the white people so long as we "stayed in our place."

I was working on Ted Kennedy's 1980 Presidential campaign when Papa died. Tina couldn't tell me and Mama wasn't able at that point. Dementia was establishing itself. So, Terry called and told me. I felt like someone had blown everything out of my head. All brain matter was gone, eye sockets hollow, nose cavity empty, no mouth, tongue, teeth gone. Papa was my anchor. Now I was adrift with only Mama to hold onto. Without Papa, my stability slowly eroded. With each passing year since his death, except for a two-year respite, I've become a little crazier. I flew home for the funeral and every night thereafter for a year, I dreamt about Papa.

Chapter Nine

I Want Mama

I could rest my head in Mama's lap when we were home.

She let me turn the living room floor into huge cities with my wooden building blocks.

She taught me how to read and write when I was three. I also learned how to read out loud really well. The Sunday School teacher always made me read the story we were given, usually a lesson about Jesus. The other kids began to hate me. They wanted to know how come I could do that, read out loud and not stumble, and why couldn't they do it. I told them about Mama, how she made me study and "get them lessons!" They still hated me. I made them look stupid. Who wanted that?

Mama taught me how to knit and combed my hair every morning on the front porch. I'd sit on the floor and lean against her knees while she plaited two shoulder length braids in the back and one on top. My hair was very thick and blue-black. Mama was so pleased because, as she often said, "Your hair is your glory." But it was also a source of pain! It wasn't a good idea to be "tender headed". Best to ignore the pain of Black hair care. Pain wouldn't change anything. Only Black women did Black hair. A difficult job but a profitable one for Black hairdressers. Their beauty shops were usually in their kitchens. Mama and I walked down 19th Street until we arrived at her friend's house who "did hair". Her kitchen was dark, but there was a chair for Mama to sit in and a chair for me. Early that morning Mama washed my hair before we went to have it pressed. After it dried, I'd sit silent for three to four hours while my hair was straightened (or pressed) with a "hot comb" that was heated in an open gas flame. More terror! Was she going to burn my scalp or my hair line or miss both and burn my face? Mama watched. She would run interference if she thought I was going to be burned.

Mama washed and ironed my clothes and made sure I took a bath every day and dressed "nicely." She wanted me to always be "presentable."

The Lawrence household always ate rice the way some white people ate potatoes. Learning to cook a perfect pot of long grain rice was a rite of passage for me. We often ate what Papa grew in his garden and a lot of seafood. Gumbo with crab legs, with shrimp, maybe with chicken or sausage. Mama would cook fried fish sometimes with a drop or two of hot sauce, crowder peas, snap beans. She bought all kinds of citrus fruit, oranges, cumquats, satsumas, lemons. Watermelon was bought from a man with a truckload driving through the community. It was always an event. The driver would "plug" the melon Mama or Papa pointed to. They wanted to make sure it was sweet before they paid him.

Mama let me sprinkle sugar on butter beans and rice and make bacon sandwiches with toast and jelly. She loved making Campbell's tomato soup, so I loved it, but Terry hated it! He ate it anyway. I've never tasted anyone's fried chicken or apple pie like hers. It had something to do with sage for the fried chicken and a mysterious amount of cinnamon in the apple pie. Her lemon meringue pie was divine. We'd get inspired to cook something after seeing a recipe on television. But salad was Mama's nemesis. I was almost twenty before I had a decent salad. She couldn't cook grits without lumps and I hated those lumps! Both of us discovered the joy of hot dogs especially with relish and sometimes Mama would cook breakfast for supper. We'd have pancakes or griddle cakes with a bit of molasses. I had a child-sized kitchen set with a table and four chairs that we'd bring into the living room. Mama would often serve my meals there if Papa was working during dinner time. Mama and I would eat while watching television often giggling at something we found silly.

The joy of hot dogs followed Mama and me to New York where we discovered Kosher hot dogs with brown mustard. They were wonderful. Mama and I would have hot dogs every weekend in front of the television and watch either the Friday Night Fights or on Saturday, wrestling! (Papa didn't like hot dogs. New York introduced him to White Castle hamburgers. He enjoyed those.)

Every now and then Mama would instruct me to never eat out at anybody's house. There was a chance they might poison you. I was horrified. I couldn't imagine why they would do that. But years later, I discovered the source of her advice. There were stories of how Native people were invited to "break bread" with white people when the west was being settled. Promises were made. A meal was served. The Native people died. Their food had been poisoned by white cooks as ordered by high- ranking military.

Mr. Jimmy King taught me an essential lesson about cooking. He was one of Papa's best friends. He'd walk down the driveway and find his way to the kitchen. Dressed in denim overalls and a blue and white striped railroad cap, he'd sit on the stoop and Mama would offer him a cup of coffee. "Yes, Ma'am, that'd be good. Miss Lawrence, when you fixed that coffee you weren't mad were you? 'Cause I can't eat or drink anything made by somebody mad. It just won't agree with me." Mama assured him she wasn't angry when she made the coffee. "Aw right, Miss Lawrence. Be sure you tell the baby. Don't cook when you're angry. All of that will get in the food…" To this day, I make sure I'm in good spirits when I cook.

Mama had one more regular visitor, Miss Rosie. Her house was off the narrow street that ran in back of ours, otherwise known as an alley. Mama and I would often be on the front porch when Miss Rosie waddled down the street, past Rials' Grocery Store, and then to our house. She reminded me of a plump gray-brown mouse enveloped in a cloud of dust. There were always two or three grocery bags she had with her. Opening the front gate, she said, "Miss Lawrence, how you doin' this morning? I thought I'd come by and get some ice." Mama nodded her head, exchanged pleasantries, and hustled to the kitchen. Miss Rosie didn't have a refrigerator. She literally had an ice-box. She also had lots of opinions about world events. This particular day it was about the U.S. sending men to the moon. When Mama came back with bags of ice for Miss Rosie, the real conversation began. "Miss Lawrence, you and the baby seen them men land on the moon yesterday?" "Yes ma'am, I did," Mama said. Miss Rosie turned, looked at me and mumbled, "Baby, how you doin' this morning?" I smiled. Didn't say a word. "Miss Lawrence, they didn't go to the moon. No...no. I don't know where they did go, but it wasn't the moon. That's too far to fly. White folks always trying to do somethin' stupid." I was speechless because she was right and wrong at the same time. Mama cleared her throat, gave a very slight laugh and said, as she always does, "Miss Rosie, you don't want your ice to melt." Miss Rosie looked at the bags of ice and stood with some difficulty. "Miss Lawrence, you know that's right. I thank you so much." She waddled out the gate and hurried down the sidewalk. Mama and I looked at each other. Miss Rosie had many theories. Mama listened to all of them with patience and kindness.

Down home, as a child I was afraid of my bed. It was too low to the ground, and it scared me even though it was in Mama's room. Her bedroom was at the front of the house. Papa had his at the back. The middle bedroom was empty – sort of. I didn't like that bedroom. I just knew Uncle George was there and didn't want to be disturbed. I think Mama knew and that's why she let me sleep with her in her bed.

But Mama had a mean streak fortified by stubbornness. She was strict, very strict. I think the phrase is "overprotective." Sometimes I felt like a prisoner but I didn't know what crime I had committed. There were a ton of things I couldn't do and I never understood why. That was the worst part, not knowing why.

I heard Mama call Papa a coward one day. For that moment, I hated her with all my soul. I wanted to run over and kick her, scream at her. How could she say that? I would learn this sharp-tongue skill was a family trait, something perfected to defend yourself. Soon it would be my turn to learn. So, I listened and watched very carefully.

Mama had some odd ideas. She was convinced gymnastics caused cancer and you could catch cold sometimes from washing your hair in the winter. And you should never take a tub bath when you had your period. It could cause a convulsion. And one more thing, never, never let a boy pull your dress up. These odd ideas scared me. Every now and then she sounded like Miss Rosie. I had many questions I had to find the answers to.

Mama had no problem hurting your feelings for a higher cause, like pursuing perfection. She never allowed me to say, "I can't." That was forbidden.

Mama and I went to church *every* Sunday when we were home. Papa stopped going after Uncle George died even though Papa laid the corner stone of our church. It didn't matter. Papa never went back.

Mama and I sat on the front porch in the summer every evening before it got too dark and every morning right after breakfast when we didn't go to town or I didn't go somewhere with Papa. Sitting on the front porch was how I learned to be a watcher. Mama made quiet comments about everyone who passed. Those comments taught me what and who were acceptable and what and who were "frowned upon". *One thing was certain; I had better not ever get fat!*

Almost every evening, Ronald, Donald or Rommie-Lee would pass and I'd hear, "Aunt Josephine! Good evening." And Mama would say, "Hey sweetheart." Maybe a grown-up would stroll by, "Miss Lawrence, how you doing?" "Pretty good," Mama would say. Someone else would say, "Miss Josephine", and nod their head in recognition. Mama would acknowledge them with a smile. Or "Miss Lawrence, you tell Mr. Will I was askin' for him." And Mama would say, "I surely will." It eventually got dark and often louder. Cars creeping down the street, music blaring. Kids running, yelling to each other. It was time to go inside and close the front door if it wasn't too hot.

We'd also go inside immediately when the white police drove through. Silence hit as they creeped by dragging the promise of trouble behind them. Sometimes they'd pull over, stop and get out. Mama had me pull the shades down. She told me it was harder for them to shoot you if they didn't see you. As soon as they drove off, you felt the entire block exhale and the noise of living started again.

Mama would tell me stories sometimes but never any fairy tales. She told me how Black children were often given used books thrown away by the white schools. Maybe that's why she made sure I always had new books. Maybe that's why I refuse to have any used or second-hand items. Or maybe it was because I didn't want to feel anything from the previous owner. I needed new things for different reasons.

She told me how some Black schoolteachers would just pass kids onto the next grade whether they had learned anything or not. Mama made sure that was never done to Tina and George.

Implicitly, I knew what I had to do, study, learn and never get left behind academically. That was not acceptable in our house. I was scared of the consequences of being stupid. My solution? Better read everything you can get your hands on.

Mama told me repeatedly, I had to learn to be independent. Marriage was not important, but education was vital. Few Black men were reliable. Few Black men were like Papa. She was right.

It was Mama who told me about the night she and her sister hid under their house when the Klan rode through. She didn't have to say much more. I could see the memory deep within her face and lurking in her eyes. She'd heard and read stories about slavery but often became too choked up to tell me any details. Decades later I ordered from the Library of Congress the testimony from freed slaves compiled in a series of soft bound books. I read the testimony of Laura Clark who said, "My mammy was de mother of twenty-two chillum." Mama and Papa had two children. Laura Clark's niece, Martha Jackson said, "She [her aunt] was er (a) breeder 'oman (woman) en (and) brought in chillum (children) ev'y twelve months 'jes like a cow bringin' in a calf. En (And) she say dat (that) whut (what) make her mo' val'ble (valuable) to her ol' Marster (Master)."

Mama said there were "*some* good white people." My pediatrician down home was one such white person. He allowed Mama to bring me to his office and sit in the same waiting room with his white patients. I never saw any other Black people there. If the white people didn't want us there or objected to "their" pediatrician having a Black child for a patient, I never knew about it. We sat in that waiting room just like we were supposed to be there. But Mama never let go of my hand until we saw the doctor.

Mama and I hated thunderstorms. They were often fierce on the Gulf Coast. Sometimes the sky would turn a terrifying shade of dark blue, swallowing the sun, during the middle of the day. The wind would pick up, and in the distance, you could hear muffled rumbles of thunder. Lightening flashed, often creating crackling sounds. Somehow instinctively we always knew when to go inside. "Get away from the window and pull down the shades," Mama would say. And then there was a clap of thunder so loud your body vibrated. During really bad storms, Mama and I would go in the bedroom and sit on the side of the bed. She told me to be quiet and held my hand while she prayed. The force that gave thunder its might was to be respected. So, we sat in prayerful silence, until the storm passed. I always wondered what would happen if the storm didn't pass.

Mama was my bridge between home and New York. I was much older before I realized how brave she was. She left everything and everyone she knew to take care of me in New York. To make sure I learned and fulfilled my potential, to protect me from her daughter and her son-in-law and all those white people!

My first memory of New York City was the old Penn Station. I was awe struck. I still see the light shooting through the windows that seemed to be attached to the sky! I couldn't imagine what we'd do in New York. How long would we have to stay before leaving for home? And just who is Tina? I found it hard to believe she was my mother. If so, where had she been all these years? She told me over and over that she came home some summers to visit me. Either she made no impression on me or I blocked her out, or she lied.

I had to wait for New York to have my patience tested by Tina's cooking and everything else she did. Until New York, I never knew that many Black people ate chitlins, pigs' feet, and chicken wings. Neither Mama nor Papa ever made those dishes down home. I hated all of them. Chitlins smelled awful while being cooked with vinegar. I wanted to gag. Instead, I stayed out of the kitchen until Tina finished cooking and Mama aired out the kitchen!

One night in New York, shortly after Mama and I arrived, I woke up and discovered my pillow was covered with blood that fell from my left nostril like a waterfall and clots the size of large grapes. The left side of my face was stained with blood.

"Mama!" Instead, Tina rushed in, turned on the lights and hovered in the doorway, stricken. My bedroom was between Mama's bedroom and Tina's. I couldn't get in or out without going through one of their rooms. One door led to Tina's room. The other to Mama's. Seeing Tina, I screamed again. "Mama! Mama!"

The other door flew open and Mama was right there, like always, to take care of me, to pray for my well-being, eyes closed, with one hand on my forehead, the other over her heart. Mama made sure Tina didn't do anything stupid. She told Tina to get some ice and call the doctor and Tina did as she was told. Obedience was a big thing with Mama.

Mother's Madness

This incident marked the beginning of a life-long battle with nosebleeds and visits to the hospital to have my nose cauterized. The bleeding was always in the left nostril. No doctor has been able to tell me why I have these nosebleeds. There was no rhyme or reason for them. But Tina was terrified, and Mama? Nosebleeds? Just another sign of having been born with a veil over my face.

There were some dissonant notes from Mama. There was something about having people over that she despised. Mama passed this attitude to Tina. They regarded every holiday with dread sustained by an undercurrent of contempt. Guests were an imposition. Holidays provided opportunities for people to take advantage of you. Therefore, no one was ever invited over for any holiday, including and especially Christmas. I still don't know where this came from. Papa was baffled as well.

Mama enjoyed an occasional can of Pabst Blue Ribbon beer. Sometimes down home she'd send me to Mr. Ivory's at the corner. You could get ice cream cones and chili hot dogs. Mama would send me to get her a Pabst Blue Ribbon from Ethel Lee, Terry's mother. She worked at Mr. Ivory's for as long as I could remember. I would get a banana ice cream cone. I loved banana ice cream! But Mama had one guilty pleasure, snuff. Mama dipped snuff! So, sometimes I'd go to Mr. Ivory's and pick up a very small can of snuff, no higher than three or four inches. It had a green and white label and it was called something like Tube Rose. If Mama and I were sitting on the porch, she'd usually wait until night before imbibing in her guilty pleasure. Dipping snuff was a messy activity. She had a makeshift cuspidor made from a coffee can that sat inside a small wastepaper basket. Spitting out the snuff in liquid form was involved.

Everything I know about strength, determination, the power of prayer, and the need for quality over quantity, came from my grandmother. Without saying a word, she taught me I always had to be ready to fight for what was important to me. I learned how to take care of people from watching her. She also taught me how to change linen on the bed and make "hospital corners". She made sure I understood the meaning behind, "We're too poor to buy cheap." There was money, so buying cheap was never a choice. I thought we were lucky. But it was my grandparents who worked to provide that "luck."

Everything I know about the reverence of God, the power of the unseen, loyalty, selflessness, being prepared, the magnificence of the natural world, the knowledge I acquired, the need for hypervigilance that's saved my life on more than one occasion, and the Motherwit that tells me the time is coming when I'll see them again, I learned from my grandparents. Because of them, I learned how to stare down loneliness. I carried all of this with me (along with Elsie) when Mama took me to New York to get an education. They bought the brownstone that was located in one of the best public school districts in Manhattan in the nineteen fifties. They paid for Bennington College, one of the most progressive liberal arts colleges on the east coast, if not the country, and during my time there, the most expensive college in the United States. It was and still is a Mecca for anyone with artistic or literary gifts and aspirations. It's a school that honors questions as well as answers, thinking as well as knowing. I didn't disappoint Mama and Papa. I had a fine education and I never stopped learning.

My grandmother died in October of 1989. I can't remember who called me. All I know is I haven't been the same since. With each year that's passed, I feel a little bit more of her creep into me.

Chapter Ten

Where Is Gulfport?

I had a white friend in college who knew where Gulfport was. Her aunt had driven them over from New Orleans and pointed out the beaches. I can still hear my friend say, "The beaches are beautiful! Now, is your place right on the beach?" Did she not know the south was segregated? Did she not know about Mississippi?

Or maybe, like so many of my other white friends at that time, she just assumed I was "different" so none of this nasty business about racism and segregation applied to me. The privilege of not having to know can be dangerous. My response? "No, we don't live on the beach."

I wanted to tell her that living on the beach was stupid. Hurricanes were powerful. Strong wind blows rain sideways. It would beat everything it touched and too often bend and destroy buildings. The wind could slam you, cars, buildings and anything not nailed down, to the ground or out to sea.

Coming from the South and coming from Mississippi are two different things. Mississippi is the belly of the beast, the worst of the worst. The perception is it doesn't get any ghastlier for Black people than Mississippi. Black Mississippians who "get out" and become successful represent a rarified species of extraordinary survivors. It should be the root of your strength. For Tina, I think it was the root of her shame.

Mississippi is the place the late Nina Simone sang about. When I was in high school, Tina took me and some of her friends to hear Nina Simone at the Village Gate in Manhattan. I had discovered and embraced all things Nina! That night I watched

Tina as she listened to Simone. It looked like Tina's hand was hugging her drink. Her eyes were half closed and she struck a pose I had often seen when she would tell someone, "I really don't care," or ask, "Who are you?" It was forced nonchalance designed to hide something. But she couldn't avoid Simone's lyrics: *"Mississippi make me so upset/Alabama make me lose my rest/But everybody knows about Mississippi/Goddamn!* It was impossible for anyone to be nonchalant listening to Nina Simone sing this.

Simone's voice sounded like a trumpet! *"Black cat crossed my path/I think every day's going to be my last/Lord have mercy on this land of mine/We all gonna get it in due time/I don't belong here/I don't belong there/I've even stopped believing in prayer..."*

I looked at Nina and looked at Tina, back and forth a few times, trying to get a peek at *who* my mother was, and some sense of *what* she was through Simone's genius. *"Yes, you lied to me all these years/You told me to wash and clean my ears/And talk real fine just like a lady/And you'd stop calling me Sister Sadie/Oh but this whole country is full of lies/You're all gonna die and die like flies..."*

Tina told me once she was born in New Orleans, *"not Mississippi!"* Every time she said this, she would lift her chin slightly and look down at you through her half-closed eyes. When she said this in front of Mama and Papa, they never said anything but they always looked disgusted and disappointed. If I caught Papa's eye, he would look at me and shake his head slightly from side to side.

When I interviewed Tina, three years before she died, the first question I asked her was, "Where were you born?" Taking her unlit cigarette out of her mouth, she leaned forward slightly and told me in an almost clinical, hushed tone, "I was born in

Hausen, Mississippi." She looked around to make sure no one else heard her. Except for my spaniels, we were alone.

The Gulf Coast of Mississippi is a world apart from the Delta where cotton is still picked and too many black people live in rundown houses. The Delta is Fannie Lou Hamer and B.B. King. It's where civil rights workers Cheney, Goodman, and Schwerner were murdered in the summer of 1964. It's where Bobby Kennedy walked (in Tunica County) to get a first-hand understanding of the poverty and gross disparities between so many Black and white lives in the Delta.

The white sandy beaches and blue-green waters of the Gulf disguised the ugliness of segregation and the occasional murders of Black people, usually Black men. Too many tourists came to Gulfport. The ugliness was kept under wraps. The only "exciting" thing that ever happened there before the casino culture took over was the death of Jayne Mansfield somewhere on the highway between Gulfport and Biloxi! Gulfport's one of those places that always gets overlooked on national weather reports when a hurricane hits the area. We hear about Biloxi, Long Beach, Pass Christian, Pascagoula, Mobile and New Orleans – rarely Gulfport.

Gulfport was home. Real home, not pretend home like New York. Approximately 90 miles from New Orleans and 90 miles from Mobile, Alabama, Gulfport was near ground zero for Hurricane Camille and Hurricane Katrina. Had the levees not broken in New Orleans, that stretch of decaying bodies between Pass Christian (pronounced Crish-stan) and Pascagoula would have received all the media focus regarding Hurricane Katrina. After Katrina finished, Gulfport looked like a war zone. The fact that our house was the only one left standing intact after Katrina is not lost on me. Terry told me almost every other home on our block while growing up was wrecked, or so seriously damaged it wasn't worth rebuilding. Devastating hurricanes and severe thunderstorms are a way of life on the Gulf Coast.

Gulfport was incorporated in 1898, eight years after my grandfather was born. It was and is the second largest city in Mississippi. It's described as a "cultural gumbo of Spanish, French, British, Native American, Acadian…" and now a large sprinkling of southeast Asians and Latinx. Lots of different people. Contending with difference was and is a way of life for me. Difference to me is natural.

If you go online, you'll discover that *"the Port of Gulfport became a working seaport founded by two white men for the specific purpose of making Gulfport a commercial harbor. Gulfport now accounts for millions of dollars in annual sales and tax revenue for Mississippi. Gulfport has evolved into a diversified community. 6.7 miles of man-made white sandy beaches, Gulfport is one of the fastest growing areas in the state, due in part to recent gaming activities. Home of the annual World's Largest Fishing Rodeo, Gulfport is a residential community that is blessed with a strong business center."*

That copy is for white people. The historically Black neighborhood where we lived is still known as "the Quarters". It was originally a derogatory term "given by white residents referring to slave quarters, given the neighborhood was mostly Black. But the neighborhood maintained its own grocery stores, drug stores and retail shops. And still does to a small extent to this day." Gulfport was no Tulsa, Oklahoma with a Black Wall Street, but the "Quarters" in Gulfport survived.

My cousin, Ronald, son of Uncle Houston, wrote on his Facebook page that, "the Lawrence Family was all in the Quarters…" (The house where he grew up was at the north end of the block from where we lived. It is now, thanks to Katrina, a

Mother's Madness

parking lot for Lockett's Mortuary across the street. In the middle of the block was Aunt Emma's house. We lived three doors down from her.)

There were jobs on the coast especially for carpenters and brick masons during the early years of Gulfport's development. Jobs my grandfather and two of his brothers, Houston, and Robert, could perform. If there were fancy white homes, hotels, and hospitals, Black women were needed to clean them.

Mama had one job in a hospital. She told me her boss, a white woman, became upset with her and threw a pail of scalding water on her. Mama managed to avoid being burned. She was fast and moved out of the way. That story stayed with me, so much so I used it in another book I wrote regarding the legacy of slavery.

Mama and I always walked to town. Town was a mile or two, maybe more. We walked because Mama was not going to ride in the back of the bus that stopped in the Quarters. We couldn't carry the groceries home, so we'd call the "colored" cab.

There was a phone outside of the A&P where we'd buy groceries. The Yellow Cabs were always lined up waiting for a fare. The white drivers approached potential Black fares and were always turned down. The sneer on their faces after being turned down and the contempt were memorable. She told me to never ride in a Yellow Cab or any cab (with the white drivers). You may not get home.

Gulfport eventually became a tourist spot because of the beaches. Usually, white folks from New Orleans drove over, checked in one of the hotels, and then planted themselves on the beach. All those men stationed at Keesler Field, some with their families found their way to the beach also. The beach was a dangerous place for Black people, but it was especially dangerous for Black women. While we couldn't go on the beach, we could walk on the sidewalk. It was Mama's niece, Mae, who told me this story.

Referring to white men, she said, "They'd see some young Black woman walking by and ask them if they would like to earn some money babysitting for him and his wife. In the beginning they'd say yes. They'd get the address and time, show up, and the men would rape them. Word got out pretty quick," Mae said. "Or some of 'em on the beach, they'd ask some Black girl walking by to come over for a minute and sit on them. As soon as the girl got close enough, they'd force them to sit, pull her skirt up and he'd stick his penis in her. Nobody cared. When he finished with her, he'd just tell her to "getta outta there. Get off the beach." They had no business there to begin with. Word got out on that too. "After a while, you didn't dare walk on the sidewalk near the beach. You forgot about the beach. It was so beautiful… It didn't look that way to us."

This was home, real home, Gulfport. Not New York City, fake home.

Chapter Eleven

So Many White People

There were lots of white people down south, but I didn't see many of them. They didn't live in the Quarters. When I did see them, fear raced through my body. Mama never had much to say about them and when she did it was simply to identify one as "a good white man". What did that mean? They would let you live. They would pay you for your work and maybe help you from time to time. But you had to be really careful about accepting their help. Often, they would lie. Mama let me know in no uncertain terms, they couldn't be trusted. I was happy not knowing them. Let them live on the beach and have their houses damaged or destroyed by hurricanes. Let them live in their fancy houses and shop in fancy stores, eat in fancy restaurants where too many of us would wait on them. Thank God we didn't live with or near them. I thought they were crazy and dangerous. If I wanted to know any more about them, I could watch television. Every now and then, a good white person would turn up on TV. I wondered if I would ever meet one.

When we came north, they seemed to be everywhere, on the streets, at school, downtown shopping and even where we lived! We were the only Black people in the neighborhood! Since I was the only Black child in my classes from first grade to sixth grade, I became as a Black friend of mine said to me much later in life, "You belonged to that special club, the first and/or the only".

A Spanish speaking girl came into one of my grades. She started a few weeks late and couldn't speak English. I remembered how she gravitated to me, probably because we were the same color and had black hair and dark eyes.

She thought I spoke Spanish and would talk to me. I'd look into my new friend's eyes, and somehow, I knew not only what she was saying but that she was scared. Everybody else thought I spoke Spanish. My teacher was amazed and delighted. (Looking back, I think she was relieved.) I invited my friend to the brownstone one day and gave her quite a few of my books. She didn't have any. Tina took them away from her and proceeded to belittle me for giving them to her. She told my friend, "You can't have these!" I remember because it was one of the first times, I distinctly felt deep resentment and rage towards Tina. I could get more books. I knew my friend couldn't. After a few weeks, she was taken out of my class and I never saw her again. I didn't realize I was already being "tracked" with the "smart kids."

Coming north marked the beginning of my other education, white people. I ended up knowing more white people than Black in the north. I watched white people. I studied their ways and learned their values. Quite a few were good, decent people, but not like the good, decent people Mama would approve of. In the North, white people didn't know what they didn't know and could get you killed in some instances, body and soul. Others practiced what I called "sneaky hate." Today they call it microaggressions. All of it was and still is intolerable, even deadly.

I discovered what many white northerners really thought about Black people. It was convoluted and full of lies, and none of them were free of the thoughts, opinions, and assumptions that automatically classified you as either stupid or poor. It didn't matter who you really were. I defied their expectations and crushed their stereotypes. I'll never forget the look on Joe Kennedy's* face when I told him my grandfather went to college. He couldn't fathom it and said in disbelief, "Is that right?!!" His face was a map of confusion.

I started hearing two phrases from white people as a child. "Oh Janis, you're different." My piano teacher kept telling me that I couldn't study jazz piano because, "You must be a credit to your race." I hated her and endured her presence in my life for eight years. The last piece I learned under her tutelage was Rachmaninoff's Prelude in C Sharp Minor. Although I love for all kinds of music from Gregorian Chants to Zydeco, I haven't touched the piano since. Yet music is as vital to me as blood is. It's my life force.

I also discovered the Holocaust in elementary school, and what it did to the families of so many of my new Jewish friends. I learned this, not from textbooks, but through their stories or from whispered, gentle first-hand accounts from their parents. The image of the tattooed numbers on their forearms has never left me. Every time there's a movie or documentary about the Holocaust, I feel I have to watch it, because I never want to forget. The fact that these same Jews could be racist and circulated a petition saying they didn't want us in the neighborhood just made everything very messy and complicated. They couldn't figure out how we slipped into the neighborhood.

Blacks and Jews, both enslaved people, both subject to ignorant assumptions and stereotypes, denigrated, spit upon, targets of ignorance that could get us killed. What sense did this make to hold each other in contempt?

I grudgingly accepted that it mattered who and what white people thought of you. My job was to defy expectations, grab their assumptions, choke the life out of their stereotypes, bury, and replace them with a truth that was more complicated, more troubling, and more defiant. I learned this by the time I was twelve while Tina was spending all her time plotting and scheming to turn me into someone I would never be.

It was the beginning of an odd, complex existence for a little girl born with a veil over her face. By the time I graduated from college, not only did I have a B.F.A., but a PhD in white folks. And all of this was for the acquisition of a top-notch education. Meanwhile, I was stockpiling my pain, fear, rage, and insecurities until my freshman year at Bennington.

Chapter Twelve

About Drora

Drora Plaut and I met in the first grade. She was my first best friend. We remained best friends through elementary and junior high school. We would have terrible fights in elementary school and wouldn't speak for weeks or months at a time. Eventually, one of us would break down. The friendship resumed and we were fine. Looking back, Drora played a critical role in how I view injustice, cruelty, and the depth of political rage.

Drora and her family lived a few blocks from us in one of those pre-World War II, New York City apartment buildings where all the apartments seemed to have long hallways. Drora, her mother, her father, and younger sister, Esther, immigrated to the United States from Israel. Her parents were Auschwitz survivors. It was one of Hitler's highly efficient death camps for Jews during World War II. I could tell by looking at her father the physical toll it took on him. He was unnaturally small. It was the kind of "small" you associated with someone who had been malnourished at a critical stage of their development, who'd been neglected, who'd never received proper medical care. Mr. Plaut was very polite, gentle, and quiet, at least he was around me. All I remember about Esther was she was cute, and impish, with a wild head of thick, brown, curly hair. She reminded me of her father because of her size.

But it was Drora's mother who taught me about the horrors of Auschwitz without saying a word. One spring day, I was allowed to go to Drora's home. We walked down the hall and stopped in her mother's sewing room. She was a seamstress. It wasn't hot but her mother had a short-sleeved dress on as she ironed. On her right forearm, I saw a long line of numbers tattooed in dark ink. As I was looking at the numbers, I saw a flurry of nightmarish images that I didn't understand. As quickly as they appeared in my mind, they disappeared. I asked Drora why her mother had those numbers on her arm. Drora told me, "It's from the concentration camp." I had never heard of a concentration camp. It sent a chill down my back, and I wondered if those images I saw had anything to do with the numbers on Mrs. Plaut's arm and concentration camps.

"Both our people have been enslaved. We have to stick together," Drora told me. (And we did until school parted us.) Drora is the reason I searched for everything I could find out about World War II, the Nazis, the history of Israel post World War II, and the history of the Jewish people in ancient times. But I also wanted to know about Coptic Christians, Black Jews, the contemporary strife between Blacks and Jews, later how Jews supported Blacks during the Civil Rights Movement, and of course, the Palestinians and what they've lost. Emotionally, the strife, the wars, the loss of life, none of it made any sense to me. I was and am sickened by it all. Is this the best civilized people do to resolve disputes? Kill each other? Intellectually, I got it. I really got it. One must defend what they think is theirs and those they care about. Drora taught me nobody's cornered the market on pain and injustice. There was more than enough to spread around.

Drora was the reason I attended art school. If Drora was going to art school, *it had to be acceptable.* Tina knew "little Drora" so art school was okay. How could they say no? After all, education was very important to Jewish people and Mama and Papa! When Drora and I attended art school, I was thirteen. Somehow, we managed not to giggle when we had to draw nude models. (If Mama and Papa knew I had to draw live naked people, they would've snatched me out of that art school so fast my feet would've never touched the ground!) But they didn't and I made sure nobody in the house saw the drawings. It was easy because no one ever asked to see them. In a funny way, Drora was my passport to the outside world, a world where art school and drama school existed not to mention concerts, Broadway plays, and art museums!

We went our separate ways when college arrived. It would be several decades before I heard anything about Drora. She returned to my life when there was a junior high school reunion of our class, the s.p.e class, not the whole school. Many of us had been together from elementary school through junior high. I couldn't go, but my friend, Fee Hun Soo Hoo, went and filled me in.

Fee and her family had escaped from mainland China as Mao was taking over. They ended up in New York. I believe her father was a professor in China. I'm not sure. Fee rarely talked about her parents' backgrounds, their lives in China. In the United States, her father opened a laundry. I think they lived in the back of it. I never thought I'd out-live Drora and Fee. But I did.

Fee told me all about the reunion, who was there, who took photos, how everyone looked after all these years. I asked if Drora was there and Fee became silent. "JP," Fee eventually said,

"I can't take it." Something had happened to Drora. It wasn't exactly clear what from Fee's comments, but I knew enough to know it was bad, more specifically, it was intolerable. If Fee couldn't take it, and she was the epitome of stoicism, something must really be wrong. She told me Drora had asked about me and Fee eagerly gave me Drora's phone number, saying, "Good luck." I called Drora and we relived an explosion of memories! The giggles we shared made my eyes water. We remembered how amazed we were when some of our classmates started to wear bras. Drora was convinced some of the girls were stuffing them with tissues! She'd whisper to me, "They're wearing falsies!"

But there was more. I had been convinced Drora was going to become one of the best fashion illustrators in the business. I remember being so impressed with her drawings, and so were our teachers. Instead of fulfilling her potential, she bounced around from one non-profit agency to another doing some version of secretarial work. All of these agencies were focused on the Jewish community.

I made the mistake of mentioning how Israel had to listen to the Palestinian point of view. A different explosion erupted. It was one of rage and bitterness. What still echoes in my mind are Drora's words, "They want to push us into the sea." She made it clear that "we" can't let "them" do that. Somehow the Palestinians had to be destroyed. There was no reasoning with her. I never mentioned it again. But she did admit weeks later that she guessed the Palestinians were human too.

One day, I told Drora she had to let go of the anger, that it would eat her up. Drora was angry at the world, not to mention a number of people who let her and her family down over the years. There were so many, I couldn't keep track. But she reserved a special place for some relative who wouldn't sponsor their immigration to the United States. As I listened, I felt my body swell with sadness and worry.

Although I knew the answer, I kept asking myself what happened? Is this, the genetic legacy children of Holocaust survivors inherit? Was trauma imprinted in their DNA? There's similar talk about the genetic trauma of slavery regarding African Americans. I couldn't argue with that theory. If that is true, it would explain so much.

"You turned out very nice for a rich person," Drora told me. I thought my eyes were going to fall out. "We all knew," she said. "And then you went to that fancy college." I was stunned. I wanted to ask her, "Who the hell are you talking about?" I didn't know the person she was describing! But I listened carefully to find out who she thought I was. She remembered my clothes, my singing voice, my artwork, and most of all, the brownstone. And then, a total non-sequitur, she wondered why Fee didn't call her. I didn't.

I now understood why Drora had few friends. I understood why Fee couldn't take it. Drora was intense and also in pain, physically, emotionally, psychically. Sometimes I felt she was carrying the entire history of the Jewish people, every injustice and slight they had endured from the moment they set foot on earth. It was too much for any one person to hold. It was too much for me to feel and hold without wanting to sob.

Drora told me she had been diagnosed as bi-polar years before we reconnected. Suddenly, so many odd things about her as we were growing up made sense. One of the most memorable traits Drora had, was this frenzied giggle. I would always laugh with her but I knew that giggle wasn't right. It felt electric and not in a good way. Maybe that was an early sign, along with the intense fights we had, of the bi-polar disorder creeping into her system.

Drora married Artie, a videographer. They had no children and lived in lower Manhattan.

She survived breast cancer while Esther was taken from this life by ovarian cancer.

One day, Drora called and told me her cancer had returned. I felt a sense of darkness descend. I put my head in my hands and tried not to cry. So much had gone wrong for her.

I wasn't surprised there was a rift between her and her father. (I assumed her mother had died. She never talked about her and I didn't ask. If she wanted me to know, she would've told me.) I didn't know what the exact problem was. What I knew was Drora was actively dying and she needed her father to understand the end was coming. And she needed to talk to him but she wouldn't call. The bridge had been burned. Quietly, she asked if I would call him for her. I didn't have to think about it. I said, "Yes. Give me his number." Drora was shocked. "You'll do this for me?!" I knew what it felt like to have no one intercede on your behalf, to leave you emotionally marooned. So yes, I agreed to do that.

I called. Her father picked up the phone. I heard his quiet voice say, "Hello."

"Mr. Plaut? This is Janis Pryor, Drora's friend from elementary school. I don't know if you remember me, but..."

He cut me off and said, "Oh, I remember. I remember." I could feel him smiling on the other end of the phone. God knows what he remembered!

"I'm calling on Drora's behalf. You know she's dying and she needs to talk to you. She's in a lot of pain." We talked for a few minutes. He had to know at some level his oldest child was in trouble.

There was a pause. "Have you thought about negotiating in the Middle East?" he asked.

We both laughed. I told him no. I was doing this because Drora was my first best friend and she was and would always be special to me.

We chatted for a few more minutes, but I think he got the message. He knew his daughter was dying. He could feel it. I just knew that. Mr. Plaut had to be in his early nineties when we spoke. There's a special curse only some parents know. Mama and Papa knew. It's that hellacious grief when you outlive your children.

"Artie! Artie! She called. Janis called!" Drora said over and over. Her thick New York accent covered every word like a blanket! "I never thought you'd do that for me. You called. Oh, my God! Nobody else would do that. Oh my God!"

We talked about her and Artie coming to see me. I told her I had a guest room and would love to see them. But Drora was growing weaker. The chemo treatments took everything out of her. I could hear it in her voice.

One morning my phone rang and it was Artie. I suspected Drora was back in the hospital.

"Janis, it's Artie… it's about Drora."

"She's in the hospital?" I asked, holding my breath for a moment. I was afraid they had her hooked up to machines, a morphine drip sliding into her bloodstream.

I could hear him inhale and slowly exhale. "No. Drora died last night."

"No! What happened?" I didn't want to believe it, but I knew.

"We had an understanding. She was supposed to wake me if she needed to go to the bathroom in the middle of the night, so I could help her. I got up this morning and she wasn't in bed. I rushed into the bathroom and she was lying on the floor. She was gone."

I closed my eyes. There was too much to think about at that moment. What was foremost in my mind, was a long chapter of my life closed with Drora's passing. From 1956 'till death do us part. Heaviness set in and I felt light-headed.

"*Artie, I am so sorry.* I can only imagine how difficult it's been for you. I know she could be a handful."

"Yeah, she could. But I want to thank you."

"For what?"

"You were a true friend to Drora. She put your photo you sent right on the refrigerator. You did a lot for her. When we place the headstone I want you to come down…if you can. It would be an honor and I never met you!"

"Artie...that means a lot to me. You have my number so if you're ever up here, don't hesitate to call."

"Thank you. I appreciate that. I really do."

When I hung up, I knew we'd never meet.

As far as Tina was concerned, the Jews were the enemy. She always talked about how they tried to rob us, us being Black people. Of course, there were exceptions to the rule, just like I was the exception for so many white people. And Mama? Kosher food was blessed. Manischevitz wine was sweet. And the Jews were God's chosen people. What more did you need to know?

PART TWO:

Meeting Tina

Chapter Thirteen

Welcome To New York – The Mid-Fifties
Tina's Town

There was another body of water that helped define where I would live nine months of every year while in school. It was a cold blue-gray color. The sun was shining and the water was slightly choppy that first morning. The waves made me think of blue-gray ribbons undulating from the shores of Manhattan to the shores of New Jersey. I would learn in school that the body of water I saw that first morning in New York City was the Hudson River, named after Henry Hudson, who "discovered" it. I could see in the distance, a bridge named after President George Washington. There was a certain functional majesty about it. I was very impressed!

The noise of Manhattan was unlike anything I'd ever heard. Whishing sounds of cars flying by. Buses groaning and hissing with speed. And why was everybody honking their horns? There weren't many birds either, except for pigeons. The sky? Bland but the sun persisted.

There were a gazillion tall buildings. Did people actually live in these buildings? So many windows! Where were the trees? And the sidewalks were so wide! I'd never seen that much concrete except on television watching police stories. And how come we were riding with a white cab driver? Would he really take us to our New York house or was he going to drive someplace, get out, and kill us? Maybe the rules were different up here.

The cab pulled over and stopped. He opened the door for Mama so she and I could get out. Carefully he took our luggage

Mother's Madness

out of the trunk and set everything next to the front door. Mama paid him. He smiled, thanked her, and left. We lived in a brownstone, 392 Ft. Washington Avenue. Years later, I found out what stunned people was that *we owned* the brownstone.

The brownstone was chosen because it was located in the neighborhood of one of the best public schools in New York City. Those were the days when New York City public schools were excellent. I had to go to the best school possible. I didn't like it. I wanted to go back home.

It would be decades before I learned that to buy the brownstone, we had to find a white lady to "front" for us. In other words, the brownstone was signed over to her (with our money paying for the house) and then she "sold" it back to us. Black people couldn't buy houses anywhere they wanted. Money didn't matter. White people didn't want you near them in any significant way unless you were serving them.

You walked down three steps to the front door. The brownstone was four stories high, three bathrooms and what was once the servants' quarters on the fourth floor. Mama unlocked the front door and brought our luggage inside.

"Lyntine?!" That's what Mama called her.

The next thing I remember is looking at this light skinned woman with short reddish-brown hair, who wore a false smile that scared me, and eyes that were more like fences barricading all those other people that lived inside of her from stampeding out and doing things I couldn't imagine at five or six years old. But I could feel it. I stood behind Mama once the front door was locked.

"C'mere, baby. C'mere. I'm your mother. Let me hug you."

I didn't budge.

With a sing-song voice, she said, "Oh, you must be shy. Don't be shy. I'm your mother."

Mama looked at me and said, "Janis, this is your mother."

I didn't care who she was. I wanted nothing to do with her. If she was my mother, where had she been all these years? Why do I have no memory of her? And who are all those people hiding inside of her?

"Mama," Tina said, "She must be tired. That's okay. She'll be okay. She can hug me later." I never hugged her, ever, and I didn't want her touching me either.

Mama and Tina brought the luggage in from the foyer, closed the door that separated the hall from the foyer, and set everything down in the hallway. This big man rushed down the stairs like a waterfall, saw Mama and said, "Hey."

Mama nodded and kicked a smile from her mouth to the corners of her lips. It was a very tight, half smile. While he was putting on his coat, Tina said, "Harry, this is the baby." He continued putting his coat on and looked for a hat. "Janis, c'mon. This is your father."

I never left Mama's side. I was frozen with fear. He walked by me like I wasn't there, barely acknowledged Mama, and slammed the front door never saying a word to Tina. Mama glared at Tina.

The hallway led to the kitchen. It was big and looked out into the backyard. The yard was punctuated with a very large tree and bordered by two apartment buildings and a synagogue. There was a driveway enclosed by a large iron gate at one end and a small garage at the other end. I had no idea how unusual this was. What I did know was all of it was grim and made me sad.

Mama looked around the kitchen. You didn't know what Mama was thinking unless you had learned to read her eyes.

"Lyntine, these cabinets look brand new."

"A-huh... I bought 'em. The kitchen needed cabinets," Tina said.

"Um-hmm," Mama responded. I remember this exchange because from the tone of Mama's voice, I was convinced she was going to slap Tina into next year.

"Mama, let me take you and the baby upstairs. You can see your bedrooms." Tina pivoted and stomped up the stairs to the second floor. Three bedrooms on the second floor. Tina's bedroom was at one end and Mama's bedroom at the other.

"Where's the baby's bedroom?" Mama asked.

"Oh! Well, it's in the middle. She can get to her bedroom. She'll have to go through one of our bedrooms to get in or out."

"Um-hmm," Mama said.

Tina opened the door to Mama's bedroom. It was huge. There was a fireplace. It didn't work. Tina had it closed. Everything was huge, windows, ceilings, but there was a little balcony, the kind you saw in productions of Romeo and Juliet that overlooked the front door and the street.

"C'mon Janis. Let me show you your room," Tina said. She opened a set of French doors in Mama's room revealing a small bedroom. Mama and I walked in behind Tina. "See, you have a closet and everything."

The room made me feel like I was suffocating.

"What happened to the windows?" I asked. This is where Doctor Radna came to see me in the middle of the night after my first nosebleed. He was a Russian Jew, with a big moustache, thinning black hair and kind eyes. This is where he would talk to Mama in hushed whispers about my nosebleeds. And this is the room I would flee from when Harry went on one of his weekend rampages.

Tina looked at me and then the windows. "What? What do you mean?"

"I can't see out of them. What happened?"

"Oh." She paused. "Those are frosted windows."

I looked at Mama and I looked at the windows. "Why?" I asked.

"Why what?" Tina asked.

"Why are they frosted?"

"So the people in the synagogue can't see in," Tina said.

"Can you open the windows?" I asked.

"Open the windows? Umm, well you can, but why would you want to do that? There's no need to open them."

"I need air," I said.

"You'll be able to breathe," Tina said. Her voice changed and I could tell she was getting annoyed.

"What's that silver thing between the windows?"

"Radiators, Janis. Those are radiators. That's how you get heat in the winter."

I turned to Mama and said, "There's no sun."

"I know, baby," Mama said.

"The closet is behind me, to the left," Tina said.

There was something opposite the closet that also had two doors. I pointed to it and asked, "What's that?"

"That's my shoe closet. That's where I keep all of my shoes." Tina smiled.

"Lyntine, you have a shoe closet? How many pairs of shoes do you have?" Mama asked. She was really annoyed. You could tell now by the look on her face *and* the tone of her voice.

"Mama, I have to put my shoes somewhere," Tina said. "I'm going to bring up your luggage and tomorrow, Janis, you and I are going shopping."

Little did I know at the time, that shopping would be one of the few things Tina and I would ever do together unless she was coerced by some authority greater than herself to take me somewhere. An authority greater than herself? Guilt was a contender, although she acted like there was *no authority greater than herself!* I didn't know then that Tina believed she knew everything! I would find out in painful, costly ways.

Shopping, the beauty parlor, ballet and piano lessons, and the orthodontist, these were the primary ways we related to each other. Nothing else mattered to her. She was determined to "fix" me. Attending art school, studying drama and the theatre were beyond her grasp. I was a puzzle to her from the very beginning. What did she care about eventually? "All that beautiful orthodonture work." That's how she referred to my braces, a rite of passage for some children.

Shopping became a Saturday ritual, interrupted only by trips to the beauty parlor during grade school or trying to recover from one of Harry's Friday night demonstrations of alcoholic madness. Fifth Avenue became my second home, Bergdorf's, Saks, an upscale shoe store, I. Miller, where Tina was known, Lord and Taylor, B. Altman's and then down 34th Street to Macy's. At that time, Macy's had an extraordinary delicatessen in the basement. I found the aroma of pastrami intoxicating. I loved pastrami on rye with brown mustard. Lox, knishes, babka, this was a form of heaven. Chopped liver with little bits of hard-boiled egg could be used for sandwiches. Fabulous food. Right up there with bologna sandwiches on wheat bread with sliced tomatoes and mayo!

But my wardrobe was Tina's main interest followed by my overall appearance. I had a problem. I was tiny. I was passing for five years old until I was eight! I was always the first or second in line at school because I wasn't very tall! What did that mean as far as Tina was concerned? All my clothes had to be altered to fit properly. And then, my feet were a problem. They were not only small but narrow, and narrow feet meant narrow heels. God forbid if the shoes slipped off my feet. Shoe salesmen would run around and find these "things" to put in the heels of my shoes to insure a better fit. I became very finicky about what shoes I would wear. Tina ignored that and bought me shoes she liked. I wouldn't wear the shoes. Eventually, she gave up and bought me shoes I liked. It was a fashion defeat for her, the first of many that would follow.

All the salespeople knew us at Lord and Taylor on the children's clothing floor. They would greet her with big smiles. "What can we get for you today, Mrs. Pryor?" She would pick out two or three things for me to try on. I hated trying on clothes. But before we went into the dressing room, she would turn the clothes inside out and examine the seams while the salesperson would sweat bullets.

"No, no," Tina would say. "This seam isn't done right. Look at this? My daughter's not wearing this."

The salesperson looked at the piece of clothing, often with a blank expression.

"We don't want this. I want something made better than this," Tina would say in a tone that made you feel like pond scum. I stood and watched. She would throw the clothes on the counter and look around.

The salesperson ran off to find some clothing Tina would like. Eventually the salesperson came back with an armful of dresses, skirts, jackets. While showing the clothing to Tina, they mustered up the nerve on this occasion to ask Tina. "Mrs. Pryor, how do you know all of this about clothes, seams, stitches?"

Tina looked the salesperson dead in the eye and answered as if she were annoyed and couldn't be bothered with their questions. It was a look that sent trepidations all through you. "Home Economics. I took Home Economics." You would've thought she was talking about brain surgery from her smug demeanor.

Ballet lessons were different. I had never seen a pair of tights nor a leotard until then. I was very uncomfortable. I felt trapped in these clothes but the ballet slippers were really cute. I got a glimpse of pink, satin toe shoes in another studio. They captivated me. I thought they were beautiful. Our ballet teacher, a lean, muscular, white man with thick, dark brown hair, told us if we worked really hard, we could dance in toe shoes one day. The toe shoes motivated me in class. Ten or twelve little girls of all colors lined up, shoulders, arms and hands extended so everything gracefully flowed, elbows just so. I still remember, first position, second position, third position and fourth. I loved ballet in all forms, and still do.

Tina asked to speak to the teacher one Saturday. I had changed into my street clothes. My leotard, tights, and ballet shoes were in a tote bag.

The teacher walked over to Tina. He smiled at me.

"Mrs. Pryor, what can I do for you?"

Tina became a detective. Her eyes narrowed and she asked almost in a whisper, "Is she any good?" She tried to smile. She wasn't successful.

"Oh, my goodness," and he laughed, smiled at me, and looked at Tina. I was nervous. What was he going to say? "Mrs.

Pryor, Janis is very graceful when dancing. She's got the perfect body for ballet if she stays lean. She has great potential even though she's started late. If she keeps working and practicing, she will make it to toe shoes, easily."

I almost exploded with joy. Soon I could get my own pair of pink toe shoes. (To this day, I still think about having my own pair of pink toe shoes!) He smiled at me again. At that moment, Tina's face turned to stone. All she said to my teacher was, "I see. Well, thank you." She grabbed my hand and almost yanked me out of the studio. We waited for the elevator. Barely moving her lips, she said, "They won't let you be a ballerina." She didn't say another word. No more ballet lessons for me. I was crushed. But I discovered the Bolshoi, Rudolph Nureyev and Margot Fonteyn, Mikhail Baryshnikov, The American Ballet Theatre and George Balanchine, Arthur Mitchell and The Dance Theatre of Harlem, Alvin Ailey, Twyla Tharp, the legendary Martha Graham, Broadway's iconic Bob Fosse, and eventually the short lived but powerful Native American Dance Theatre. Going to a dance concert is akin to a religious experience for me! I never got over my longing for pink toe shoes nor my love of ballet. I never saw any ballet dancers of color while growing up. There was a lot of talk about how black female bodies weren't "built right..." for ballet. Too big. But I wasn't big. When Misty Copeland came along, I almost exploded with joy. I felt vindicated.

Ballet was just the beginning. I had other surprises for Tina and she understood none of them. But what I grew to understand was Tina thrived in New York, soared to heights in the North that were impossible for her in the South. Tina embraced New York City with a ferocity that reminded me of a starving animal finding food. Black Mississippians who "get out" and become successful (as defined by white people) represent a rarified example of surviving. It should be something to be proud of. It should be the root of your strength. After all, we're the descendants of those who didn't die in the Middle Passage. For Tina, it was the core of her shame.

Mama and Papa taught me I had to be smarter and better than white people, and *maybe* you could be anything you wanted to be. But it was Tina who made sure I knew that white people would never let you be all that you can be. And they would never pay you what you deserved. Tricks, lies, and deceit were everywhere! So, one had to be pragmatically persistent, hard-working, focused, and right with God, morally centered if you were going to survive as a Black person in America. You had to learn how to "cope."

Remember, with all of that Mama never allowed me to believe or even say, "I can't." Mama's solution was, "You can, with God's help."

Tina told me in a thousand different ways to never trust a white person, *never* expect them to understand, *never* expect them to treat you with decency and consideration. "They'll *never* operate in your best interests," she said over and over. Tina was angry, bitter, and at best ambivalent on good days. She hated them for thwarting her ambition and envied them with their privilege afforded by color. Often people said things around Tina not realizing she was Black. She knew what white people really thought about Black people. I watched her interact with white people in New York. She smiled and laughed and listened to them attentively, much in the same way Mama would. But the minute they turned their backs and walked away Tina's pleasant, attractive face transformed into one full of contempt. It was unsettling to watch. She was going to make sure I could hold my own with any well-to-do white person. They were the only ones that counted. She dismissed from consideration anyone of color regardless, and she didn't trust anyone who was poor. Poverty, as far as Tina was concerned was a cardinal sin and a character flaw.

I would make the painful discovery, over and over, as I grew up, that Tina was right about many things. To this day I'm finding out she's still right in various and unexpected ways. Her rage was justified. Her bitterness honest. I would discover before she died that her responses to the monster of racism were jaw dropping.

Chapter Fourteen

School

When I started elementary school, I knew how to read and write. Mama and I had our first serious conflict when she taught me to write. She put a piece of lined paper in front of me one day, along with several pencils. She asked me to pick one up. I reached for one with my left hand.

"No, no. You mustn't use your left hand, baby."

"Why?"

"That's bad," she said. "Use your right hand."

I was almost four years old and livid. I wanted to ask her, "What's wrong with my left hand?" But I didn't. I continued to seethe (for the rest of my life) and defied her when she wasn't looking. To this day, I am partially ambidextrous. I can draw with both hands and write with my left if I have to. It's not as good as my right hand, but you can read what I've written. I'm told my handwriting is quite distinctive. Every time I hear that I say to myself, "Not as distinctive as it would've been with my left hand!"

I walked into P.S. 173 ready! Tina would go to Barnes and Noble and buy the reading textbooks used in class for me to read at home. Doing homework was attacked with great passion, discipline, and fierce determination. When I finished, I had to go over all of it with Tina and Mama every night, reading, arithmetic, spelling, current events. We had to select a story from the newspaper, cut it out with a photo preferably, and give a verbal summary of the story the next day. Tina constantly told me I would stand out in class, so I had to be twice as smart. She was right.

Grade school in the mid to late fifties and early sixties was quite different from what it is today in the 21st century. Early on, we started taking the IOWA tests and a battery of exams to measure our reading comprehension. It became an unspoken rule that you had to be at least three grades ahead in your reading. Anything less was unacceptable. We started reading the New York Times in the fourth grade. I can still see our teacher standing in front of the classroom giving us a lesson on how to hold and fold the Times if we were reading it on the bus or subway. It was important to know this so we wouldn't hit other people in the face with the paper. I've been reading the New York Times ever since. I remember teachers telling us how we had to prepare for college as early as the third and fourth grades. Eventually we heard about the dreaded annual tests in New York State, the Regents' Exams. You had to pass them. School was no joke nor was breakfast.

Our fourth grade teacher went around the room *every morning* asking us what we had for breakfast! You had to be specific. She believed breakfast was the most important meal of the day. To this day, (and until I die), I have breakfast! When I started working in political campaigns, breakfast was the only meal I could count on. Double reinforcement about the value of breakfast!

I always got good reports from my teachers during the parent-teacher conferences. Tina would come back, talking as if she were the student who'd received these accolades. The teachers liked me. The one troubling comment was, "Janis can be withdrawn but her work is very good. We know she's listening." During the first and second grades my teacher would stop by our house on the way to school, pick me up, and we would walk four blocks to P.S. 173. Mama and Tina felt honored by this. So, each morning, Mrs. Geveritz and I went to school. She was a short, plump lady with dark hair who wore glasses. I liked her.

During one of those elementary school parent-teacher conferences, early on, maybe the second or third grade, something changed. Tina walked into the brownstone with a very odd look on her face and almost raced to the kitchen. Her face looked like a roadmap of bewilderment, fear, and shock. She wasn't happy, that much I knew. I was terrified.

Mama was standing in the kitchen preparing to cook. Looking at Tina, she asked, "What is wrong?"

Tina put her handbag down while I stood fearfully in the door so I could hear. Tina, wide eyed, in almost a whisper, told Mama, "She's got a high IQ." She paused, unbuttoned her coat, took a breath and said, "Creative... The tests show she's creative, something visual... gifted. Reading comprehension excels. Mama, it's a high number, way above average."

Wiping her hands on her apron, Mama said, "Lyntine, that's wonderful. We want to keep that up. George was smart like that."

Tina stared out the window. I was confused. Mama looked happy. Tina looked stricken. Was it bad to be gifted, to be smart? I thought that was what they wanted. That's why I'm here in this awful city. I had caused Tina's world to radically shift just by being born. Now this. It felt like I was the cause of something wretched. More trouble for me. More difficulties trying to get along with this woman they wanted me to believe was my mother.

Sensing my presence, Tina turned around, slapped a smile on her face and said, "Hi, baby! The teacher says you're brilliant. Hot dog! Brilliant." Tina, the Proud Parent, had just made her first disingenuous appearance. This version of Tina wouldn't appear often in my life, perhaps three more times before she died.

Tina was thrown by this development, but she recouped quickly. She thought my intelligence made me a problem free child. She would have nothing to worry about. I would be compliant. She could control me. If she said jump, I would ask, "How high?" Everything would be smooth sailing, when in fact just the opposite started to unfold. Aside from the talent and intelligence, she discovered another quality in me that intimidated her. She never imagined her daughter would have such strong opinions ever, much less in a child's body! And I could be unnervingly stubborn like Mama. As long as Tina felt she knew more than me, she felt in control. Tina had roughly twelve years to feel superior. I was Tina's square peg that she kept trying to fit in the round hole of her dreams for me. I started to fight for my life. She got the wrong daughter.

One of our first battles had life-long consequences for me. Tina came home one day, beaming, and announced that she was going to enroll me in Jack and Jill. All I knew then was Jack and Jill was a nursery rhyme! For African-American middle-class families, it was much more than that.

Given that I had no Black friends in New York during elementary school, Jack and Jill was the perfect solution as far as Tina was concerned. In her own way, my mother was trying to do the right thing. I overheard her talking to Mama. Tina had an almost desperate tone in her voice when she asked Mama, "But who is she going to marry?"

Jack and Jill, Inc. is a non-profit organization founded on January 24, 1938 in Philadelphia by Marion Stubbs Thomas and twenty African-American mothers with children between the ages of two and nineteen. The purpose? To bring together "children in a social and cultural environment." The formal goals, all of them noble and honorable, are itemized on their website. The informal goals were and still are to provide a social network for middle-class, well to do, African American children so they could meet the "right kind of people," their "own kind" and eventually, potential marriage partners. Jack and Jill gave their children the social skills and familiarity to navigate the upper-class white world.

Mama expressed nothing but disdain to me and everyone else about marriage. I should never aspire to that. She told me over and over, "You can get an M.R.S. degree anytime. What you need to do is get your education and you won't have to depend on anyone." Every time she said this, she would close with, "You must be independent." That was her mantra. As a child, I wasn't really sure what marriage entailed, but whatever it was the tone of Mama's voice scared me. The tone said, "Forget marriage!" And I did. Add to that what I witnessed almost every weekend between Tina and Harry, forgetting marriage wasn't hard. It was and never has been a priority for me.

But it was a priority for Tina. It would give her an opportunity to show off and demonstrate to her peers just how much she could give to her daughter. Tina promised me "lots of Cadillacs" for my wedding. Joining Jack and Jill was the first step down the aisle. I couldn't hear Mama's response to Tina's ideas. What I saw was Mama glaring at Tina and then turning her back on her daughter. That was enough for me.

Later that evening, Tina marched over to me and said, "You're going to join Jack and Jill."

I looked up at her and said, "No I'm not." I knew Jack and Jill was a trap and I wanted nothing to do with it.

"What do you mean, no you're not?! You'll do what I say you'll do," she shot back.

I held my ground and told her, "No, I'm not. I'm going to ask Papa if I have to join and if he says no, I won't go." Tina didn't know what to say. Her mouth hung open slightly. I left her standing and staring at me. Papa was in the living room. I told him, "Tina wants me to join this group called Jack and Jill, Papa. I don't want to do it. It sounds silly."

Papa and Tina talked for a few minutes. I never heard anything about me joining Jack and Jill ever again. Looking back on that incident, I think Tina stopped seeing me as her daughter, and started seeing me as "the enemy," a rival that either had to be controlled, defeated and/or destroyed so I would never pose a threat to her again. All of this animosity was expressed whenever she called me, "You little red bitch!" The older I became, the more often I would hear that when she wasn't calling me, Red. She said, "There's too much damned red in your skin." We were part Native American. What did she expect? My teachers saw it in my face!

What gave me the boldness to defy Tina? After all, as someone said, she *was* your mother. No. She was my grandparent's daughter and she had to answer to them, just like I did. They were the final authority in my mind, not her. Tina was a make-believe mother, a fake, someone to present to the public, a pretend mom, who said all the right things in public…with charm. Someone to serve as an interlocutor on behalf of Mama and Papa. Tina knew this and she knew that I knew also. She had not one clue as how to raise me. She floundered with every attempt, like a fish out of water, flapping, desperate, terrified.

I was slow to make friends in elementary school but by the time I graduated, I had a gang of friends, all of them white. We marched into Junior High School 115 and took over! We were the smart kids!

The only prolonged or meaningful contact I had with children who looked like me was when I went down home and even that was highly curtailed.

I was becoming a foreigner among my own people, a cultural freak, and more inexplicable to Tina with every book I read, every piece of artwork I created, and every independent trip I made to Saks, Bergdorf's and a store she knew nothing about, Henri Bendel's. The results? I was a fashion beast! By the time I was in my early thirties, I was a heat-seeking missile when it came to designer clothes. I had a particular fondness for Armani. I could spot his clothes a mile away, never needed to see the label. I thought he was and is a master of elegant, understated, beautifully made clothing. I understood what made Armani's clothes so extraordinary, but the sound of his name frightened Tina. By the time I was fifteen, I understood the difference between style and trend and valued timeless design over fads.

I was becoming a very good student in every subject but math. Art, drama, literature, and creative writing became my specialties. I could fake my way through science, but math was a problem that resulted in poor grades. And a poor grade was really a big problem. Tina had an idea to help me with math.

"You know," she began one day, "your father is very good in math. He can help you."

I froze. How could I get out of this? I was going to have to be around this man. I'll never be good at math. And I wasn't.

Tina's plan was ingenious. She thought I could learn math by playing cards with Harry. I can't remember how many sessions I had with him. The three of us would march down to the "rec room" in the basement, sit at the bar while he dealt cards. I looked calm, but my brain shut down, my stomach knotted, my breathing was shallow and my heart felt suspended in motion. I was certain he was going to erupt into rage right in the middle of playing Blackjack or Pit-A-Pat. He didn't, and he didn't say a word to me either. He barely looked at me. It was almost as if I wasn't there.

Tina's ingenious plan had very limited results, so she found a tutor for me. Her name was Edna Sahl, and she lived within walking distance of our brownstone. She was the first person who really believed in me without qualifications or obligations. Our relationship was life-long. Whenever I face disappointment regarding my work, especially when it came to writing, Edna Sahl's distinctive voice of encouragement comes to mind. She was so patient with me. We'd sit in this wonderful room in her apartment. It was filled with books neatly arranged. Mrs. Sahl also introduced me to Gouda cheese! She'd slice the cheese and put a piece on a cracker for me. I loved it! And one week, we had Muenster cheese. There was nothing like this at the brownstone. Every now and then, Tina would come home with this huge, rectangular block of yellow cheese she'd taken from the school.

Learning math with Edna Sahl made sense. Everything about algebra, geometry and later, French, was clear as a bell when we worked together. The minute I took a test, my brain shut down. I managed to just pass those exams. Math became interchangeable with Harry. Anything that has to do with numbers still poses an emotional block greater than the

Canadian Rockies. If I become really upset, I'm unable to do simple arithmetic, no adding, no subtracting, no multiplication. I can add a column of numbers and get several different answers! My brain goes on lockdown. It would not be an exaggeration to say when it comes to math or simple arithmetic, I have PTSD. The condition was diagnosed by a doctor decades later. This is Harry's legacy to me.

Chapter Fifteen

Payback, Psychics, and Junior High

When Mama and I were down home, I wasn't allowed to go to anybody's house alone. No activities for me (and that included church activities.) I sat on the porch and read. In New York I did get a few invitations from classmates to come to their homes. Mama and Tina were very skeptical. They didn't think the invitations were sincere coming from white people. Why would they want to invite me? Tina often told me, "They don't want you in their homes!" Then Mama reminded me about the chance you took eating at other people's homes, especially if they were white. "Remember, they might poison you," Mama would say softly. "You don't know, baby. You can't trust 'em."

It was easier for me to invite kids over, sort of. During Junior High, I had several parties in the "rec room" in the basement. One friend from that time, still remembers them! The concern expressed by Mama and Tina had to do with the children's safety. If anything happened to them while they were at our house... As Black people, what would their parents do to us? Would we be sued? Run out of the neighborhood? I was reminded of that petition that went around when the neighbors heard a Black family was moving in, and not just anywhere, but the brownstone!

Having kids over was dangerous. Sleepovers or pajama parties were out. Every time I got permission to have friends over, I now knew that represented a huge risk because we didn't have the same rights as white people. We wouldn't be given the benefit of the doubt, so nothing better happen to those kids while they were in our care. I spent a lot of time alone and learned to absorb disappointment on a regular basis.

Since going to a friend's house or having friends over required something akin to cross-cultural negotiations that went on for days and always resulted in somebody getting mad, it was easier convincing Tina to take my friends and me out. That way I got to play with my friends and no one had to worry about me getting poisoned or my friends getting hurt at the brownstone. It also allowed Tina to show-off and demonstrate that she had enough money to treat these white children to an afternoon out. She loved it! So, for most of elementary school there was the annual trip to Palisades Amusement Park in New Jersey. Before going, Mama warned me about the Ferris Wheel. It was dangerous and I shouldn't get on it. What if I fell out or it got stuck? And don't even think about the roller coaster. Keep your feet on the ground. Let the earth serve as your root.

Tina was baffled by everything about me. One day she asked me, "How did you get to be around so many white people?"

I looked into her unhealthy, slightly yellow eyes and said, "You put me there. I didn't choose to live in a white neighborhood."

Her lips parted slightly. With great reluctance, all she could say was, "Oh."

The balance of power was beginning to tilt in my favor, so I thought. Tina felt superior for six years. Once I set foot in junior high things changed. We had been playing "checkers" in elementary school. Now, we started playing "chess." We'd have these verbal fights that would almost paralyze her. The only defense she had was cruelty. She was a master of humiliation while I used silence to unnerve her.

One day while looking for something in Mama's bedroom closet, Tina marched in, glared at me, and announced, "Your grandfather doesn't love you. You're just a tax write-off for him with all those trust accounts. That's all." And she marched out! Didn't she think I would tell Papa what she said? *That was the exact moment I decided to make her pay for hurting me.*

Every time she indulged in this craziness, I shopped, and charged everything to her. The more she hurt me, the more I charged. This practice lasted well into my adult years. She compounded matters because she would tell me to go downtown and buy, "…shoes, coats, pants, dresses", whatever she felt I needed. When the bills came, she couldn't remember if it was a purchase she ordered me to make or one of my revenge sprees. That distinction determined whether or not the purchase would send us into destitution!

It didn't help to have Mama or Papa point out, "Lyntine, you told her to go downtown and buy those things." Or as Papa often told her, "Tina, you can't buy her affection." Mama became very cross over these incidents and Tina's declaration of impending destitution. Mama would call me into her bedroom and tell me, "Don't worry about money. Don't ever worry about it." But I did. I became frightened of money. The PTSD regarding numbers that established itself with Harry became deeply rooted when it came to money. It still is.

I'd hear Mama chastise Tina about her ranting and raving regarding money. Tina ignored Mama and I ignored Tina's feigned distress. As time slid by, she became more and more dramatic. She'd walk around the house, usually with a drink in her hand, bemoaning how we're all going to go on welfare because of me. I was going to be the cause of the family's downfall. No matter how much money Tina had, it was never enough. This became her mantra. "You're going to make us go on welfare, Janis. Yes, you will." That meant, "Janis, there'll be less money for me."

When she wasn't forecasting our financial doom, she wrapped herself up in sacrifice and martyrdom. The scene was always the same. I'd come back from downtown and she'd inspect my latest acquisitions. She'd look wistfully at the shoes, pants, suits, whatever, and say in her most pitiful voice, "That's okay. I don't need anything. I can go buy something cheap. I don't need much… Why would I need ___?" Fill in the blank: shoes, dresses, blouses. Unfortunately, this never extracted the response she wanted from me.

I'd wait until she finished, look at her and say, "That's stupid. You should buy yourself something." And I'd walk away with my new purchases. I never let on that I knew she was racking up jewels and furs. I watched this until I left for college leaving behind her madness that often whiffed of Chivas Regal. I think scotch helped her endure my other act of revenge. I would jump out of a coat closet I knew she'd be opening and try to scare her to death! That really shook her up and made me laugh until it hurt.

She squelched ballet while I was in elementary school. I terrified her in junior high school. I became totally incomprehensible. She didn't count on drama, the visual arts, and the scariest ability of all from her perspective, writing. She asked Mrs. Grover during one of the parent-teacher conferences when I was in the seventh grade if I was college material. I know this because Tina told me. She was taken aback when Mrs. Grover said, "Of course she is!" Once again, Tina was stricken, stunned and told Mama. Mama looked at her, bewildered by her daughter's response.

Everything my teachers told Tina about my gifts, she dismissed. None of this was what she wanted but she would manage to take credit for my accomplishments, as if the accolades were for her, to smile graciously when I received compliments, as if I wasn't there. Maybe she thought she could steal them and render me useless. She didn't understand why writing, art, drama, literature came so easily to me. Her frustration was palpable. And she couldn't steal the veil. She didn't dare try. That genuinely scared her. Every now and then I'd catch her glaring at me.

"What's wrong?" I asked.

"Nothing. Mind your business."

Every spring in junior high there was a play or a set of skits performed by the students. Auditions were held. Somewhere I had picked up the talent of imitating people. At the time, the Jets were the new guys on the football scene. A quarterback named Joe Namath was getting a lot of publicity. New York City was ecstatic! A series of commercials started to run introducing the team to the city through the persona of "Jet Set Janie." I became Jet Set Janie, high pitched voice, excited and thrilled by the Jets. I wrote a skit based on Janie's commercials, auditioned using the skit, and was chosen for the annual drama production. Mr. Schmitt was our coach, director, and teacher.

I was funny and he said I had a great sense of timing. I got the lead role in the longest skit. But there was also a skit straight out of musical theatre. I was enchanted. I felt like I had discovered a brand-new world. *Another opening/another show/from Philly, Boston and Buffalo...* The best part? It wasn't boring. There were three skits. Three casts received enthusiastic applause with the

Mother's Madness

leads featured. When it was my turn to step forward and take a bow, many people stood, clapped and yelled. It was great. Tina came and when we walked home, several people congratulated me. Tina said, "Thank you so much." As we were walking, Mr. Schmitt caught up with us. I introduced him to Tina.

"So nice to meet you," Tina said, oozing charm. Mr. Schmitt smiled. Before he could say anything, Tina asked him, "Is Janis any good?"

I remember him looking surprised and slightly dumbfounded. He had a beige sweater thrown around his shoulders, a pair of cream-colored gabardine pants and tan nubuck shoes. He readjusted his sweater before saying anything. When he did, he looked her directly in the eye and said, "Oh my God, yes! She should think about trying out for the High School of Performing Arts." He looked at me and smiled before continuing. "She has a great sense of timing. Performers kill for it. She'd make a great comedienne."

"Really?" Tina said, her voice jumping at least an octave. You got the impression that this information harmed her in some way. The quiet before the storm of adolescence just arrived.

He quickly scrutinized Tina, looked at me again and said, "Janis, great performance." He winked his eye at me and crossed the street. Tina didn't say a word. As soon as his back turned her smile fell, the eyes froze, her skin was a blanket of contempt. Monstrous. Her eyes reminded me of Edvard Munch's painting, The Scream. Tina was where the scream originated. We walked the rest of the way to the brownstone in silence. I knew what the problem was. The applause, the compliments and the recognition, none of it was for her.

I often thought about these moments with Tina. What happened to her? Did Mama and Papa give all the attention to

George and none to Tina? He was "the son". He was highly valued. The expectations were huge. I could sense that listening to Mama talk about him. She rarely spoke of him, but when she did, you had the feeling that the world had been robbed of a young black man with amazing intelligence and foresight. Not Tina. Mama only "mentioned" Tina and when she did it always referred to something Tina messed up. As far as Mama was concerned, Tina was a bitter disappointment.

As for me seeing the dead and other things she couldn't explain, Tina pretended she wasn't bothered by it. She was paralyzed by it. Tina couldn't kill that, or even make an attempt without sentencing herself to hell in a room with her name on the door. Hell, as in fire and brimstone and eternal damnation. That was her version of hell. My version of hell was living with her.

I slowly began to realize what I knew intuitively when I first met her. All those "people" hiding behind her eyes were dark elements in Tina's personality. It would be decades before I discovered how dark.

One Saturday morning, Tina informed me that we were going to visit a psychic. I had heard Tina talking about her to Mama. Mrs. Jordan had special powers, insights, and gifts. I must have been thirteen or fourteen when Tina took me to see Mrs. Jordan. She was blind. I remember she had jet-black hair that was neatly curled. She wore dark sunglasses and an off-yellow cotton dress. Her skin was the color of Hershey's chocolate.

Mrs. Jordan lived in a walk-up. So up the stairs we went. When we got to her floor, there was a long line of people in the hall. Tina walked to the front of the line and knocked on the door. A young African-American woman cracked it open. Tina whispered something to her and I heard the young woman say,

Mother's Madness

"Come right in." I was trying not to stare at the people standing in line. There was nothing wrong with them. I simply hadn't been around that many Black people outside of junior high school. Northern Black folks were different from Southern Black folks. These people in the hall were tense, nervous, some felt desperate. I felt as if I were being suffocated by their emotions. I felt everything they were feeling. The dimly lit hallway didn't help. I wanted to leave.

"Janis, c'mon," Tina said.

I turned and followed her into the apartment. It was tiny. Two women were seated in the living room. One was smoking. She never lifted her head to look at anybody. The living room had one window. Opposite the couch were closed French doors. Once again, I felt like I was being suffocated. I really wanted to leave now. This trapped sensation was washing over me.

Suddenly the French doors opened revealing an older African American woman seated in a recliner in front of her bed. She wore sunglasses. I could feel her kindness. There was a gentle quality about her that put me at ease. The young woman stood next to her and lying at her feet, was a German Shephard, alert, watchful, somber. He looked at me and slowly wagged his tail.

"Tina, you came. You bring your daughter?"

"Yes ma'am," Tina said to Mrs. Jordan.

"Oh, Tina! I'm so glad you could come and you brought the baby. I'm so glad. Tina, give me your hand." Turning her head slightly towards me, Mrs. Jordan said softly, "Give me your hand, darling."

I remember her slightly squeezing my hand and then smiling. She held Tina's hand also. Mrs. Jordan turned her head towards Tina and said, "Oh Tina. Yes, yes, yes… she is the older one here."

Tina looked perplexed and slightly anxious. "Oh Mrs. Jordan, no, no. I'm the mother. She's the daughter. I'm her mother. I'm older than she is!" Tina's eyes darted between me and Mrs. Jordan.

"Hmmm, no, no, Tina. I'm not talking about that. Of course, you are the mother, but your child is the old one here. She understands. She knows. Your child walks in many worlds already. She can go deep and far, on both sides of the veil. You must listen to her…"

"No, no. That can't be. I'm the mother…"

Tina was cut off by the Mrs. Jordan again. "You are not hearing me. This little girl is an old soul, a very old soul. She sees things you cannot see. She knows things you do not know. You must listen to what she says." Mrs. Jordan was still holding my hand. *"She's here to teach you."*

Tina looked at me, panic stricken, trying not to appear shocked and stated, "Well, we know she's very smart, very…"

Mrs. Jordan, cutting her off again, looked up at Tina, still holding both of our hands, and said, "Tina leave us. I need to talk to your daughter."

The corners of Tina's mouth dropped. Her face turned to stone and her eyes hardened. For a moment, I thought she had stopped breathing. Tina tried to smile and left the room.

"I'll be right outside," Tina said.

Mrs. Jordan looked up at me from her chair. She appeared old yet ageless. Her eyes may have been blind, but it felt like she was looking through my heart and beyond. Maybe she saw my soul and maybe it was behind my heart. I didn't know. She smiled at me and held my right hand tightly. I felt like I was in a state of suspended animation. Her hands were soft, warm, and tingled slightly.

We didn't spend more than a few minutes together according to the clock, but I had the sense that we had spent hours together. What happened between us has no words. It can't be talked about nor written about. We don't know how to communicate this kind of exchange, and I'm not sure we should. It can only be experienced and felt at some profound and unfathomable level. It was clear to me that we had gone somewhere and when I left her room, I had the same sensation I had when I was a little girl and saw Uncle George seated at the foot of my bed. I never forgot that experience and I never forgot those moments with Mrs. Jordan when time seemed to stop.

As Tina and I left the building, she asked me, "What happened?"

I looked at her and said quietly, "Nothing." Tina looked at me out of the side of her eye. I told her, "You should keep seeing Mrs. Jordan. She's an amazing lady."

Standing next to Tina, I wanted to run. I knew what Mrs. Jordan was telling me. I felt it and realized I had to remain silent. I also believed if Tina realized I understood the full import of what Mrs. Jordan said, she'd throw me in front of a moving car.

We stood on the sidewalk. Tina pretended to look for a cab but she kept eyeing me. I could tell she was immensely irritated by my response. Once again, I wouldn't do what she wanted me to do. I thought she was going to cry. Her jaw and chin were trembling. Tina finally hailed a cab, and we went downtown to shop. She never spoke of our visit to Mrs. Jordan. Every now and then, Tina would convey greetings from Mrs. Jordan but that was as far as it went. Tina wanted nobody to know what Mrs. Jordan had said about me, and that included Mama, but Mama already knew. She'd known since I was born.

Chapter Sixteen

Meanwhile

I was still being tracked in school. So many of the friends and classmates I had in elementary school were the friends and classmates I had in junior high. I was in one of the "S.P." classes, special progress. There were three S.P. classes. One was S.P.E. – Special Progress Experimental. That's where I was, always an experiment! We ruled junior high. We were the kids always going on trips, always studying special things, like earth science, seeing movies that enhanced the books we were reading, like *Wuthering Heights*. For some reason that was probably connected to history, we saw *Lawrence of Arabia*. I was awe struck! It was an exquisite film. The cinematography was resplendent with a beauty unique to film. I became hooked on the movies.

Miss Terzanno, one of our English teachers, taught us how to diagram sentences. We were offered French or Spanish as a second language to study. Our homeroom teacher, Mrs. Grover, championed us! We were stars! For many of us, she was also our English teacher one year. She gave us a party at her house in New Jersey at the end of the year! That was a very big deal for a teacher to invite her students to their home.

Tina was one of the parents who came to "chaperone." She was delightful, smiling, chatting, watching me like a hawk. Everybody kept telling me, "Your mom's great! She's so nice." I never said a word. I smiled. Our Social Studies teacher also came, Thomas Pappas. We adored Mr. Pappas, so much so we won a special "Good Guy" sweatshirt for him that was offered on WABC radio with the deejay, Cousin Brucie. We were big fans.

Mother's Madness

The students, parents, Mr. Pappas and Mrs. Grover gathered on her patio that was surrounded by her yard. The only other time I had been to New Jersey was to visit Palisades Amusement Park. The fact that real people lived in New Jersey was just a theory until we went to Mrs. Grover's house! My friend, Sonia, and I danced. We enjoyed dancing with each other because we loved to dance. She was the only student shorter than I was so we looked perfectly matched. The boys? They hung out near the food! They didn't dance but they gawked at us from time to time. I could feel them praying that no one would make them dance. When we got back to the brownstone, all Tina could talk about was Mrs. Grover's house. It was as if there was no party for our class at all. Tina had been on a house tour!

There was something about *holidays and celebrations* and having people come over that Mama despised and she passed this on to Tina as well. They loathed every holiday and birthday whether it was down home or in New York. Guests were viewed as a burden, an imposition. Holidays provided opportunities for people to take advantage of you. Therefore, no one was ever invited for the holidays, including and especially Christmas. Yet Tina always wanted to throw a party! The minute Mama and I left for home the parties began. Mama would always find out and Papa would always be dismayed and repulsed. The parties stopped when Papa moved north.

I associate holidays primarily with food and music. Those were the only things that distinguished Christmas, Thanksgiving, and Easter, except for the resurrection of Christ. I knew that was real. I didn't care what anybody said.

Listening to Tina made my head hurt. By junior high school, I was a headache master! I was nine years old when headache hell started. The first time it arrived was on my birthday when I was down home. I was stretched out on the living room couch with my eyes closed, trying not to cry from the pain. Uncle Jim and Mama looked puzzled. Mama had a frown on her face. Eventually she gave me a cold rag to put on my forehead and two children's aspirin. It's hard to heal what you don't understand.

I didn't know what was happening and neither did Mama. The pain gripped the left side of my face. Noise was magnified. I was yet to be diagnosed with acute hearing. I couldn't stand bright lights. The intensity of the overhead living room light made me want to scream. The light felt like knives stabbing my eyes, running up to my brain! Mama thought my request to turn out the lights was foolish so she kept them on. I knew my brains would explode. I wanted to cut my head off. It was a full day and night before the pain subsided. When it did, I quietly focused on the new typewriter Papa gave me and began writing stories.

After this experience, I dreaded my birthdays. Preparing for my birthday seemed to be an unpleasant chore for Mama. What she loathed was inviting the cousins over for my party. She considered them a necessary evil in the configuration of my childhood. Eventually, my birthdays were celebrated by giving me a check. One year when I was twelve or thirteen, Papa opened a checking account for me in my own name at one of the banks he did business with down home. He taught me how to fill out a check and balance my account. A check was a written contract for the amount entered guaranteed by your signature. Then he taught me the value of my signature and to never let anybody copy it. I think that's one reason I made my handwriting so distinctive. The other reason? My great-Aunt

Elizabeth had beautiful handwriting and she always wrote with a fountain pen.

My birthday and migraines are permanently linked in my mind. To this day, I still associate my birthday with unbearable pain. It would be several years before I was treated for these headaches. I learned to live with migraine pain on a weekly basis for decades.

Junior high school was a forecast of my social life for a very long time. I wasn't allowed to go to what few parties I was invited to, and there were no invitations to anyone's Bar Mitzvah. There would be no dating...ever! But I could go to the theatre and shopping. I could go to museums, wander through Rizzoli's bookstore, and attend concerts. That was the advantage of growing up in New York City and having the money to do these things. I often went alone. Thank God for matinees. I saw Richard Burton in Hamlet and Equus, witnessed Ethel Merman bellow out, *"There's no business/like show business/like no business I know/everything about it is appealing..."* Pearl Bailey delivered Hello Dolly a thousand miles away from the style of Barbara Streisand and Streisand was – is phenomenal! The theatre became my refuge from family craziness. The stage provided my soul with sustenance along with every book I could find. I read searching for an explanation, anything that would either help me make sense of the immediate world around me or unlock the secrets about the other side. It would be decades before I found *some* answers, not all. I'm still reading.

Chapter Seventeen

One Dance

This is what I remember, a junior high school dance, but it wasn't after school. It was during school. Several classes were led into the gym, a huge, beige room absent of any character. It was purposeful and institutional. There was not enough crepe paper in the world to transform the gym into something pleasant.

All the S.P. classes along with ones and twos were on one side of the gym. For example, if you were in the smartest eighth grade class you would be in 8-1, the second smartest would be 8-2. The special progress classes (S.P.) were at the very top of the heap. We were the brainiacs, the scary, bright children. On the other side were different kids. They were all kids of color. I looked at my side of the gym, all white with the exception of me and by then, my friend, Fee, who was Chinese. I knew something horrible was about to happen.

Standing between the two lines were several of our teachers, including Mr. Papas. Miss Flanagan was there too, a very heavy set, dark haired, rotund woman with cream colored skin. Her upper arms were huge and looking back, she was young. Miss Flanagan was not to be toyed with! When she walked down the hall everybody stood back to let her pass. It was like the Humboldt Junior High School sea opening for Moses Flanagan.

And then the music started. At first, nobody moved. Then one by one, couples formed and started to do what passed for dancing. There was no crossing over. Everybody danced with "their own." No one counted on me because the smart kids were always white. What happened when one of the smart kids was

Black? Nobody danced with me. And then, one brave, short, Black boy stepped across the divide and asked me to dance. Everybody froze. I didn't want to dance with him, but I felt I had to. It was one of the most awkward, distressing moments of my young life. I didn't want to touch him. When the music ended, he went back to his side of the room, and I went back to my side. I buried the moment but never forgot it.

A Caveat on Precariousness

The precariousness of my existence was taking shape in my mind like the ominous vibration of an earthquake.
It didn't feel right. It felt dangerous. It felt crazy.
Clearly Tina and Harry were not right. There were times when nothing felt right in any way. My life started to gently rattle, like the initial rumble of an earthquake.
Everybody was at risk.

I started to wonder, and still wonder, how are you surviving this? What's holding you together?
As Oriah Mountain Dreamer asks,
What's sustaining you, from the inside, when all else falls away*?
I'll tell you what I've come to realize.

I was never really alone.
There was always a protective presence of something or someone. I have to believe it was God's breath.
It compensated for what I didn't understand.
Looking back – From the age of five to the age of 17 I lived in constant trepidation.
Sooner or later, something shifts, something cracks from the inside,
Just like an earthquake – the sidewalks move. The earth opens. The noise? A memory never forgotten.
And you run for your life.

The Invitation, by Oriah Mountain Dreamer

Chapter Eighteen

What Does Tina Do?

No matter what happened the night before or over the weekend, Tina managed to get up, get dressed, and go to work, leaving "weekend Tina" buried in the brownstone, with a bottle of scotch. Mama was proud of Tina's work. I heard Mama say countless times to friends down home, "Oh, Lyntine runs a big school up in New York." Or pointing to Tina's framed graduate degree that hung over the piano purchased for me to practice on while I was down home, Mama would say, "Lyntine got her master's degree. See, it's up on the wall. Columbia University."

Tina's graduate degree helped her become one of the first Black Directors of what would become a landmark daycare facility in New York City. Her appointment had to be sometime during the early to mid-fifties. Deep down, she always believed it was her color that got her the position. I say that because she constantly denigrated dark skinned Black folks! They weren't smart. They weren't "cultured". They had big feet. They were too loud. They were ugly, and it always came back to their intellect. Referring to some exam required of her teachers, head held high, eyes narrowed, she would tell me, "Us can't pass the tests. Everybody else can pass. You can train everything but a nigger."

When Tina talked about race it was as if she was the only one in the house impacted by racism. Her experiences, as far as I could tell at this point, seemed to be indirect and ominous, and always involved her work, but she would never elaborate. She had a way of talking in shadows. She never gave any specifics, just bitter references in passing. I could sense the hurt. It was tangible and alarming. You can't hold all that hurt without it taking its toll. I would find that out.

Every now and then when I had a holiday, usually in the spring, she would take me to her school. I remember the layout and how cold it seemed, flat teal blue, beige walls, artificial floors, maybe linoleum. No matter what they did that institutional feeling seeped through. It made me uncomfortable. I kept thinking that the walls held secrets, bad secrets and something was going to happen. Confusion hung in the air. What did these walls witness?

(Indigenous people are taught that everything holds spirit, animate and inanimate. It didn't matter. All those inanimate objects most people ignore, like stones, buildings, rooms, have a spirit that you can interact with if you know how. So, walls, and furniture, trees, witness and absorb our activities. The expression, "If these walls could talk," has truth.)

Tina's office was small. I don't remember seeing a window. What I remember is the dreary beige color of the walls and a set of file cabinets to the right of her desk. After leaving my coat in her office, she would take my hand and I'd be "shown off." We'd stop in every classroom and at least one teacher would say, "Oh my God! Mrs. Pryor, this is your daughter!" The teacher would turn to the others and repeat that, as if they hadn't heard her thick New York accent announcing my arrival. The fawning would begin. "Oh my God, she's so cute and so tiny!" Tina would turn to me and dictate, "Janis, say hello."

"Hello." I looked around. There were clusters of small tables and chairs designed for preschool aged children. There were toys and cubbyholes, and each classroom had a bathroom with child-sized toilets, washbasins with step stools so kids could reach the faucets, and those horrible beige paper towels.

There were bright, harsh colors in the classrooms. Cerulean blue seemed to be everywhere. I also noticed that there were lots of Black and Latinx children. I had never seen so many in one room. I found myself wondering, what were they like? What games did they play? What stories do they know? Did they like hot dogs? Why did people, including Tina, think they were so different, destined to grow up, and become dangerous?

Walking back to her office she would always make some derogatory remark about them. She described one little boy she had just hugged as, "That little spic, his mother's a dope dealer. *Takes* drugs, too." I wasn't quite sure what a dope dealer was at eight or nine years old, but I knew it was bad from the tone in Tina's voice. Or, she would point to a Black child and say, "See how black he is? He ain't gon' be nothing." I often felt a lump in my throat when she said those things.

Every time Mama and I returned down home Tina would give me strict instructions to stay out of the sun. "You don't want to get too dark." Sometimes my throat felt like it was going to close up or I wouldn't be able to breathe when she said that. What does she say about me when I'm not around?

Eventually my throat would loosen, and my voice returned. I asked her, dumbfounded, "Why do you say those things?" Tina was perplexed.

Looking down at me with a frown on her face, she would always say, *"What are you talkin' about? What's wrong with you?"* She looked at me like I was crazy.

I spent most of those visits to her school drawing in the staff lounge, or in Tina's office wondering when we were going back to the brownstone. Teachers would come to her office and ask questions. She responded always sounding in charge. I watched her interact with the children. She smiled too much, held them too tightly. The kids would squirm while she called them honey and sweetheart.

Over twenty years later, I went back to the school with her (in a bigger facility and location) and watched her again. She did all the same things and I realized what bothered me as a child when I saw her with children. Tina didn't like kids! All the affection and emotion she demonstrated towards them was fake. My head started to throb. How did she interact with the parents? I asked her.

Tina said, "I didn't do a lot with the parents and I didn't do a lot of support for parents. Interacting with parents is too hard because the parents are resentful. They're on dope. I'd be afraid they might hurt you. A spic'll cut you. *But they wouldn't slap a white lady.* I'd rather not deal with parents one on one. I can threaten teachers." She paused for a minute, staring off into space while I sat opposite of her, astounded.

She continued, stating that she had, "...all minority teachers with the exception of a few. The white ones pass the exams. 'Us' can't pass 'em. I tell 'em, if you don't get it now, you never will. White folks rarely help Black folks unless you were so good, *so good*, you had something they wanted and I had something they wanted! You can impress people with your power."

It hit me while listening to her, the school was her kingdom. It made the following statement she proclaimed over and over more significant. *"This is my school."*

Chapter Nineteen

Preparing For War

The decision to attend the public junior high school was fraught with drama. The good news was junior high was also within walking distance from the brownstone. The bad news was Tina didn't like these conveniences. She marched in one day and said, "The elementary school principal said he would put us down as a 'hardship case.' I told him we owned our home! We weren't a hardship case! The teachers made the school, so you *will go* to the assigned junior high school!" That's how I ended up at Humboldt Junior High 115. The alternative? A fancy private school. In Tina's mind, I was going to the public junior high to prove we weren't a hardship case. This ridiculous thinking process she employed, I called "Tina-Think."

Again, I learned from her (and from quite a few white folks) that to be Black was to be considered automatically poor, and stupid wasn't far behind. Tina wasn't wrong about that. You were treated as if you were worthless and useless, capable of little to nothing because you were ignorant, excluded from the privileges the world offered the well to do who were mostly white. If you were Black, you were more than likely, a burden to *white society*. There wasn't an abundance of well-educated, prosperous, sophisticated Black people known to white people in the fifties and early sixties. White people couldn't imagine that Black folks could be anything but poor unless you were an entertainer, athlete, or movie star. We were a radical anomaly for most white people during the fifties and sixties. They didn't understand that there were Black middle-class people, much less affluent ones until *The Cosby Show* came along.

All those children of color in junior high horrified Tina. I kept hearing one of Mama's favorite admonitions, "Association brings on assimilation. Be careful who you associate with!" There I was, isolated from my people because the intellectually elite were a better fit for me. It's a conundrum that still eats away at me.

New rules were put down. The storm of adolescence was forming on the horizon and creeping towards shore. No dating. No parties. No socializing especially with Black people at this school. The party at Mrs. Grover's house was fine. There was no attending a party at another student's house. If I questioned her about these rules, the mantra of my adolescence fell out of her mouth, "I'm the mother. You're the daughter." She used that phrase a great deal until the day I stopped her with roughly six or seven words.

Tina asked about the kids in my classes. She was especially curious about the Black children, but would preface her questions proclaiming, "You don't know who these people are!" There were *never* many Black students in my classes if any! So, I had to scan the hallways when we were changing classes so I could have an answer. She wanted to know, "Well, what do they look like? Are they dressed well? Where do they live, Harlem?" When she spoke during my early adolescence, her words were lethal weapons hiding on her tongue, waiting to attack. They rushed out through her mouth, ready to fight, ready to engage in a rope-a-dope maneuver if need be. Each word was fueled with the beers she drank during the evening. As my adolescence progressed, so did her drinking. (And where was Harry during my junior high years? Upstairs, I guess when he wasn't out. The real answer? I didn't know where he was. He'd come in late during the week and leave before I was up for school. Having Harry in the house was like living with a time bomb.)

Tina would return from work, change into a house dress, an ugly fashion invention allowing you to take off your "good clothes" and then toss on one of those house dresses. Tina often found a pair of anklet socks and then she would plant her feet in her house slippers, little satin, embroidered slippers from Chinatown. The slippers would decisively flap, flap, flap with each step she made. Her reddish hair was thinning, and she hated it. It wasn't the same hair she had as a young woman. I think Tina believed she was going bald. I would swear on a stack of Bibles that Tina believed she "caught" baldness from Harry. Like everything else about Tina, I couldn't quite figure out what happened. One thing was certain, I never knew what color her natural hair was, probably black. But who knows?

Over the years, Tina acquired dozens of blonde short haired wigs. She wore them with definitive defiance. She dared anyone, with a look that could kill, to ask her if it was her own hair.

Within the first five minutes of her arriving at the brownstone from work, she would open a can of beer and then the wig would come off! There was a choreography to the removal. Head held high, eyes closed, with one swift motion her right hand quickly rose, and the wig was removed in seconds. She often threw it on the dining table, with another smooth, flick of the wrist. She made a drink and glided up the stairs while shouting, "I'll be back, Mama. I'll help you with dinner."

Chapter Twenty

Some Things Tina Told Me (and Terry) Some Things She Insisted I Have Some Things I Observed...

Tina knew how to lie well. She turned it into a stunning art form. The big lie technique was one of her favorite devices. Two of her lies stayed with me, minor in comparison to what I later discovered, but nevertheless jaw-dropping.

"If you cut your hair it'll never grow back."

"Only lesbians drive SUVs."

Tina told Terry, "...if you lie constantly, you need a good memory." You don't have to struggle to remember the truth. The truth often interfered with Tina's plans.

She managed to weaponize questions, making you feel like a complete fool. The sneer in her voice was inescapable.

And she could fabricate information on the spot to suit her purposes or make herself feel better. "Your father's an engineer." (That was a lie.)

"Janis shows her work at the Zabrieske Gallery in Manhattan." (That was a bigger lie. Why the Zabrieske Gallery because she knew nothing about art? One of my art teachers in college showed her work there!)

Tina had unusual requests and expectations given my work in politics.

Mother's Madness

"I want you to get Jesse Jackson to come to my retirement party." I ignored her request... She never retired.

Shortly after I moved to Cambridge from Boston, Tina called one Saturday morning. She sounded unnaturally perky.

"I want you to make a baby," she said.

"You what?"

"Go have a baby. I need to have a grandchild. You're not doing anything for nine months or so. Have the baby and then give it to me. All my friends are grandmothers. I could raise the child. You won't have to do anything."

"Tina, I'm not going to have a baby so you can be a grandparent. That's not happening."

She began to rant and rave, stating over and over that she needed to be a grandmother. What was she going to tell her friends about me? How would this make her look? For a minute I thought I was going crazy.

Quietly, I said, "I gotta go now." I hung up and continued with my day. I was told she went ranting and raving around the house, muttering, "Why won't that red bitch make a baby?" She never asked me again to have a child, but she did have one more plan.

After her request to supply her with a grandchild got nowhere, she sent me a small package. There was a note in the box that said, "Wear this!" It was a diamond ring. I called her.

"Tina, I can't wear this. It looks like an engagement ring!"

"It's so pretty, isn't it? Such a cute diamond. It's perfectly cut."

"I can't wear this!"

Her voice dropped to a whisper. "Why not?" she asked.

"Because it looks like an engagement ring!"

"So, it looks like an engagement ring."

"But *I'm not engaged to anyone*, Tina."

"Well, you should be," she said.

"But I'm not…" I was almost shouting as if that would help.

"If you wear it, you will be," she instructed. "People will think you will be and you should be. It's none of their business otherwise."

This was another episode of "Tina-Think." I felt like someone had scrambled my brains as I tried to follow the logic that didn't really exist.

"Sooner or later people will want me to produce the fiancé and there will be no one!"

"It's none of their damned business. You'll have the ring. Wear the ring, Janis. Why're you always defying me?"

"Look, I'll send this back to you."

"Oh no you won't, little lady! *Don't you send that ring back to me.* Do you know how much that cost?"

"Tina, I didn't ask you to buy this ring!"

Viciousness creeped in her voice and she ordered, "You *better not send that ring back here. I mean it*!"

My head started to throb. I paused, took a deep breath and said, "Okay. But I'm going to have it reset. I will not wear it in its current setting." This was my concession. Otherwise, I had a vision of her descending from the sky in a black cape with fire shooting from her eyes, ready to do God knows what!

"Do whatever you want," and slammed the phone down.

This was not an unprecedented conversation. We had a similar exchange regarding skis when I was in college. She wanted me to buy a pair of skis. More Tina-Think.

"But I don't ski, Tina."

"So? You can just have them."

"Have them for what?!"

"For show…"

I never bought a pair of skis. Fastening two long boards to your feet, wrapped in boots that couldn't really bend, and race down a hill often in below freezing weather with the hope that you wouldn't crash into a tree and do irrevocable damage to yourself made absolutely no sense to me. I'd rather sit by an open fire and knit like Mama taught me.

Holding a lit cigarette in one hand and a drink in another, she looked me up and down one day and said, *"You know, your grandfather set houses on fire for a white man."* I felt my eyes widen and my brain curdle. Once again, I said to myself, "She's damned crazy!" The thought of challenging her would've been evidence of my own craziness at that point.

In my late twenties, she gave me a Blackglama Mink coat and expected me to wear it to work. This was after I sent back the first one she bought me that was more befitting some grande dame who lived on Park Avenue and wore too much make-up! When the fur swap was all over, I had a Blacklgama, and a full-length raccoon coat, with the expectation I would wear the raccoon coat to work. I could get away wearing raccoon. It was "kinda cute," a fun fur! Not so with black mink. But *she wanted me to have everything "the rich white girls had…"*

During her early teaching days before she went to graduate school, she told me, "I'd come home and work on those lesson plans. I'd sit in the living room on the floor, writing these proposals and things and read them to Mama and Papa. Of course, they didn't have the intellectual capacity, the intelligence that I had... but they could encourage you, you know." I was speechless.

"Those dirty so and so's put everything in your way to make you fall and stumble. Three or four years ago was the most cruel moment of your life! Disrespectful! Running over you!" She never elaborated on what happened. I had to piece together information from various comments, complaints, conversations overheard. What became clearer was the impact of racism on her life. What was also clear was her arrogance, her sense of superiority. Of course, she never received the regard she thought she was due. I found all of it stupefying. What I discerned was it was true, her arrogance, her sense of superiority, and the racism.

Tina related another story to me about her early work experiences in New York. "After I became Director, some inspectors came over to the school and asked for Pryor. I walked out and they said to me that it was rumored..." Tina paused before going on. *"They said, 'We thought you were a Negro all this time!' I looked at them and said, 'What do you think now?'* The Inspector smiled at me and I asked, 'How can I help you today?' I knew everything they wanted, how much square footage per child, including furnishings..." I tried not to stare at her. What was I supposed to say that would make any sense to her? Did she tell them she was Black? I didn't ask. I was afraid of her answer.

She wanted Mama, Papa, and me to know how difficult white people made it for her constantly. Who else would she talk to about this? I didn't know. These comments usually came during the beer phase of her evening. I heard her tell Mama, "They don't want you to get ahead! *Ask you to do something that they don't ask anybody else to do! They'll keep their foot on your neck, so help me God!* Dirty, rotten bastards! Some fool called from downtown. I said to him, 'Do you know who you're talking to?!" She was becoming more and more agitated.

This is when I'd hear Papa's voice from the living room. "Take it easy, Tina. You do the best you can. Work hard... That's all you can do." She wasn't buying it. Something was brewing deep inside of her. Mama and Papa told her that white people would wait for you to make a mistake and then take everything away from you. This was not some paranoid delusion. This was a fact of Black life in America. Double standards, betrayal, treachery, enforced oppression everywhere. How could Tina not understand that? Maybe she didn't believe it. Maybe she *couldn't* believe it. If she did, it might kill her. She would repeat, "You don't have the same privileges white folks have. They're always watching you, dirty, rotten bastards! *They* can steal but you can't! *They* can get away with things, but you can't! *They* making all the money!" By this point, she was shouting.

I looked at her once after she'd gone through this nightly rant and asked her, "Why would you want to steal anyway?" In my mind, I could hear Mama and Papa say, "Thou shall not steal."

Tina glared at me so intently, I felt like I was shriveling. She spit the words from her mouth and said, *"Shut up! You'll learn."* Before I could ask her any other questions, she left.

Sitting in his recliner, Papa slowly shook his head, and said, "Don't listen to her." He would pause and quietly say, "Don't ever think you can beat the white man the way Tina thinks. The white man is the Master Thief here." I knew Papa was referring to the land. "There are other ways to deal with him. You have to be smarter than he is," Papa said. He looked at me, paused and said, "Go to school and learn."

This particular evening took place when I was still at Music and Art. Papa watched Tina warily. Her behavior had two faces. We were sitting in the living room watching television, an activity based on how much homework I had that night, which was most of the time. If I had a lot of homework, I would rarely see Tina and I could forget television.

If she came looking for me, Mama would firmly say, "Janis' got her head in those books, Lyntine. Let her do her homework!"

Friday nights were different. Mama, Papa and I watched television. I also had a front row seat to see which one of Tina's personas emerged. Would her drinking bring forth the little girl with the high-pitched voice who sat in the corner of the couch, one leg crossed over the other swinging it back and forth? There was always a lit cigarette in her hand and often she was chewing gum to cover up her scotch breath.

This particular evening, she strutted in the living room, drink in hand and asked, "Whatcha y'all doing?" The little girl had arrived and flopped down on the couch.

Mama and Papa didn't answer. They never did. I would hear my voice state the obvious, "Watching TV, Tina."

"Ohhhhh," she said with wonder. Mama might get up and go into the kitchen and ask Papa if he wanted anything. I might go and get a Coke. Tina sipped that tumbler of scotch until it was all gone or until the eleven o'clock news came on. Television provided something for us to talk about without getting into a fight.

The Bitch Goddess was Tina's other persona. She was belligerent and miserable. The Bitch Goddess strode into the living room, greeted everyone in a voice that was barely audible.

Her face was stiff, her eyes both sad and angry. There was no conversation, no commentary. Where was Harry? Gone out or upstairs. I didn't know and didn't care. Keeping him away from me was all that mattered.

One night, something happened that cemented the dynamic of my relationship with Tina, something I assumed Miss Jordan helped Tina resolve. We were watching *Star Trek*, the original series with William Shatner. I loved science fiction, and *Star Trek* was one of my favorite shows.

I can't remember the storyline, but I felt it was quite predictable. I started saying the lines of dialogue before the characters said them. The first two or three times, Tina laughed. When I kept on doing this, her eyes grew wide, her mouth drawn and tense. She clutched her glass of scotch.

"How did you know what they were going to say?" she asked.

I shrugged my shoulders. "I don't know. It's obvious. Simple storyline."

"*It ain't obvious,*" Tina said staring at me. Tina looked at Mama for help. Mama smiled. Tina took another sip of her drink and said to me, "You oughta put a rag around yo' head and make some money."

"What?" I asked.

She didn't respond. Tina looked at Papa and asked, "Didn't you hear her do that? What is that?" Tina didn't wait for Papa to answer. "She's got that way about her," Tina said and poured herself another drink while mumbling, "Born with a damned veil over her face." She glared at me. "You scaring me."

"Tina, take it easy," Papa said. "Calm down. Nothing's wrong."

Tina's glare was fixed on my face. I could sense she was really afraid of me. I felt like I was being circled by a predatory animal.

With all that for Tina to hold, the racism, her dysfunction, her drinking, her inability to control me, Tina somehow soared in the seventies. On May 22, 1975, Tina's school was named after her. She invited me to the dedication ceremonies for the "Leontine L. Pryor Day Care Center." I declined. Mama and Papa went. I have the photo taken that day. Papa stood looking stern. Mama looked uncomfortable. Tina beamed like a child who had won a prize for a great accomplishment. And that's exactly what she was at that moment. Maybe now, Mama and Papa would hold her with the same regard they held her brother, George, when he was alive. Harry? No evidence of his presence.

Tina sent me a program from the event. I could tell by the tone and the errors, that it was written by her. There was a section on the history and another on the construction of the school. It was one-of-a-kind in 1975. Preschool and kindergarten students with disabilities would be accepted along with able-bodied children. Three classrooms were for the exclusive use of disabled kids. Each of these classrooms would have twelve children, *"...along with appropriate staff to guide them in their daily activities. For example, speech therapists, occupational therapists, psychologists, a social worker, registered nurse and teachers in special education. The remaining classrooms will be used for group day care."* Tina's school grew out of the Parkchester Bronxdale Day Care Association, which began in 1942, originally located in a small storefront building.

Tina wrote, "*Due to the astuteness of our director, a contract was signed with Mental Health and Mental Retardation Services providing additional staff and consultation services.*" She described herself as, "*exuberant, aggressive, and understanding of the needs of families and staff as she was in mid-1952, perhaps more so.*" (Perhaps more so, was one of her favorite phrases.)

"*The Board of Directors, Parents, Community, and Staff of Parkchester Bronxdale day care association are the beneficiaries of Pryor's dedicated and creative labors as an outstanding educator and administrator of our mutually beloved centers.*"

These were Tina's words and this is how she viewed her world. How could she possibly take care of all those children with special needs, and me?

Referring to Mama and Papa one day, she screamed at me and said, "*These are my parents. Not yours.* I'm the mother. You're the daughter. When are you going to start treating me like your mother?" She'd been asking me that for years. I finally answered. "*When you start acting like one,*" I said.

With a drink in her hand, her lower lip was trembling. She stared at me for a long minute and then walked away. I continued to read, but I knew it wasn't over.

Every now and then she'd firmly tell me, "Don't you ever let me catch you doing any volunteer work. They already got free labor from us through slavery. That's enough. Make 'em pay you." She would end by swearing under her breath and snickering, "Volunteer work. Ain't that a blip?!"

I was invited to China by the State Department and The Young Political Leadership Council to be part of a *formal delegation* to China given the normalization of relations between our countries. Once again, I took her breath away. I had come back to Riverdale to tell them. Papa's health was failing. Tina looked at me and said, "If your grandfather dies while you're away, we won't tell you." I remember looking at her and growing cold. I heard someone or something say, "Walk away. Walk away." Thankfully, I did.

Mother's Madness

PART THREE:

Conflict

Chapter Twenty-One

Blood and Rage

My life and the life of everyone in my generation forever changed on November 22, 1963. The Cuban Missile Crisis was a warm-up. JFK's assassination was the first of a string of events that would always be recalled with the question, "Do you remember where you were when...?" It became the rite of passage for us. There would be many more.

The details of that day are still sharp in my mind. We were returning from gym class. I noticed the halls were empty and fearfully silent as we walked into our home room. Everybody sat down and then we were told. The finality of the event transcended our need to understand or make sense of it. JFK was gone – period. Everyone was sent home. I was stunned and touched in places I didn't know existed inside me.

JFK's assassination provided one of the few subjects Tina, Mama, and I could have limited but compatible conversations. Mama and Tina were huddled in the kitchen when I returned from school. I heard Tina mutter, "You know Johnson had something to do with it. A peckerwood...shot that young man." Tina never liked Lyndon Baines Johnson and was too eager to accuse him of taking a role in JFK's assassination. There was no proof, but that didn't stop her nor did it stop many Black folks from casting a hairy eyeball at LBJ. No matter what he did, and he did a great deal to improve our well-being in the United States, primarily through the Voting Rights Act and his declaration of the War on Poverty, LBJ was always suspect among many Black folks we knew.

Along with the rest of the country, we were in suspended animation, shattered, shocked. Everything stopped for four days. And yes, as so many print journalists and television professionals would say, "This was television's finest moment."

"Mama! Mama! Somebody shot Lee Harvey Oswald." Mama ran into the living room from the kitchen, dish towel still in hand. She looked at the television, shook her head and muttered to herself. Her words were followed by that "Black dialect" that consisted of sounds and tones and not words. I heard her say, "Ummm, um, umph." The emotion and meaning were clear.

I sat on the living room floor glued to the screen trying to absorb this nightmare and the name Jack Ruby, who shot Oswald. It was Oswald who was accused of assassinating John Kennedy. The next thing I knew the police tackled Jack Ruby. How did he manage to get that close to Oswald? So many questions popped up on November 22, 1963. To this day, none have ever been satisfactorily answered. My generation is still haunted by these questions and the indescribable loss that began. We were baptized with JFK's blood. Little did we know what awaited.

(At some point during these four historic days in American history, Tina walked in my bedroom, threw a booklet on my bed about menstruation and ordered, "Read it!" My mind was awash in the blood of assassinations. I read this booklet and tried to grapple with the fact that my body would be bleeding every month and it's considered "natural", even "normal"! Would the blood from assassinations become "natural" or even "normal" also? JFK's brains were blown out, spilling onto Jackie's pink suit. I was enraged and horrified! I had a feeling that this monthly bleeding routine was going to get in my way. This was the closest Tina came to "having a conversation" with me about the dreaded subject of sex. It was much easier to talk about the assassination of JFK.)

The country started to crumble on November 22, 1963 and continues right up to April 20, 2021, when a white policeman was found guilty on three counts of murdering a Black man, George Floyd. *Maybe* now some form of rectification will start. But as I write this the country is grappling with the memory of the Tulsa Massacre that took place at the beginning of the twentieth century. Black Wall Street was burned to the ground by white folks angry and jealous of the prosperity acquired by these former slaves and their descendants. Three hundred Black folks that we know of, were killed and dumped in a mass grave. It took a hundred years for recognition of this nightmare. And who knows how many more massacres there are? You're forced to revisit the concept of "progress."

It makes me remember the importance of faith and the words of a former boss. "The work goes on...the cause endures...the hope still lives and the dream shall never die..." Some may not want to admit it but those words and intent serve as fuel for some of us. Thank you, Bob Shrum for writing these words for our one-time boss, the late Senator Ted Kennedy.

In some ways, the era that came to be known as "the sixties" began (for me) on that fall afternoon in November of '63. Like so many young Americans then, I had been touched by Camelot* and all that it stood for, the honor and necessity of public service. (The glamour and youthful qualities of the Kennedys helped!) John F. Kennedy's tenure as President taught me about the power of a gesture, the complexity of leadership, *the art and science of it*, and the pervasive might of politics. I thought that maybe, one day I could work for the Kennedys, maybe even in the White House. The fact that I was way too young and no one knew if any other Kennedy would ever want to continue in public life given the assassination didn't dawn on me. I just assumed they would go on and they did into the 21st century when the unthinkable happened. A Kennedy lost an election.

JFK's assassination planted a seed of conflict in me about what to do with my life. The battle began between the head and the heart. My head and upbringing demanded that you "serve", that you contribute to make this a better world. That was the Virgo in me and the echo of Papa telling me, "To whom much is given much is expected." My heart cried and begged me to develop and fulfill my potential in the arts, to feed that hunger for expression. That was the Leo in me. The conflict continues to this day.

Two years after JFK's assassination, Tina suddenly had a connection to the Kennedys! At least that was what she wanted you to think. Bobby Kennedy visited Tina's school campaigning for the United States Senate seat from New York. Everyone was breathless with anticipation. I took a photo of him working the crowd. Tina was not far behind. She beamed with pride. He approached me and I extended my hand to him. As he took my hand, he turned to Tina.

"Your daughter?" he asked.

She nodded her head, smiled coyly, and said, "Yes."

"I can see that. I can see that," he said. I was 15 and his campaign for the U.S. Senate would be the very first political campaign I participated in. Fee and I were given signs to hold at a rally for RFK at 181st Street and Broadway in Manhattan. I was hooked. (Much later in life, I had that sign framed.) There was just something about this man. That was the day I became a "Bobby person."

One thing became absolutely clear to me. On November 22, 1963, JFK's assassination initiated a generation who came of age in a frame of nuclear uncertainty, christened by more blood, church bombs, and high-pressure water hoses, demonstrations leading to cracked skulls and bruised faces, broken ribs, and throats full of rage screaming, "Hey! Hey! LBJ, how many kids did you kill today?" and "No Justice! No Peace!" not from *one national tragedy or crisis*, but close to *a dozen* starting with the Cuban Missile Crisis and it still hasn't ended as indicated by the evolution of the chant. "No justice! No peace! No racist police", with the haunting melody of "We shall overcome..." barely audible.

With all this, there was also the lingering trauma of Emmitt Till and the deep, bellowing sounds that defy description from countless lynchings of Black people, with an overlay of too many white people who considered lynchings to be some perverse form of entertainment instead of it being their shroud of shame.

White children attended lynchings. Postcards were printed of the "event." The smell of burning flesh and the evil behind it were ignored. Combine that with denial. Too many white people decided selling their souls to live with evil was a small price to pay to secure their "power over" in America. I write this in the shadow of George Floyd's murder seen around the world thanks to cell phone cameras. America's "troubles" continue targeting those of us who are red, yellow, brown, and Black because many white people refuse to accept the coming changes. A critical mass is doing everything they can to turn the clock back. We're headed for a major conflict, the likes of which haven't been seen since the Civil War. I hope I'm wrong.

Many of those people, with such a limited, simplistic vision of the future, brought us the insurrection of Jan. 6, 2021. We, who are not white, carry fear, faith and insecurity every day in a variety of forms along with seething rage. Whether or not it's warranted is almost irrelevant. I often wonder if this *lasting faith many Black people still have* is also part of the genetic imprint of slavery.

When I first wrote this, we were approaching the fortieth anniversary of JFK's assassination. Today, well into the twenty-first century, I'm less able to cope with that loss and the subsequent assassinations of other political and activist leaders from that era, than I was then. As I watch injustice metastasize, I'm more haunted by that wrenching question, "What if he had lived?" He, by now referred to John F. Kennedy, Bobby Kennedy, Reverend Doctor Martin Luther King, Jr., and Malcolm X. What if? Would we be in the strangle hold of Donald Trump's authoritarian imposition as he spreads lies and plots his return to the White House gutting democracy in the process?

Some readers may wonder right now, is this a personal story or socio-political treatise? *If you are a person of color in this country, the minute you leave the womb, your life is already a combination of the socio-political realities of the United States, along with the personal specifics that shape your authenticity. It's that simple and that complicated. It's not either-or, but both-and. This is part of what Dubois coined as having, "double consciousness." We have no choice.* Only white people have that choice, and usually they choose not to see any of this, and so they don't.

Tina and I made radically different decisions when it came to our political and personal rage against injustice and racism. I was experiencing and understanding racism very differently from Tina. What I would come to do in life astounded her because she had no control over it and couldn't fathom how I did what I achieved. I worked for and with people she would see on the nightly news. Created "things" that were televised and sometimes broadcast on the BBC or countries she knew nothing about. Won some awards and nominations that intimidated her.

What Tina did, horrified me, *but I eventually understood why she did most of the things she did.* I wish I didn't. I wish she'd lived long enough to see Derek Chauvin, the white policeman who killed George Floyd, convicted on three counts of murder, or witness the towers falling on 9.11, or find herself speechless over the election of Barack Obama and the fierce gracefulness of Michelle Obama.

I often wondered if the assassination of JFK marked one of many divergences between us. As I grew older, I couldn't understand why Tina seemed to be so surprised by injustice. I expected racism and all of its ripple effects, just like I expected the sun to rise each morning. It was a fact of life if you weren't white. And if you were not white *and from Mississippi,* you'd be a fool *not to confront racism and figure out how you would handle it before it handled you.* But I didn't look "almost white." As a friend said, "You're a little mocha." I was tan! I was "not white." Looking *almost white* in the United States, can nurture dangerous delusions if you're not careful and grounded.

Racism is treacherous "up North." It's everywhere and nowhere. Tina was always on guard once she left the house. Her instructions to me? Never let them know that you know what they're really thinking deep down about you. White people were to be kept at arm's length. Doing this on a daily basis can wear you down. Maybe *this* is why Tina was so worn out at the end of the day. Maybe this is why she needed that drink, which became several drinks by the time she went to bed. Too many times, I saw her wrapped in confusion, bitterness, and bewilderment after a day at work.

There she was dancing on the color line with no real hope of having white people see her for who she really was or thought she was. I always had the feeling Tina believed she could skip racism the way kids skip a class. When she realized she couldn't whatever hope she had, died. Fighting racism for Tina was akin to being ambushed by history. Any Black person, especially African Americans, ambushed by racism in America, was evidence of pathological denial.

Chapter Twenty-Two

It's On

Regardless of what happened, anywhere, school remained a prominent reality and priority in our house. I would be the third generation going to college. For Mama and Papa, it was never a matter of if I would go, but simply, where I would go. Anything that had to with learning was okay with Mama and Papa and eventually Tina. After all, going to art school with Drora helped me create and refine a portfolio of work (along with excellent grades) that were accepted by the High School of Music and Art.

There were specialized high schools in New York City, Music and Art, Performing Arts, the Bronx High School of Science, Hunter High, and Stuyvesant. Kids came from all over the city to attend these schools. I took a bus and the subway to Music and Art. Never thought twice about spending an hour on public transportation to get to school.

Music and Art, aka M & A, aka "Castle on the Hill" was then located at the top of a hill on the campus of City College, the poor man's Harvard for New Yorkers, long before the days of open admissions.

We were a pretentious bunch who attended Music and Art, way too sophisticated for our own good! If some of us decided to cut school for a day, we headed downtown to the Museum of Modern Art. We were very impressed with ourselves. We chose not to have a prom, and graduation was held in the Waldorf Astoria. I barely remember it. I didn't want to go to graduation, refused to find a dress. Papa dragged me downtown and made me pick out a dress while he sat in a chair and waited. We weren't going anywhere until I picked out a dress and made sure it fit! Eventually I found one, an off-white, cream-colored cotton dress with just a bit of embroidery across the top.

Once I was admitted to Music and Art, drama school was next! I should have auditioned for the High School of Performing Arts. (Today the schools are combined.) Tina felt the academic program was better at the High School of Music and Art. What that meant, was she understood what went on at Music and Art. She was clueless about the High School of Performing Arts. Therefore, it was no good.

I found a drama school I could attend on Saturdays. That freed me from the trauma of shopping with Tina and only one day of the weekend to endure her! Along with the other students at drama school, we studied acting, improvisation, dance, speech, and voice. Some of us talked about eventually going to the Actor's Studio. Method acting was intensely discussed.

Saturdays were absolutely glorious. I became very good at improvisation. My friend, Beth, and I bonded almost instantly. We were great singing duets, or at least we thought so! After classes I remember the two of us linking arms and often skipping down the street singing, *"We're off to see the wizard, the wonderful Wizard of Oz!"* I think we embarrassed our friend Hedy, who loved ballet and Prince Charles! Did Beth and I cause stares? Nah! It was New York City! Nobody cared!

Tina never asked about drama school. She hated the very idea of it. Mama and Papa? They didn't understand. Everybody was concerned. Tina constantly told me that acting was a ridiculous pursuit for me. She made it very clear over and over. Eventually, her contempt was unavoidable

"Nobody's going to hire you to act! What is wrong with you? You ain't gon' be nobody acting. How many Negroes do you see acting?" she would rhetorically ask. (I could say, she was trying to protect me, looking out for me. Successful Black actors were few and far between. But it didn't justify her scorn and condescension.)

Having survived being the only Black kid in so many classes during elementary school, I wasn't bothered by the odds. But her words crushed me. I didn't understand why I couldn't try, so I continued. To hell with Tina.

Reading Variety one day at drama school with friends, I found an ad for an open call to audition for The Young People's Repertory Theatre. It was an off-Broadway venture that would perform modern and ancient classics. The difference would be the cast. You couldn't be over twenty-five. I auditioned and I was accepted. Tina was sick with shock. She tried to pretend that none of this was happening.

"Who are these people? They've accepted *you*?" she asked.

I showed her the letter and the background material on the company. Two women were the founders, Terry Hayden and Stella Spence. Tina's face was a storm of emotions, panic, fear, frustration.

"What will you have to do?" she asked.

"What do you mean? I'll act!" I thought to myself, *"Why does she ask questions like that? They make no sense!"*

"You have to go to rehearsals?" she inquired coldly.

"Yeah, Tina…" Again, I thought to myself, *"Is she out of her mind? Of course, I have to go to rehearsals! What is wrong with her?"*

"Well, I don't know…" she said quietly and looked down at me while throwing the letter of acceptance on the dining table.

Another battle during the war of adolescence was on.

Chapter Twenty-Three

Bloodletting

Mama and Papa were wary about this acting business, but quite proud of me. Tina? Her anger seethed just below the surface. She tried her best to hide it in public. She failed.

My participation in the Young People's Repertory Theatre became a flashpoint. Tina placed all her energy in getting me to give up the theatre. No matter how hard she tried, she couldn't control who I was becoming and that enraged and frightened her. So, she launched a new reign of emotional terrorism.

"What makes you think these people want you?" she asked every time I got ready to go to rehearsal. "They don't want anything to do with you. They're just using you."

I never responded to these taunts, but a cold fire burned like dry ice inside me fueling more migraines, digestive problems, and anxiety that made me tense and always on edge. I felt like a trigger being pressed to shoot. I kept trying to address her comments with logic. "What would these people be using me for? Why?" But Tina had succeeded in planting the seed that grew into a tree of doubt, with me believing, "I'm not worth anything." Relief was instant the minute I got out of the house. I tried to dismiss Tina's comments and all that they implied but I never quite succeeded. The longer I stayed around her, the less worthwhile I felt. I wasn't good at ignoring her, but I was good at *pretending to ignore her*. Our bond had become what's labeled as "negative bonding."

If you're an artist you could say, I was Tina's "negative space." Negative space is "the space around and between the subject(s) of an image."

Vicious verbal explosions began when invitations were issued to a cast party or dinner by one of the co-founders, Stella Spence, at her home. I would ask for permission and the battle would begin. Tina's opening salvo was looking at me like I was crazy.

"Go to a party? Where? *Why do you want to go to the party?*" She was baffled and almost indignant. Mama and Papa trusted no invitation from white people. Papa would shake his head from side to side. No, was his message. The real drama began.

Tina grabbed a drink. She started to march back and forth, from one end of the house to the other, free arm swinging while deliberately muttering to the threshold of yelling, so I would hear what she had to say. "*You've got to be a goddamned fool! You ain't going to no party! You little red bitch! They want you? Hell no. You're going to disgrace all of us! All this money we're spending on you and you do this? This is nothin' but mess.*"

I wanted to put my fist through her face. Papa watches. Mama goes to her bedroom.

"When are you going to learn how to talk to me? You'll do what I say you do." She slams her drink down on the table. It spills slightly. Droplets of scotch and water fly upwards from the glass and then onto the table. Eventually, a small puddle of scotch and water surrounds the glass.

I look at the scotch puddle and then at her. I fire back with, "Not in this lifetime. I'll never be what you want me to be! You keep trying to turn me into somebody else. Keep doing that and *you'll never win!* I don't care what you do. And God knows, I don't want to be like you. Ever!" Her face seemed to tremble but her eyes were paralyzed, fixed on me. She never knew what to say after that. Her hand grabbed the glass and she retreated upstairs.

Some version of this happened on a regular basis. It was becoming our primary form of communication. The first time this eruption occurred regarding the party, I walked over to the phone, called Stella, and told her Tina wouldn't allow me to come to her home.

Stella responded with, "What?! You have to come. Let me speak to her." I shoved the phone in Tina's face. The metamorphosis begins. Tina becomes the model of grace, charm, dignity and courtesy. In a matter of seconds, she transforms into someone else. The voice, the posture, all of it changes, except for the look in her eyes, terror.

In a high-pitched, weak voice, Tina says softly, "Hello. And you are?"

Who knows what Stella said? All I saw was Tina's face harden like a trapped animal. "Well… of course. That's so very kind of you to want Janis. Oh! Aren't you nice! We're all very happy she's participating. It's wonderful you think she has so much talent! Really? She what? Has the lead?! Oh, for heaven's sake…" Tina pauses for a second or two and then lets out this silly little giggle that makes the hair on my arms stand on end. "What?" she asks with her saccharine voice dripping in pretense. "Of course, she'll be there. I'll tell her. You're so very kind. Yes, it's nice talking to you too." Tina hangs up the phone. Her smile disappears. Tina the Tyrant reappears and her voice returns to "normal."

I glare at her.

"Don't look at me that way," Tina ordered. I continue to glare at her.

She picks up her drink, and says with a sneer draped over her mouth, "She's sending a car for you. She must be rich. You can go."

Mother's Madness

Tina turns and walks out of the room, then stops, and comes back. "Do you know where she lives?" She took another sip of scotch.

"She lives on Fifth Avenue," I said.

"Fifth Avenue?" Tina gagged. "You've been invited to somebody's house on Fifth Avenue? Well, wow, wow, wow. Aren't you the little something?"

I was trying to suppress the desire to choke her or find a way to push her down a flight of stairs at my first opportunity. She never acknowledged I had the lead in "Antigone" but she came on opening night, beaming.

After the performance was over, Tina showed me the Playbill. "Your name isn't even in here."

"Oh, it is. It's right there, Christina Lawrence. I changed it."

"Why did you do that?!"

"I thought you didn't want to be associated with 'your daughter the actress' who was being made a fool of, simply being used by these people. Now you have nothing to worry about. You won't be embarrassed because nobody will know."

Most of us were carrying a double load of going to school and working in an off-Broadway repertory company. When summer came, I chose to stay and work, and not go down home with Mama. Tina was disgusted. She didn't know what to do. On one hand, she was elated that I wouldn't go South and become darker. On the other hand, I would be doing something she still thought was foolish, offensive, and denigrating. She wanted me to believe pursuing acting reflected poorly on me, and more importantly, on her. If she said that once, she said it ten thousand times. She'd always manage to get the following in, *"You don't have the good sense to know you're not wanted there.*

They're never going to accept you. Did you forget? You're a Black gal. Grow up!" Tina never understood why I persisted with this. She was "vexed" by my determination, much in the same way Commodus was (in the movie *Gladiator*), by his inability to kill Maximus. Like Commodus, Tina kept trying. And like Commodus, even though she tried to disable me, much in the same way Commodus stabbed Maximus before their last battle, she would lose and die, leaving me "victorious" without laying a hand on her. The Lord works in mysterious ways.

"It's not who your mother was,
it's who you remember her to be."
Anne Sexton, poet

Chapter Twenty-Four

What Tina Taught Me

Every now and then, I'm asked, "Didn't Tina do *anything* for you?" Another question was, "Don't you have *any* pleasant memories of her? There had to be *something*." So, what did Tina teach me besides only lesbians drive SUVs and my hair wouldn't grow back if I cut it? What did she do for me?

She saved quarters to give me for the tollbooth.

She made sure I had lots of clothes that fit well and good shoes. She had a particular abhorrence for cheap shoes. She believed they reflected "bad character."

She expounded on Mama's lesson that we were too poor to buy cheap. Buy quality items and we could. Tina helped me understand what quality was, especially when it came to clothing, and anything that had to do with my appearance. She kept telling me, all through my childhood "the price of beauty is great baby."

As I grew older, I realized Tina was right about the price of beauty. My realization had nothing to do with appearances or expensive face creams. I discovered art was expensive. That was my beauty.

When I was eight or nine, I received specific instructions about how to wash my face and the necessary upward motions that were needed to prevent wrinkles or sagging skin. It was a nightly ritual. Going for regular facials as a young woman was part of my normal. Found one aesthetician, Cheryl Ferrari, and stayed with her for a very long time.

Tina taught me how to organize. Being organized was key to accomplishing your goals, however modest they may be. It was important to lay your clothes out the night before so you wouldn't waste time in the morning figuring out what you were going to wear to school or work. Time is precious and wasted time could result in being late. Being late was something white folks expected from us; Black people were always late. What Tina didn't know was almost all ethnic people were characterized as being late. She didn't care. If you couldn't manage your time, you'd never get anything done. She was right. She just never imagined I'd take what she taught me about organizing and apply it to organizing people, doing advance work and planning routes for motorcades, working with the Secret Service, managing television production crews, creating edit plans, and on some days, simply getting from here to there.

She wanted to know everything about the people I worked with after I finished college and left Riverdale. She took on the persona of a confidant and saw no reason why I wouldn't tell her everything. I decided to be quiet and let her talk. And she did. Each story, worse than the one before, all centered on *letting no one take advantage of you*. She was upset if I worked with white people and upset if I worked with Black people. White people would try to destroy you and Black people's jealousy would drive you crazy.

She taught me to wear bright colors in the summer and dark colors in the winter. She was an advocate of wearing white between Memorial Day and Labor Day – only! And don't go out of the house looking like you fell out of bed. Consequently, my appearance was inspected every morning. She kept her eye peeled for a wool pleated black skirt I liked. Eventually, I'd hear, "You're not wearing that black skirt *again*, are you? People will think that's the only thing you own." Back up the stairs I went to change skirts and too often every other thing I was wearing so I looked coordinated.

She taught me manners – indirectly through her criticisms of what she observed in others. She'd mutter to me while watching someone else. I'd hear, "Ain't that a blip! Don't you ever go out to a restaurant and order the most expensive item if somebody else is paying." Or, "This is the first time you're going to their house you better bring them something. Don't go there empty handed and don't go there lookin' bad. Let me see what you're going to wear." Or "Don't pry into their business. If they don't bring up a subject, don't you dare ask anything about it. White folks are too damned nosey anyway."

"Don't be afraid to tell them if they ask anything that it's none of their business. And don't ever discuss money with them or anybody else." Some version of this serves as the backbone of what's known in the Black community as "good-home training". It's how to act in public, in private, with white folks, with black folks, with your boss if he or she is white and if he or she is Black, how to survive with polish and how to act with polish so you're accepted in places where they don't expect you. Good Home Training!

Tina wasn't completely wrong about white folks ignoring (your) boundaries. I showed one of the very early drafts of this book to a white friend who was also a psychologist. I was deeply interested in her comments. When she finished reading the early draft, her first question was, "Where did the money come from?" I smiled and never answered her. I never forgot either.

Tina also taught me something quite dangerous and maybe evil, certainly malicious. I learned by watching her. She had an uncanny ability to spot anyone's weakness. It was chilling to witness. The message was multifaceted and blinding making your soul squint: don't cross her, don't disobey her, don't stand up to her, don't dare demonstrate your individuality. The last lesson? *Don't ever let her see your vulnerability nor discover it.* Tina taught me how to destroy people without lifting a finger or pulling a trigger. The ammunition? Words.

She taught me to keep my emotions hidden, especially from her. If I let them out for any reason, she'd work to break my will, like a cowboy breaking in a horse.

I am a quiet person. Don't mistake this for shyness or insecurity. I could be sizing you up, waiting for the perfect time, considering the best phrases that will cut your heart in two, leaving it and you, bloodless and motionless. I watched Tina. Wounding is for amateurs. There are many reasons I go to church.

Tina taught me to set traps for people to determine if they would really treat you fairly. All those "friends" who said you were just like family, were you? And all those people you worked with who promised to "do right by you", would they? How many smile in your face and then rob you blind hoping you won't notice? You may have to sacrifice something pursuing that knowledge, but that was okay. Find out because people can't be trusted. People have betrayed me thinking I didn't notice. I found that out as recently as eight to nine months ago. They don't know that I know. I set a trap for them. I can afford to do this. I have an evil patience. Don't let my size or my smile fool you. I was taught by an expert.

Tina weaponized money, using it to manipulate, humiliate, demean and control people, including me, especially me.

She sent Terry up by plane to bring me a dozen hot dogs from the Skyview Deli in Riverdale. Brown mustard was included. Terry was instructed to turn around and take the next shuttle back to New York from Boston.

Tina sent Carrie, our housekeeper in Riverdale, to help me clean whenever I moved into a new apartment.

Tina let me know that white people will always expect the worst from you and jump to false conclusions. Don't ever expect them to do the right thing because *they really don't care about you.* Too often she was right, especially if they could commodify you and get something monetary in return.

Tina taught me anybody could be pushed to the breaking point and kill. She helped me realize I could kill her. But "Thou shall not kill…" keeps playing in my head on an endless loop. Thank God, because I've seen the inside of a medium security prison. The noise is beyond articulation. The aesthetics are unpleasant. I wouldn't last.

I saw a sweatshirt I wanted to buy. It had a saying sewn on the front, something like the following, "I'll throw you in the trunk of a car, lock it, throw away the keys, and join the search party looking for you… Do not mess with me."

Tina introduced me to my dark side.

Chapter Twenty-Five

Moving

Shortly after I started Music and Art, Tina told me we were going to move. It was 1965. Mama and Papa had decided to sell the brownstone to the synagogue next door. Mama reached this decision reluctantly. She thought that one day the brownstone would be a gold mine, and she was right. But the brownstone was also becoming too much for her to take care of. The brownstone had 16 rooms with three baths spread out over three floors, not counting the basement with the "rec" room. Every now and then, they'd rent out a room to a Black graduate student, usually from Columbia University, who couldn't afford room and board. Yet with all those rooms, Tina and Mama railed against Papa's siblings who wanted to come and visit. Harry's mysterious family was never a consideration. I understood that. But Papa's family? I found it very perplexing.

Tina was angry with the realtor she contacted. "Do you know where he's looking? The dizzy bastard, he thinks we're going to move to the Polo Grounds! Ain't nobody moving there with them niggers. Is he crazy?!" Right hand holding a drink, left arm swinging back and forth, she stomped out of the kitchen and up the stairs to her bedroom.

Papa told Tina he didn't want Harry moving with us. Once again, Papa offered to pay for a divorce.

"No, it'll be okay…" she said. When Mama expressed similar thoughts, Tina told her, "This is none of your business."

I prayed Harry would leave. I was tired; tired of the yelling, fighting, broken furniture, clothing he ripped to shreds, and the profanity. That was something I never heard from Mama and

Papa. I was also tired of being scared all the time. It wasn't safe with Harry around, regardless of where we lived. He never apologized while he was alive. Harry barely spoke at all. I wanted him gone.

It would be decades before any studies were done regarding children who witness domestic violence. But when the research was conducted, they found out what I already felt and knew. "...exposure to domestic violence affects children in a range of deleterious ways. It affects their emotional development, their social functioning, their ability to negotiate intimate relationships as adolescents and adults," according to Betsy McAlister Groves, author of, *Children Who See Too Much.* I had already seen enough.

We moved to Fieldston Road in Riverdale. It's an interesting community in the northwest corner of the Bronx. There were high-rise apartment buildings, the massive residence behind guarded and gated entrances for UN employees from the (then) Soviet Union, there were one or two residences for ambassadors. Private schools served as bookends on Fieldston Road. At the northern end, The Riverdale Country Day School. At the southern end The School for Ethical Culture, and the Horace Mann School. The Architectural Digest section of Fieldston Road had cobblestone streets, big lawns, big houses, and big New York money, which meant it was obvious money, but in this case, tastefully used.

The middle-class section, that would've been big money anywhere else in America at that time, is where we lived. There were two family homes, side by side town houses, a modern apartment complex and another complex that reminded me of the Dakota Apartment building where John Lennon and Yoko Ono would live one day. There were one or two other black families on Fieldston Road. We never met them. Tina said, "Why would I want to meet them? They ain't got nothin' I want!" I hated Riverdale. I hated the house. This was another version of fake home, complete with Harry.

Minutes before the moving van arrived, Tina and I had our first Fieldston confrontation. I saw her fly by with some of my things. She stomped up the stairs and I asked her, "Where are you going with my stuff?"

"I'm taking your things upstairs. You'll be staying with me and Harry."

I raced up the stairs and said, "Wait a minute!"

She turned and looked at me, her eyes full of fear but defiant. "What?"

"I'm not staying up there with you. I'm staying downstairs with Mama and Papa."

"Oh no, little lady! We're your par..."

I cut her off and repeated, *"I'm not staying up there,"* while thinking to myself, *"You've got to be out of your mind!"* The van pulled up. "You want me to go ask Papa?" I asked firmly.

Her face became stone, and there was a pause for two or three seconds. "Do whatever you want, Janis," Tina said. Her voice was flat.

"Give me the boxes, Tina." I took the two small boxes with my name on them, turned and walked down the stairs. We entered a new era.

I found the house in Riverdale to be claustrophobic and stuffy. Tina never liked to open the windows. That meant she'd throw a fit if anyone even cracked one open. Mama and Papa grew more and more disgusted with their daughter's marriage, and Tina? Her drinking increased but no one said anything and our relationship went from bad to worse.

There were so many fights between us, fights I didn't understand, fights that I've forgotten, but not the pain. I still live with that damage every day. I always felt I was fighting for my life around her. It was hard to know Tina's pain. She started doing things that alarmed me, caused me to panic and avoid her, which was harder to do in the Riverdale house. Her behavior became inexplicable, an elusive web of irrational and startling responses that often ensnared you, left you speechless or mortified, if you weren't very careful.

The Riverdale house was her newest victim. She spent more time maintaining appearances and keeping things in order. Plastic slipcovers were ordered. They became her obsession. She never asked Mama if she wanted plastic slipcovers. One day some man arrived to take measurements. Mama was shocked but gave in to Tina's plans. Papa didn't care so long as his recliner was left untouched. After the slipcovers, plastic runners went down crisscrossing the carpet she had installed to cover the hardwood floors. Tina instructed us to walk *only on the plastic runners*. Papa ignored her. I walked wherever I wanted, and Mama simply said, "Um-hmm." Tina decided we were no longer to use our porcelain dishes. She began to siphon off plastic dishware from her school and insisted that we eat only on them to preserve the "real china". Mama refused on the grounds that you couldn't get plastic dishes clean. Tina was shocked! Plastic dishes stained easily according to Mama, so we continued to eat on "real china". Tina was left standing in the dining room with her mouth open.

Tina's disregard for the delicacy of china, crystal goblets, and wine glasses baffled me. She just threw the crystal into one of the buffet cabinets. The crystal and wine glasses landed any ol' which way. She wrapped half-eaten pieces of toast in plastic wrap and refrigerated them. Fresh food was suspect, and too much trouble to cook. She railed against Papa's garden in the backyard. Everything Papa touched blossomed. It required tending beyond opening a can, and that was all Tina wanted to do. She viewed cooking with a hostile eye. She had several cramped, pot bound but neat plants, screaming for larger pots. I could hear them. These plants were interspersed among her artificial ones.

I rarely saw Tina eat anymore, only drink. She would cook Harry's dinner, wrap each portion of food in aluminum foil and then wrap the whole plate, set it over the stove's pilot light and leave it for him. Eventually the plastic plates burned.

No room on Tina's floor was untouched by her decorating and that included her bathroom. It was carpeted (as was her kitchen). Both the kitchen and the bathroom carpets required covering yet again to "save" it. The solution? Scatter rugs.

I found her sense of color insulting! It was in its full glory in her bathroom. The walls, tiles, tub, basin, toilet were mint green. The bathroom carpet was hot pink with a matching fluffy cover for the toilet lid. There was a gold étagère over the toilet to hold her cosmetics. Pinned on the hot pink hand towels was a note in her handwriting that said, "Do not use these towels. These are for decoration only." Then there was the Saturday I considered to be a frightening, turning point.

Mama, Papa and I heard her yelling. It was a Saturday morning.

"Oh my God! What the hell has he done? Oh my God," she bellowed.

(We didn't know if Harry was gone. He usually dressed up and left early to head down to Harlem and meet his buddies or worse.) Papa was reading the paper. He looked up at me. I said to him, "I'll go find out."

Mama walked in the living room and asked, "What is wrong? Is it *him*?" She was referring to Harry.

"I don't know, Mama." I was a little afraid to go upstairs, but I did. When I walked in, Tina was stomping out of the bathroom and heading to her kitchen.

Quietly, I ask, "What's going on?"

Ripping off several paper towels in the kitchen, she turns and looks at me. Almost hissing, she says, "The dizzy bastard! He got the tiles wet."

"What do you mean, he got the tiles wet?"

Walking past me, deep frowns digging their way into her forehead, she tells me, "He took a shower!"

I stood there a few seconds thinking, "How do you take a shower and not get the tiles wet?" I walked to the bathroom, stood in the door and watched Tina. She vigorously wiped the tiles dry that surrounded the tub, all the while swearing under her breath.

When she wasn't worried about the wet tiles, the choking plants, or somebody daring not to walk on those plastic runners, she was worried about my safety. I remember her calling a cab for me so I could go downtown to shop, of course. It was a cab service we used frequently in Riverdale. They knew us by name.

The cab pulls up. It was one of those old-fashioned, boxy Checker cabs with two jump seats in the back. The driver is accompanied by another person. As I walk to the cab, Tina comes running out shouting, housecoat tightly wrapped around her. Chinese satin slippers flip-flopping up and down like bird wings. "What is going on here?"

I turn and look at her. "What are you talking about?"

"There're two men in there," she says. Her face is drawn up so all of her features now form a frown. The suspicion in her eyes is palpable. She grabs me by the arm and whispers, "They could take you off somewhere and kill you." She immediately let go of me and runs to the cab. The passenger window is lowered and she sticks her head in to talk to them. "I'm not letting my daughter go downtown with two of you."

I could see the driver's stunned look. I hear him say, "Mrs. Pryor, this is a new driver. He's just going around with me today to see how things are done, the routes, you know?"

"I don't care. Come back with one driver," Tina orders. And that was the end of that. The cab pulls away. Tina turns around and walks back to the house telling me again, "They could kill you."

I stand there thinking, *"The only one who could kill us is Harry!"* As I walk back to the house, I think about Mama and the white cabs down home and wait for Riverdale Taxi to return with only one driver, who may or may not kill me.

A Word About Rio...as in Brazil...and Tina

I'm not sure when this began but Tina started accumulating jewelry from these trips to Rio, diamond rings, gold bracelets. I'd overhear a sentence, maybe a muffled paragraph from a phone conversation. Then somebody got sick and off to the hospital she went, sitting by somebody's bed. I'd hear Tina mumble about someone's wife she would meet at the hospital, something about visiting in shifts. And then I remember concentrating on all that I heard. I'd stare into space reviewing everything as if I were watching a movie with missing scenes. That voice said, "She's having an affair. Just wait. She'll tell you." I could see Papa shaking his head. I inhaled and exhaled slowly saying to myself, *"Oh, for God's sake."*

She wanted to give me some jewelry with semi-precious stones. I remember being annoyed and asked, "Tina, where did you get this from?"

"One of my trips to Rio," she said as if I should've known. "I've had this relationship... He takes me to Rio, and he..."

I cut her off with, "I really don't want to know this."

Her voice jumped an octave. "Oh, my goodness! Aren't you sophisticated! Wow, wow, wow! His wife and I..."

"I don't want to know, do you understand? And it's got nothing to do with being sophisticated."

Eyes wide and quite bewildered, she pulled back the corners of her lower lip. "Oh..."

Whoever this man was, he died and left her some money. The trips to Rio stopped. No more jewelry. And no more affection for Tina.

Chapter Twenty-Six

Enter Dr. Gaynor

Dr. Greenstein was my pediatrician in New York. I remember him as a nice man who spent a lot of time listening to Tina. I have vague memories of his waiting room. There were copies of back editions of Highlights Magazine for children. Maybe that's how my passion for magazines started. His office and examining room were some odd color of pale pink with more than an undercoat of beige.

As I crossed the Rubicon of childhood into adolescence, Dr. Greenstein announced I was getting too old to have a pediatrician. I needed a grown-up doctor. Tina called the pediatrician assigned to her school at the time, Dr. Karen. Dr. Karen suggested Dr. Arthur Gaynor. He was an internist and cardiologist at Montefiore Hospital in the Bronx, not too far by car from where we lived in Riverdale if you took Mosholu Parkway. Tina made an appointment, and we went to see Dr. Gaynor. His waiting room was crowded, and he was running late. I remember immediately liking Tillie, his nurse-secretary. I don't think people like Tillie exist anymore. The practice of medicine has changed so much. She made you feel seen, acknowledged, and considered.

When I met Dr. Arthur Gaynor, he made me feel seen, acknowledged, and considered. He had a very soothing, comforting, presence that was totally foreign to me and he listened to what I said and didn't say. It was almost as if Tina disappeared in his presence. Revisiting that day in my memory, I discovered something rather shocking for its significance to me.

Aside from Papa, Dr. Gaynor was the only other person with whom I felt safe.

He diagnosed my headaches as migraines and found it a little troubling that I had them to begin with. He asked me when I had the first one. I told him I was nine. Although the expression on his face didn't change, his eyes did. That's how I knew migraines at nine were not a good thing. He had to wonder what was going on that would generate migraines in a child and on into her adolescence. How often did I have "these headaches" he asked? I told him every week. They'd start on Fridays usually. I couldn't stand loud noises or bright lights. There has been a new migraine drug developed at Montefiore called Fiorinal. He wrote a prescription, and I got some relief if I could take it when the migraine first presented itself, or if I could get out of the house. The third option was decapitation!

We discovered that Dr. Gaynor lived maybe three blocks from us on Mosholu Avenue. Tina was resurrected by this. She emerged from her slump of indifference and I heard her say, "Oh for heaven's sake!" I clearly remember thinking, *"Oh thank God he's nearby. Maybe I can visit."*

I want to tell you about every minute I spent with the Gaynor family because that's how precious it was to me.

I want to tell you about the first time I visited their house and met their children, the relief I felt when I realized there were no plastic slipcovers on their living room couch, no plastic runners on the floor. Going to their house the first time was a very big deal from Tina's perspective. She supervised every item I put on. There was a gift I had for them and there was a long list of things that I was not to do when I got there. As a result, I was over dressed and not very relaxed at all. That was something the Gaynor adults picked up. I could see it on their faces.

I want to tell you about the extraordinary meals I had with them and came to realize that some people actually had conversations and good food at dinner. The Gaynors invited friends over from time to time. They sat down and talked and laughed with each other over a great meal! I felt like an alien from another planet observing the human species.

I want to tell you how they became my shelter from the constant emotional upheaval that was my life on Fieldston Road, and how I practically moved in, much to the disappointment of Mama and Papa. I remember it being a gradual process. Leaving home for any other reason than going to school constituted breaking one of the rules of Black solidarity.

I stayed with the Gaynors for long stretches during college. I shamed the family, humiliated them. Tina was panic-stricken. Mama and Papa were devastated. But I was safe with the Gaynors.

I have to tell you I was full of insecurities and thought the Gaynors didn't want me around. That's what Tina kept saying, but I was desperate. I had to ignore her as she shouted, "They're Jewish. They don't want you!" But they opened their home and their hearts to me.

I want to tell you about Evelyn Gaynor, M.D., hematologist, who gave me another model of motherhood. Evelyn was a hot ticket! I never saw her demean her children. She seemed to enjoy them! Tina never enjoyed me.

I want to tell you about their three children, Alison, Chris, and Jenny in that order. Chris and I share the same birthday, and he said recently, "We shared a father." He was right. Arthur Gaynor was the closest thing I had to a contemporary father.

I want to tell you about the terrible jokes Dr. Gaynor would make that always teased the borders of being politically incorrect. What I remember is groaning when I heard one, or looking at him and saying, "You can't say those kinds of things!" One time he went too far at work! I remember Chris and Alison telling me he was seriously reprimanded at the hospital.

I want to tell you he made *the best scrambled eggs* I've ever had.

I want to tell you Evelyn and Arthur Gaynor drove to Vermont for my college graduation and how joyful I was. I can still see them standing and smiling.

Were they perfect? No. There were fights and moments that bordered on total chaos especially at the dinner table. I remember looking up once, just in time to see Chris throw some food at one of his sisters. He was so defiant in ways that made me crazy and hysterical with laughter at the same time. I watched Chris more than Alison and Jenny. Maybe it was because we had the same birthday. I don't know. Maybe it was because I detected an intensity that was familiar to me, that I'd seen in other people. When he was around eight, I knew his secret. I'm not sure when he knew, but it's his story to tell, not mine. It made no difference to me but I did worry and still do. As I write this, we're living in crazy, hateful times. Chris and I are targets.

I want to tell you they gave me an opportunity to see love in action framed by the full range of vulnerabilities and imperfections, big dysfunctions and little dysfunctions. I didn't need perfection. I needed some version of healthy love that wouldn't destroy me. They had that!

All three children were remarkably beautiful, with stunning combinations of their parents' features, high cheekbones, gorgeous skin and shiny dark hair. Jenny was the reason I decided age three was the cutest age. When you looked at her, you knew she was Arthur Gaynor's daughter, just as Alison was Evelyn Gaynor's daughter. And Chris? He magically morphed into both. It was amazing to witness.

I want to tell you how Evelyn's death from cancer, when I was in my early twenties, shattered something inside of me that's never been repaired. Their friend, Liz Russo, whom I got to know and liked, called me at work to let me know Evelyn's diagnosis. Liz explained that Evelyn had been given roughly six months to live. It was incomprehensible.

Mama and Papa were deeply saddened by the news. Tina was terrified. She kept saying, "Cancer? Oh my God. She's got cancer." Mama and Papa felt I should spend as much time as I wanted with the Gaynors. Tina, fearing death, was all but immobilized. She was amazed that I was not afraid. Fear was the last thing on my mind.

The last time I saw Evelyn in mid-May, she was home in bed upstairs. She opened her eyes, looked at me and said, "There was so much I wanted to do."

"I know," I said, standing at the foot of the bed.

"I need you to help me," she said and motioned for me to come closer.

I walked over. She pointed to a box of bath powder lying on the bed.

She asked if I could sprinkle some on her. I did, and in the process saw the scar that had replaced her breast. Several years before, she had a radical mastectomy. I think she had passed the five-year mark, but perhaps the pain from her congenital arthritis masked the symptoms from the recurrence of cancer.

Evelyn was a beautiful, vibrant woman, wonderful cheekbones, smooth skin and bright eyes. I helped reposition her in bed so she was more comfortable. She was surprised at my physical strength. While my arms held her, she said, "You're strong!"

I smiled and fluffed up the pillows for her. By this point, tears slid down my cheeks.

Her face was crying out, "I want to live," not with words, but with make-up! There was too much of it! The softness of blush became the harshness of rouge. Eye shadow resembled eye paint. Her features were exaggerated, but the beauty shined regardless.

"JP? I want you to promise me two things."

"Okay."

"One, don't spend your life sleeping alone, and two, watch over Alison for me." Saying that much exhausted her.

She was afraid I'd go through life never knowing what it was to love or be loved. She made me promise that wouldn't happen.

She wanted me to stay connected to the children. I nodded my head. I would have promised anything if that brought her any comfort. I wiped my eyes.

At one point, she heard the kids raging downstairs. She got up, grabbed her cane, and went after them. Her gown flew behind her like wings! There was no stopping her. She returned to the bedroom muttering, "I'm not gone yet!"

I helped her get back in bed and position herself again. I don't know if I said goodbye. I said something. I got in my car and drove back to Boston where I was living at the time. I didn't think it was possible to cry as much as I did while driving back. The sobs came from some mysterious place inside me that I knew nothing about until then. The Merritt Parkway was my witness. I planned on coming back the following week or so. I told myself, she wouldn't die until I saw her again. She couldn't die, but she did in early June. Liz called me at work to let me know. With Evelyn gone nothing would be the same, nor should it be.

By the time I got to the first set of tollbooths on the Mass Pike, driving back to Riverdale, I was numb. That shattered space in me became a hole in my heart. It's still there and always will be. I wondered if Evelyn knew what a significant force she was in my life. I didn't realize its magnitude until she left.

I remember the depth of Jenny's sobs and how Dr. Gaynor scooped her up in his arms at the Temple when the service ended. It felt like Alison disappeared when her mother died, kidnapped by grief, adolescence, and rage. I've always wondered how alone Chris felt without his mother. And Dr. Gaynor put on a good front until the evening before the funeral.

He was talking to someone on the deck and broke down. Nobody was doing well. Yet, everything looked so "normal" to anyone passing by while a tragedy was going on inside the Gaynor home.

Losing Evelyn required therapy of the highest order. I wasn't easy to treat. But I found a miracle, Dr. Harvey Schein of McLean's Hospital in Belmont, Massachusetts. McLean's was infamous among a certain group of Bennington graduates, many of whom belonged to the "Crazy Mothers Club." You could say McLean's was a form of "graduate work" or a mental health "finishing school" for some of us. I was so relieved after talking with Dr. Schein. He was someone who "got" the complexity of my life. I remember him saying, "I think I can help you." He was very smart and I wouldn't be able to con him nor dismiss him as an idiot. The Bennington mind was not going to be a stumbling block for him but a stepping-stone. Healing was nearby. McLean Hospital had sheltered and helped many artistic, tortured souls over the years. It seemed perfectly natural I'd find my way there too. Harvey Schein was hope.

Several days after our first meeting, a colleague of his called to let me know Dr. Schein had died of a massive heart attack. Whatever his colleague said after that I didn't hear it. Word spread that Dr. Schein committed suicide. Who knew? Heart attack or suicide, he was gone. I tried not to scream.

It would be years before I felt strong enough to go back to the Gaynor house. I wasn't sure I could stand it without Evelyn there. Dr. Gaynor eventually remarried a kind, sweet woman, named Elizabeth. I couldn't help but think of her as an intruder but she made him happy and that's all I cared about. Tina neglected to tell me about the wedding until it was over. She sent photos. She had gone to the wedding.

Dr. Gaynor, Elizabeth, Alison and her husband, Gordon, came for some holiday dinner at my house in central Massachusetts decades later. Ironically, Alison and Gordon lived in Grafton, MA, not too far from me at the time. I had some other friends there, one being a very important person in my life, my mentor, my idol, my pal, my true north, Rose vonThater Braan Imai, former Director of Education for the University of California Berkley Center for Particle Astrophysics, Director of Silver Buffalo Consulting, and most importantly from my perspective, Tuscarora/Cherokee Elder. I still want to grow up and be like Rose!

Dr. Gaynor's hair was now steel gray. Age had taken an inch or two from his height, but he still had that dangerous, politically incorrect sense of humor. He almost did something that would've insulted Rose and left me speechless. I remember hissing quietly, "Stop that!" He had that grin on his face. He knew what he was doing! Thank God, Rose was out of the room.

He hugged me tightly when he left. I hugged him back and smiled. He stepped into Alison and Gordon's car. I waved as they pulled out of the driveway.

I walked back to the dining table, sat down, and started to cry. Rose asked, "What's the matter?"

I told her, "I don't think I'm ever going to see him again."

I didn't. A few years later, Chris called and told me the father we shared had died after a long illness. I had been expecting this for some time, but it didn't make it any easier or less painful. I was silent. All the air left my body, everything stopped, at least that's how it felt. Eventually, I found my voice and said, "I'll call you back." I was outside when Chris called, far north in Jackson, New Hampshire, nowhere near Riverdale or metro Boston. It was cold. I sat down on the steps, took a deep breath, folded my arms on my knees and put my head down. There was nobody left at that time who loved me for just me, without all the bells and whistles I managed to professionally acquire that made so many white people take renewed interest in me once introduced, and so many Black people view me with suspicion and jealousy. Arthur Gaynor, M.D. was gone. I was no longer safe.

Chapter Twenty-Seven

Vermont

You could only apply to three colleges when I was going to High School. And one of those schools had to be your "safe school". The safe school was City College. There was no way I was doing that. The thought of spending another four years in New York, in Riverdale, and commuting to City College where Music and Art was then located was absurd. My so-called Guidance Counselor thought I was insane. She was a tight little white woman with her white hair pulled back in a firm bun. She kept trying to convince me to apply to City College. I kept saying no. This woman knew nothing about me except for my transcript.

"I think it's foolish not to apply to a safe school," she said somewhat annoyed.

"I'm not going to City College," I told her, and that was the end of it. I'm sure she thought I would change my mind. I didn't.

Tina had another memory of the safe school issue. According to Tina, she told me that when it was time to apply for college, we would both see the guidance counselor. "She wanted you to go to City College. *I told her no. They wanted to know why I didn't go to City College. Why I had to go to Columbia!*" The only place Tina saw the guidance counselor was in her mind.

The guidance counselor wasn't the biggest hurdle. Tina was. I wanted to visit the campuses.

She told me, "Oh, we can't do that. We don't have any money to do that."

"What? I've got to see these places, Tina. I'm not spending four years at a place I haven't seen."

"Well, we can go to Sarah Lawrence. You should really be accepted there because you could commute. You wouldn't have to stay on campus, and we could save that money for dorms and things…"

I remember staring at her like she had grown another head. I said, "That's insane."

"You must think money grows on trees here. I can't take off from work and go with you to see these colleges. What is wrong with you? Maybe Sarah Lawrence… but I can't go to Vermont or Pennsylvania to that other school, and you can't go alone. Oh no."

"Well," I said. "Somebody better go with me."

"Oh, for God's sake, Janis. I'll find somebody to go with you to Vermont, but not that school in Pennsylvania. I don't know why you want to go there anyway. And you're applying to Bennington, too? That's a very exclusive school. Only *brilliant* people go there…"

I gave her a hard stare and said, "Yeah… your point?"

"Oh my God, wow, wow, wow – so exclusive," she mumbled. Then with great exaggeration, closed her eyes tightly before opening them because she couldn't see me there!

Mama yelled, "Lyn'tine!"

Tina almost jumped and answered, "Yes ma'am! I'm coming!" She quickly walked to Mama's bedroom. I waited a few seconds and then followed her.

Mama was seated on the edge of her bed, frowning. Tina walked over to her. Her back was to the doorway where I was standing. "Yes ma'am?"

Mama looked at Tina and said, "Look, there's money for Janis to visit her colleges. You shouldn't be telling her that you don't have the money! What do you do with your salary anyway,

Lyn'tine? You and Harry working, and you can't find money for this?"

Tina sent one of "her" teachers with me, a young woman named Faye. Going downtown to shop on Saturdays was one thing but taking time from her job was something else. What remains with me after all these years was how annoyed Tina was at the expectation that she should accompany me to see the campuses of Bennington and Carnegie Tech.

Carnegie Tech's drama department held auditions in Manhattan for applicants who were considering a major in drama. I did a piece from Chekhov's, *The Seagull*. There were three faculty members seated behind a folding table. Nothing glamorous about the surroundings. When I finished, they asked a few questions. One of them asked if I knew who Beah Richards was. I didn't. He smiled and said, "You remind me of her. Go look her up." I did. She was one of a handful of Black actors at the time. I had an English teacher in high school who said I could be the next Lorraine Hansberry. I began to wonder where the "next me" was located in all these comparisons.

It was obvious to anyone who knew me why I applied to Carnegie Tech! I applied to Sarah Lawrence to get Tina off my back, and Bennington College for their progressive approach to education. Their art department was legendary. Tina was convinced I'd get into Sarah Lawrence. When I received a rejection letter from Sarah Lawrence, Tina was devastated. I was delighted and relieved.

I wanted to see the Bennington Campus. I had never been to Vermont and the idea of getting out of the city made me drunk with anticipation. Tina kept wondering why I wanted to see the campus. There was just something about it that she found insulting or offensive. I was now at the stage where nothing she said or did struck me as odd anymore. Odd was her normal.

My first impression of the Bennington campus was I could breathe there. I had been aching for open spaces and beautiful scenery. That was Bennington. Everything about it, I liked. The first thing I said to myself was, *"This is the place."* There it was, hugged by the Green Mountains, set up like a small New England village with approximately 300 women. Bennington remained a women's college until my junior year. There were always some male students who were dance fellows. Three hundred gifted, driven, intense, highly intelligent young women selected to explore, create, experiment and most importantly, embrace the finer points of learning how to think. It was Mecca for creative students, heaven for dance majors with all the angst, pretense, and pain that accompanies talent. We had access to professors. Classes were small, almost like tutorials. My mind could breathe at Bennington. It was unlikely I would get bored.

When I came back home and told Mama and Papa about Bennington, they liked it. Papa was quite pleased that the students could wear jeans to class. Mama was pleased that it was a women's college. She didn't want me getting distracted and "make the mistake" of getting married.

It was also far enough away so Tina couldn't easily get there.

The letters arrived in early spring. I got accepted to Carnegie Tech and Bennington. Tina was dumbfounded. She wanted to know if it was cold in Vermont. That was her only question.

Like a mantra, Tina kept repeating when I was in earshot, *"I really didn't think you'd get accepted. Wow… very exclusive. Only brilliant people go there…"*

I looked at her from time to time and said, "Always a kind word."

"Shut up," she said.

Mama made a point of letting me know over and over, "Not to worry about the money. Everything is taken care of." They never lied to me. I believed them and didn't worry.

Before Bennington, I had to endure high school graduation. Senior year had been an exercise in enduring boredom! Although I was dangerously bored, I was also a nervous wreck! There were two more hurdles to clear, taking and passing the Regents exams, and suffering through graduation.

The pressure of the Regents was extraordinary. Although I had good grades, I didn't do well on exams. I remember staying up all night studying for the Regents. I was so tired by the time I had taken all of them during senior year I fell asleep in the shower one morning!

There were a certain number of exams one had to pass in order to get an academic diploma. No academic diploma put your college acceptance at risk. Come hell or high water I had to pass, otherwise Mama, Papa, and Tina would kill me. The other wonderful thing about Bennington at that time? There were no exams and no traditional grades. You wrote papers and received comments from your professors. If you could read you could write, and if you could write you could think, and if you could think you were automatically "value added." Hallelujah! You were almost home free.

Chapter Twenty-Eight

The Day the Earth Stopped

The day before my last English Regents Exam, Tina and I had a bitter exchange. It was late afternoon, shortly after she arrived home from work. I can't remember what the argument was about. What added fuel to my outburst was the poisonous tone in Tina's voice. It had enough venom to make a rattlesnake recoil. I had two options: fight back or die. As I walked downstairs, she shouted, "I'll have Harry come down and take care of you!"

Harry lumbered into the living room. To me, he looked twice as big than he really was. He walked over to me and said, "Your mother…" and then he hit me. It was a wallop right across my face. I almost lost my balance and fell. That's when the earth stopped moving.

Tina stood behind him smiling and smug.

Papa was on his feet. Mama came rushing in. Papa told Harry, "Lay another hand on her and I'll kill you."

"Old man, sit down. You can't do nothin'!"

"I'm not too old to pull the trigger of a gun," Papa said, "and blow your brains out. Don't you ever lay another hand on her."

"William, be quiet," Mama said. "Stay out of this."

"Get him out of here Lyn'tine," Papa shouted! "Get out of my house and stay out. I mean it. I'm tired of him."

"Papa, I…" Tina started to say.

Mama rushed over to Tina and said, "Do what your Daddy says, Lyn'tine. Get him out of here right now."

Harry had already left. I stood there watching all this as if it was on television. I was disassociated. Mama walked over to me and asked, "Baby, are you alright?"

I looked at her and said, "No."

Tina fled up the stairs. Papa shouted, "Lyntine! Come down here." His voice sounded like thunder. He walked back to the living room and sat in his recliner.

Tina came down the stairs. Her steps were deliberate and loud. She walked right past me, her eyes darting around in every possible direction. She knew she had crossed a serious line. The tension bounced off her body like ping-pong balls.

With the meekest voice she could find, she asked, "What's the matter?"

Mama let out one of those intonations of outrage. I continued to watch.

"I want him out of here, Lyntine," Papa said.

"But Papa..."

"I want him out of here. Now if you want to go with him, you can git gone too. Let me give you a guarantee, he will *never* touch that child again."

"Papa, Janis won't talk to me with any respect, at all. I told Harry to come down here and fix it."

I was barely breathing. Mama was standing behind me holding my hand.

"He's no good. He's never been worth anything. I don't want to see him in this house again."

"Daddy, he has nowhere to go," Tina whispered.

"Ummmm-um-umph," Mama said. "Listen Lyntine, you heard what your Daddy said. I don't know why you hold onto Harry anyway. What is wrong with you?!"

"You can pack up some of his things and leave 'em at the front door. I've had enough," Papa said as he looked for his pipe.

Dramatically blinking her eyes, Tina walked past me, never looked at me, never said a word, and stomped up the stairs.

"Baby," Mama whispered to me.

"I'll be okay," I muttered. I went back to my bedroom, and sat down at my desk, trying to forget what just happened. I had to focus. I had a Regents exam to take the next day. I opened a book, picked up a pencil with my left hand and realized my hand was shaking. I grabbed my left hand with my right hand, hoping the shaking would stop. No one had ever hit me. I swore to myself that if he or anyone else ever hit me, I would kill them, and it wouldn't be right away either.

I had a tough time studying for the rest of the evening. No one ever mentioned this incident. Silence ruled. It was as if it never happened. I passed the Regents and secured my academic diploma.

What stands out about high school graduation was this forced photo Tina made me take with Harry on one side, Papa on the other, and me in the middle. Everybody looked miserable. Mama refused to be photographed with Harry. I'm gesturing at Tina asking rhetorically, "Why are you doing this?" when Tina took the photo. When the photo was developed, I looked at it and told her, "You can't show this to anybody."

Another Caveat

High School

What I find sad about M & A (Music and Art) is how few memories I have about those years and how few friends I held onto after graduation. Only three friends do I remember, Alexis, Dulce, and Gary. Weren't those supposed to be *the best years of your life?* Not for me. Maybe the most boring years of my life, but not the best!

There weren't many teachers who were better than books I could read on the subjects they taught. However, there was a painting teacher I'm eternally grateful to for introducing me to one of my favorite artists, Nicolas DeStael. Our painting class went to the Guggenheim to see an exhibit of Vincent Van Gogh's work. Beyond Van Gogh on one of the upper levels was DeStael. He's still not very well known here. I often tell people his work changed my life.

"How?" people ask. "What do you mean?"

I *looked* at things differently, shapes, colors, movement. I *see* more specifically. It was like being reborn. DeStael painted a bowl of lettuce. I thought it was one of the most remarkable things I'd ever seen. I've spent most of my life honing that skill, *learning how to see and knowing exactly what you're looking at. Being an artist demands that you become observant.*

The same painting teacher took us to MOMA*. Jackson Pollock was the reason. Standing surrounded by these large canvases reminded me of the movement you'd see looking through a microscope at some new life form scurrying about. And then our teacher spoke.

"*Jackson Pollock freed line from configuration to carry color."*

These are my strongest memories of high school.

Mama and I couldn't get out of New York fast enough after my graduation. My college money was in a bank down home, far from Tina's reach. Papa stayed in Riverdale. Believing in always working, he had found a job when we first moved to Riverdale, managing a laundry at a rest home at the far end of Fieldston Road. I worried about his safety. Tina had let Harry slink back.

My coping skills during high school had just about worn out. Keeping up a front for the public was draining. As far as the outside world was concerned, our household was exemplary. No outsider ever witnessed the fights. Harry's violence (privy only to the police), Mama's despondency and rage much less Tina's behavior, all of this, hidden behind closed doors. Her actions were becoming more and more conflicted, hostile, erratic, and unpredictable. There was something very wrong with Tina and everybody pretended she was just fine, except for me.

*MOMA – Museum of Modern Art, Manhattan

Chapter Twenty-Nine

I Went to Bennington

When it's all said and done, what did Bennington *do for me*? It taught me how to think, how to process information, how to embrace the legacy that you never really stop learning, that you could do anything you wanted to do! Bennington was the last place that knew all of the intellectual and gifted me. The comfort that provided has never been found outside those gates that introduced me to the remarkably beautiful campus.

What did it *give me*? A profound love of art created during the residual impact of post-World War II artists like Marc Rothko, Helen Frankenthaler (a Bennington graduate), Jules Olitski, Robert Motherwell, the pervasive influence of the Bauhaus and LeCorbusier, Ellsworth Kelley, Barnett Newman, Rodin's drawings, Turner's oil paintings, and the extraordinary influence (on me) of Claude Monet, the "Godfather" of color field painting as far as I was concerned. And color field painting was and still is my first love. Bennington prepared my intellect to recognize decades later the genius of the late architect, Zaha Hadid, with something close to reverence because you never stop learning! Bennington gave me a community I've never been able to replicate.

Aside from the visual arts, Bennington was an oasis for modern dance, the tone, talent, and standard established by Martha Graham. Her presence hovered in every dance studio on campus. Dance students lived in a world unto themselves, leotards, stringy but strong muscles, and constant concerns about food. They challenged the very definition of dance, not to mention adjectives of "odd" and "intense." What we, "the others" learned, was dancers unlike visual artists, writers, and musicians live on borrowed time. Their bodies will eventually give out. Then what?

The Drama Department was way out there as far as I was concerned. The theatre, for me, was off-Broadway, Broadway, and Lincoln Center, not the Living Theatre with naked performers jumping down into the audience gathered in the Carriage Barn! I was not ready for that. But watching them perform remains one of the most memorable experiences I've had – ever!

Those of us who wanted to be writers, found some challenges at Bennington. The intensity was extraordinary! The professors? Familiar to anyone who reads the Book Review in the Sunday Times or The New York Review of Books. Along with that came faculty egos, genius, arrogance and a little bit of madness that would drive most people over the edge, not to mention students. Bernard Malamud was particularly "difficult." Stanley Edgar Hyman was a gift as far as I was concerned. I will never forget his analysis of the first pages of *Portrait of An Artist As A Young Man*, by James Joyce. I gained a visceral and sophisticated understanding of literary analysis thanks to Stanley Edgar Hyman. It was a history professor, Arnold Ricks, who was responsible for my grasping and appreciating abstract thinking.

Bennington was not a four year walk in the park. It was a monster, as some of us would call it, consisting of heady conversations, creative pursuits, and exploring new subjects. It constituted four years of a slow, agonizing, but necessary death, resurrection, and refinement of the mind for me. Parts of my brain were put to work that I didn't know existed! What this complex experience gave me, I wouldn't fully appreciate or notice until years after I graduated. As I struggled with the amazing reality of "B-town," as some of us called it or "the cage," I just assumed that everyone I had known in high-school and junior-high was receiving the same extraordinary education where thinking was as highly valued as learning and questioning everything was respected and held in high esteem. I was wrong.

There we were, three hundred intense young women, in competition only with ourselves. You wrote your way through Bennington unless math and science were in your curriculum. (It was decades before laptops were invented!) As mentioned earlier, papers were the way you demonstrated your understanding and knowledge. Paper Week, especially during the spring terms, was always highlighted by the sounds of students typing. The click-click-click sound flying through open windows. The all-night study room in the library becoming your second residence if you had a roommate who needed to sleep or if you couldn't resist the lure of your own bed. The dark circles under your eyes and that single-minded, creepy appearance that evolved from those papers being your world until they were completed was your "look." The formula for success was "simple": read, write, think. Remember, if you could read, you could write. If you could write, you could think. The three were intertwined. There was no escape. There would be hurdles and speedbumps, failures, and setbacks, the dreaded request for an incomplete, but that came with the territory.

Somewhere in all this, you'll find reasons for the high dropout rate at Bennington. Every year, usually in the spring, there was either one fatal car crash and/or one suicide, but you carried on. That was another skill Bennington gave you. They call it "sticktoitiveness". I don't think that's mentioned in the catalogue or college literature. Nor was it mentioned, anywhere, that there was a critical mass of young women who had crazy mothers. We were sisters in the struggle to survive their influence. It's hard to know if we were drawn to Bennington in search of one another or Bennington drew us to it like the star of Bethlehem the night Christ was born.

This was the era of Vietnam, assassinations, the emerging Women's Movement, the Gay Movement, Kent State, Chicago '68, Black student protests, Woodstock, drugs, sex and rock and roll. How much of this crept onto campus at Bennington? Not much compared to other institutions. Remember where we were, the Green Mountains of Vermont not Harvard Yard, NYU, Columbia, nor Berkley. We were *remote* but not out of touch. My political voice and identity began to emerge.

We had teach-ins. Everything stopped for a few days to examine these issues, to think about where "the college" stood. And what was this uproar to establish something called Black Studies? Bennington's nod toward this "request" from those of us non-white students was a remarkable, Black musician/professor named Bill Dixon. That was it. He shouldered the burden. There was no one else of the same or equal caliber until Milford Graves arrived – a genius whose obituary in the New York Times described him as an "exceptional drummer, an inventor and polymath." The Times revealed he was also a "botanist, acupuncturist, martial artist, impresario, college professor, visual artist and a student of the human heartbeat. And in almost every arena, he was an inventor." Milford Graves belonged at Bennington. He was one of us.

My class? I was one-half of the Black students for my class. It was me and the late Barbara Abercrombie. We were very different. She was practical. Barbara became a doctor. She studied at Harvard Medical School and did her internship at Montefiore. She met Dr. Gaynor. And some of her siblings attended Tina's school. That sent a chill down my spine. Barbara and her family were impressed and grateful for Tina's service to their community.

(While writing this in 2021, one of my friend friends from Bennington called to tell me Barbara had died in 2020. An internal earthquake erupted inside me. We weren't very close but being "the only two" in our class created a bond that couldn't be transcended nor broken.)

Barbara didn't frighten Tina. Barbara did what she was supposed to do. She embraced a profession that Tina understood, medicine. Barbara married another doctor, and they had one daughter. Somewhere in all this, Tina weaponized class, money, and privilege. She used it like a scalpel when it came to accepting Barbara's presence at Bennington. Barbara and her family grew up in the projects. That's all Tina needed to know to justify Barbara attending Bennington. She represented to Tina, a form of academic charity.

Some of us took great pride in our verbal abilities. We loved verbal sparring and used sarcasm like an automatic weapon! Dinner was show time. This was our form of intellectual entertainment especially during my junior year. The new dining room became our domain. Usually, we sat at one of the round dining tables with director's chairs. There had to be some kind of magic going on. The round tables were meant to comfortably accommodate six people. Often ten of us found ways to squeeze in, eat, and partake in the verbal festivities.

Sunday brunch was the other forum on a smaller scale. My friend Eileen and I had the habit of reading the Sunday Times to each other, often at the same time with individual commentary, while eating. It drove people crazy! Too often, they didn't know which one of us was talking. Eileen and I were fine. One Sunday morning, a mutual friend who was brave enough to sit with us and try to participate in this information ritual couldn't handle it. Suddenly we heard her all but scream, "Stop it! Stop it! I can't tell which one of you is talking!!!" I remember Eileen and I looking at each other, pretending to be baffled by our friend's confusion. We knew what we were doing.

There's something about those of us who went to Bennington. Too often to be a coincidence, and too unnerving to dismiss, sometimes we can spot each other years later without having known one another at Bennington. Often, we weren't in the same class. I can't tell you what *it* is or where you can find it or develop to make it your own, but we do find each other. Roughly twenty years after I graduated from Bennington, I was speaking at a conference in Boulder, Colorado. At the end of that day's lectures and presentations, there was a cocktail party. Small clusters of people talking and sipping wine with laughter that was compatible to your intellect. I was not enjoying myself and barely remember what we were talking about. I turned around and saw another woman, a little older than I was, on the other side of the room looking at me. I looked back right into her eyes. I walked slowly towards her. We were maybe three feet from each other when we said simultaneously, "Bennington! Oh my God!" We laughed and hugged each other. The recognition was instant and comfortable. I didn't know her name, didn't know what year she graduated, and the fact that she was white didn't matter at all. Her husband, a very well-known musician, chuckled and said, "I've seen this before. I'm going over there while the two of you…talk." He headed for the bar. My

Bennington Sister smiled and asked, "When were you there?" The recognition produced relief and the safety of familiarity. We are an unusual bunch with a wide range of eclectic skills and knowledge. The Bennington difference often takes people aback. I've seen it. I've been the object of their surprise.

For some reason (maybe it's age) I scan the obituary pages now. If you read the obit pages in the Sunday Times, you'd think nobody Black ever died unless they were "important" like Milford Graves. On May 9, 2021, there were a few photos on the obit page. There was one of a white woman that grabbed me. Her short, dark hair was slightly disheveled, and she had high cheekbones. I stared at it for a few seconds and decided to read the obituary that was written by her children. I felt like I was searching for something, driven. A third of the way down, I found what drew me to her obit. "…Otis studied sculpture, zoology and writing at Bennington…" It's a little spooky but so are we.

All of this was easy. I call it the public life of Bennington. It was the private life of Bennington that was dangerous, who you were when you shut your dorm room door. I almost died.

Chapter Thirty

The Taconic to Routes 9 and 7

Tina had a family friend, Blackie, drive us up to Bennington. I found myself studying Tina's face as we drove through the huge, iron gates of Bennington. Cigarette in hand, her eyes slowly oscillated from left to right with the rhythm of a porch swing. We found our way to my dorm, Leigh House. She observed everything with a disturbed look on her face. I've never forgotten it. She was out of her element. I think she was intimidated!

My years at Bennington were the most complex and revealing times of my life. Tina didn't understand because she didn't want to understand. Whether it was true or not, Tina now felt I was smarter than she was. It was another element of control that slipped away from her. Bennington destroyed whatever wish she had for me to conform to her standards, to fulfill her imaginary image of "her daughter". That image was nowhere to be found at Bennington.

The campus shocked her. It had a large Common or green area that overlooked a beautiful backdrop that so many of us never took the time to appreciate while we were there. The dorms were clapboard houses, each with roughly twenty rooms, several bathrooms, a kitchenette, a living room with a fireplace, a "phone booth", a small sitting area on the first floor and there was an attic. Narrow roads ran between each cluster of dormitories. As we walked around the campus later that day, she said to me, "Eventually, you're going to need a car." She continued looking around and said, "Ain't nobody Black up here."

"It's Vermont, Tina," I said.

"This is the woods," she said. "Ain't nothin' up here."

I repeated, "It's *Vermont*, Tina." No matter how often I explained that Vermont was overwhelmingly white, she kept looking for a Black beauty parlor. She saw another Black couple walking down the street in the town of Bennington later that afternoon and asked them, where was the Black beauty parlor. I watched the interaction. They all laughed for a minute and shook their heads. Tina told me what I had already told her. "There're no Black beauty parlors here. Ain't that a blip?! You'll have the wig if you can't get home to have your hair done."

Blackie smiled and said, "This is rarefied air up here. Baby, you're among the elite of the elite." Blackie had gone to college and got a degree in social work. He couldn't get a job as a social worker. They weren't hiring Black social workers when he graduated, so he became a bartender. That's how he met Tina, and I guess that's how she met Harry. Harry met Tina in a bar.

The second thing Tina said *again* was, "I'm glad I bought that wig for you 'cause there's nobody up here to do your hair. You'll have to come back to get your hair done. I told you you'd need matching luggage." I never used the wig.

We found our way to Leigh House. I wasn't happy. Tina intruded on my thoughts and announced, "Papa said to open up a bank account here so we could deposit your allowance. Can you cash checks on campus?"

"I think so."

I was totally unprepared for the social trials Bennington posed. I had never gone to camp. Never shared a room with anyone. Never had to worry about noise, other than Harry's drunken rages. Never had to share a bathroom. Never allowed to iron or cook. Never allowed to prepare projects for school if it involved "messiness" like glue or cutting out shapes. I went to maybe three parties in high school, all affiliated with the repertory company I was in. What the hell was I going to do?

I would be living in a dorm with other young women where I had no control over noise, a big issue for me. I was diagnosed by my pediatrician after taking a hearing test, as having "acute hearing." I learned quickly the fine art of telling people to shut-up or turn the record player down in a hundred different ways! I got so good at it after a while I didn't have to say anything. I could simply look at somebody and they knew.

My lifeline (and a tenuous one) was a shared set of values and expectations. Not just a passing familiarity, but a deep understanding due to an upbringing that exposed me to many of the standards, beliefs, stores, cultural events, behavior and vision of the well-to-do. I knew what was expected of me in certain situations with wealthy white people, especially those from New York, a breed apart. I knew what fork to use, the top vacation spots, the trends before the trends, the difference between shopping at Bendel's versus Bergdorf's, the flattering joy of a Pucci dress, and why (at the time) we all genuflected in front of Bloomingdale's! I also understood that this part of my existence had no place down home.

Meanwhile, I shocked some peers at Bennington while others didn't think twice about who they thought I was, Black regardless of the Choctaw and European aspects of my heritage, with all the breeding and mannerisms of the upper class. It allowed me to blend in and stand out. I had some white people tell me, "You don't act like you're Black. You're more like us!" And "us" was white. Thank God, I didn't look white. Bad enough with straightened hair, I had the "classic third world face" according to some art teachers in high school. (I had one teacher who was riveted by my looks. He made me nervous.)

My first roommate slept with a black leather glove on her right hand. What was I supposed to think?! Eventually, we switched roommates. I moved down the hall and shared a room with Sharon Parnes. She didn't sleep with a black glove on her hand. She came from some place in Massachusetts called Leominster. She was low-key, interested in history and had a dry sense of humor. My kind of roommate!

Many of the young women at Bennington had social lives that were foreign to me. I started to hear stories about boyfriend "Tom" or "Richie". I didn't have any stories about boyfriends or dating. And I had no desire to pile into a car and head over to Williams College with a gang of Bennington women prowling around for potential boyfriends. It seemed ludicrous to me. I would find out years later that for too many Black women attending prestigious colleges, they went through four years of college without one date, while longing for a boyfriend, a romance, an evening of young love.

Listening to conversations about "fun-filled" weekends from everybody else was unbearable. This aspect of "having fun" seemed like such a waste of time. I approached everything as an opportunity to deepen my understanding of the human condition. What did fun accomplish? What's the point? There was something wrong with me.

I spent many weekends going back and forth between Bennington and Riverdale running from one hell to another. At least I was familiar with the dysfunction on Fieldston Road. "The devil you know is better than the devil you don't know." The devil I didn't know waited for me every time I stepped outside of a class or headed for my dorm. I felt trapped in a foreign, hostile country. Bennington was a new threat wrapped up in a socialization process I knew nothing about and never participated in. *I was socially ill-equipped and emotionally unqualified for this phase of life. It had nothing to do with money and nothing to do with intellect. I had run out of places to hide from the larger world. I didn't have a clue. I was lost with nowhere and no one to go to except for one Political Science Professor, the late Don Brown. He and Dr. Gaynor had the same birthday and the same kind of soothing voice. A storm was forming inside me.*

I missed Mama and Papa. Sleeping was a growing problem. With darkness came emptiness, desperation, feeling unprepared and stranded, needing things I couldn't or wouldn't identify. I wasn't just tired, but insanely weary. And then there were times I was so tense and anxious I would jump at the slightest noise. I knew I was depressed, but so many of us were depressed at Bennington, that I didn't consider this unusual. I didn't understand the depth of my depression nor where it was leading me. I'd get up in the morning and keep going.

I found a group of friends who became critical to my well-being at Bennington and after Bennington. Many were young women who also had psychically wounded mothers as well. We, the daughters of crazy mothers, formed a special sisterhood. We had a bond, a common set of references and characteristics, sharp intellects, a sharper, darker, often side-splitting sense of humor, and shared pain that manifested in dozens of self-destructive ways. We had unnerving perceptive abilities and a passion for analysis. These were the women I considered my "soul sisters." None of them were Black.

It was December 1967 of my freshman year, and I was fighting off a migraine that particular weekend in Riverdale. I was filled to the brim with despondency. I wasn't good describing what I was going through. When I tried, I was dismissed. I grew up never being allowed to show or express feelings beyond a simple smile or enjoyment watching television. I knew nothing about the daily reality of depression nor how dangerous a condition it is. When I walked in, I felt like I was returning to a house already in flames. That weekend, I had no idea I wouldn't return to Bennington until September of 1968.

Mama and Papa were in the living room watching television. By now, I was suffering from the mother of all migraines. Tina came downstairs and peered in my bedroom. The lights were out. The shades were drawn. Standing in the doorway, arms crossed, shoulders hunched, Tina was baffled as if I had some mysterious ailment no one had ever heard of.

In a half whisper, she asked, "You hurt, don't you?"

I wanted to throw something at her. Yell, *"What do you mean, I hurt? You think this is a joke?"* Instead, I said, my voice barely above a whisper, "Yes."

"Poor thing," she said and walked away.

The pain was so bad I wanted to cry. At one point, I passed out from the pain. Mama thought cough syrup would help. My pajama top was stained with sticky, red cough syrup.

By the time I recovered from the migraine, the semester would be over in days. My roommate turned in the work I had completed and left at Bennington. Professors mailed me my comments. In the midst of all this, we were hearing more and more about a country in Asia named Vietnam.

It felt like the whole world and everybody in it was changing except in our house. There was never any discussion about these world events. They were happening somewhere else, perhaps another planet! Two of Terry's brothers fought in Vietnam. I felt like I was being ripped open by social and political change, watching it from above, as if I was having an out of body experience.

Tina was ranting and raving upstairs in her domain. Harry was nowhere to be found. I remember dragging myself upstairs to talk to Tina. I needed help. After all, Tina let us all know, she was the intelligent one in the family. She knew everything. She was seated in what she called the "music room." It was about the size of a large rectangular closet. There was an accent wall with black and white striped wallpaper. It was background for a red, leather couch. Across from the couch was the bar filled with bottles of liquor. Some were empty because they were just "for show." Next to the bar was Tina's chair with a window behind it. The shades were drawn. She was seated and eating dinner.

I don't remember what I said to her or the question I asked. What I do remember is her looking up at me and saying, "I can't take this anymore, dammit!"

She slammed the fork and knife down on the plate, yelling, then threw her plate of food up in the air. Tina's face looked like it was coming apart. The edges of her mouth were drawn down, her eyes too wide and her cheeks appeared as if they were becoming dismembered from her cheekbones. Shocked, I stood there as she yelled at me. The food was everywhere. She continued to yell and scream. Words like suffocation, drowning, explosion, disconnected, and dying came to mind.

When she threw that plate of food in the air, it might as well have been me. Something broke. Each piece of food represented my desperate and unrealistic hope that Tina would somehow transform into a reasonably sane woman, perhaps a mother. I equated her failure, her inability to be a mother, with me being worthless. There had to be something wrong with me. She had just thrown me away... again. Up in the air I went. This time Mama didn't come to the rescue and Papa thought I should be able to "shake it off," pay no attention to Tina. But I couldn't.

In the first draft of this book, written during the 1980s, I found the following passage. "Tina walked to her bedroom, leaving the food and the plate on the carpeted floor. As she pushed me aside and walked by, it felt like she was running. Just before she got to her bedroom door, I grabbed her by the shoulders and slammed her up against the wall. She didn't scream. She whimpered and started calling, "Papa! Papa!" I abruptly let her go afraid that I would kill her or at least try. I had had enough.

"Oh my God," she said. "Oh my God. You must be crazy. Where's Papa? Oh my God! What are you doing to me?"

Maybe it was the next night or a week or two later when I knew there was no way out. Things would never change. I wasn't quite sure what all those things were, but I couldn't fight it anymore. They say suicide is a permanent solution to a temporary problem. They also say suicide is murder inverted. There was nothing temporary about what was going on. Brushing past the flames of homicide, I knew we would all continue to be at the mercy of Tina. Her madness had created a hellish environment for all of us. I was tired of it."

There was no point in living. So, I attempted to kill myself later that evening after everyone had gone to bed. Obviously, I failed but not from lack of trying.

A Caveat

Tina's Reflections on Suicide

Maybe a year before she died, I asked Tina, "After all these years, do you know why I attempted suicide during my freshman year?"

She looked me directly in the eye and said, "I thought you attempted suicide because you didn't like the dorms. The girls there had boyfriends who perhaps didn't wear their robes in the hallways and maybe that was the problem. You didn't come from an environment like that."

I was speechless. She continued to talk but I didn't hear her. *"You thought I didn't like the dorms?!!!"* I was on the verge of losing control, and although Tina and I continued to talk for another half-hour or so, nothing registered with me. I wanted to fling her across the room.

Staring at her, I took a deep breath and asked, "Why did you object so to joint therapy? Why? When that was a way to help me?"

Her eyes darted about, "Oh every time we went to that mess, we ended up fightin' like cats and dogs!"

"I stayed in the hospital three months! What were you thinking?" I was shrieking.

"You were tired, Janis! I don't know. I don't know. Why do you want to go into all this? You're a grown woman now." She was flustered and frightened. If she had the strength to run away, she would have.

"I wondered why you never married," she said.

My brain felt as if it had gone through a cognitive whiplash. "Why didn't you ask?"

"I thought you were disappointed in romance..." and Tina stared out the window, softly mumbling something incomprehensible.

Mother's Madness

PART FOUR:

Saved

Chapter Thirty-One

Stream of Consciousness

What I still remember after all this time is the relief I felt. I was safe and Tina wasn't allowed to see me, nor was Harry. I didn't have to worry about Mama and Papa. They were pretending nothing happened, that I was "away." Maybe it was just a cold that required hospitalization, but not their granddaughter's suicide attempt. That was impossible. I would never do that and I'd be home soon. Papa called after a few weeks to let me know that I needed to come home right then. Enough is enough. Once again, I had broken the unspoken rules of Black solidarity and domestic dysfunction simply by being me. But this?! Whatever pain I was feeling, whatever hurt, even if Tina betrayed you, *you say nothing to nobody*. So, I was instructed by Papa "to come home soon."

I think soon for Papa meant, a few days. Soon would be three months. That would give Tina enough time to decide what kind of lie she would tell people about my "absence." She wouldn't tell the truth. What would people think of *her*? She decided I had a severe case of mono, the quintessential ailment of overworked college students at the time. I had mono. It was easy for her to remember. All she had to do was make sure I didn't tell anyone the truth and disgrace the family or, more importantly, disgrace her.

I was rushed to Columbia Presbyterian Hospital. Six young, white, male doctors talked to me. After spending what felt like an eternity at Columbia Presbyterian, somehow it was determined I should go to Roosevelt Hospital. By the end of the day, I was admitted. I was exhausted.

I have no memory of how I got from one hospital to the other. I think I was on the ninth floor of Roosevelt Hospital. Wherever I was, it was attractive, more attractive than I thought a psych ward could ever be. There were no hospital beds. Each room had four twin beds, each with its own "area". When you put your head down on your pillow, you saw no one else. You were separated by a long divider that ran the length of one side of your bed. Maybe the divider was wood. Maybe it was vinyl. This divider was roughly two and a half feet higher than your bed and wide enough to place a few books and other small items. For some reason, I remember the color red orange was used somewhere in the room. My bed was closest to the door. Bedroom lights did go out at a certain time, but the door was left open and the hall light intruded, but not enough to keep you awake.

One morning, another patient (who ended up going to Bennington because of what I told her about it) gently shook me until I opened my eyes.

"Janis, Janis. There's someone on the phone for you."

It took me a few seconds, but I managed to stumble to the pay phone in the hallway.

"Hello?"

"Pryor?"

"Miller!" It was Braunwyne, a sister from another mother, an amazing friend from Bennington. What made her amazing? I trusted her. We spoke the same language and had the same sense of twisted humor. Shared the same politics and the same perception of Bennington. She was a year ahead of me, the House Chair of Leigh House. I said in the eulogy I read at her

Memorial Service that she was the older sister I never had and needed.

"I got your letter. Are you okay?" She had such a unique voice and pacing of her words. What a relief to hear.

"No. I had to get out of that house," I said.

"Your mother should be in a hospital," Braunwyne said. "She's fucking crazy."

The reason this has stayed with me so very long is Braunwyne *knew*. She understood. She got it. She embraced the painful truth of my suicide attempt with concern and affection. I would visit suicide one more time. That's an awful lot to hold but I didn't trust anyone else enough at Bennington or anywhere else to know the whole truth. Braunwyne never betrayed my trust, never judged me, never made me feel sorry for telling her, and never left me, even when she transferred back to Seattle in her junior year. It was Braunwyne who rescued me from Fieldston Road that summer. I flew out to Seattle and spent some time with her and her family at their country place in Issaquah, Washington. Now, many decades later, Issaquah is a suburb of Seattle.

There's so much I could tell you about my time at Roosevelt, the doctors who treated me, the nurses who befriended me, the patients, the day room where we ate dinner and watched television, occupational therapy where everybody discovered art was more than a passing interest of mine. One of the attendants, Ian Wharton, lived in Riverdale, knew "the neighborhood." He took time to care.

I stayed as long as the insurance allowed, ninety days. The night before I was released, the Head Nurse and a colleague walked in to talk to me in the bedroom. It was the Head Nurse who "escorted" Harry from the floor when he attempted to visit. Tina never came to Roosevelt after dropping me off like a bag of groceries.

Every doctor I spoke with while hospitalized had rarely, if ever, encountered a Black family like ours. The cast of characters in my family, especially Tina, puzzled the doctors, all of whom were white. They had never had a patient like me from a family like mine. There were numerous ways I could tell. I had to keep educating them about the assumptions they made. They didn't understand how racism factored into all this and were quietly shocked when I told them Papa went to Tuskegee. They had no clue about the color caste system, or how we could afford to pay our bills! They understood dysfunction, mood disorders, pathology and violence. The depth and breadth of racism in America? Not so much, but they understood the vulnerability of children and the problems presented by "very bright articulate" children who were often harder to help. The doctors' and nurses' messages were very simple.

"You're the only one sane enough in your family to have a break down. Stay away from your mother."

That was the second warning I received regarding Tina. The first doctor told me, "You must stay away from your mother. She's too domineering, too controlling. Get out of your house and stay away from her."

"You've got to stay out of your house if you want to survive," another nurse said.

I was taken aback. I asked the nurses where would I go?

"Anywhere but there."

Some Words About Suicide, My Constant Companion...

Forget what you see on television or in the movies. Have you ever noticed that ninety percent of the time when you see the person it's after the deed has been done? Blood is everywhere sliding down the bathtub or smeared on a nearby wall, or there's an empty bottle of pills next to half a glass of water.

Sometimes the person is already hanging from a rope or bedsheet like a rag doll.

Maybe they will show someone jumping from a bridge, but you never get a sense of what the impact does to the human body unless they jump from a building. You'll see the person leap and then there's a shot of him or her lying on the ground in a pool of blood.

Sometimes the person will be "saved" if it's a drug overdose. Someone rushes in, slaps the person's face or drags them to their feet, forcing them to stand or walk with the hope they'll regain consciousness.

Maybe you'll see foam bubbling from their mouth indicating it's "too late."

Trying to kill yourself isn't easy. It isn't painless, and it's not an "exact science." Real life is different.

Cutting human flesh is not like cutting a piece of paper. Your skin really is thicker and tougher than you think. I heard or read that your skin is the largest organ in your body.

You have to make *a deep slash* on your wrist(s), and it stings. It might surprise you, even shock you.

It shocked me.

There are so many ways committing suicide can backfire, and leave you worse than dead. That's why men have a higher percentage of killing themselves than women.

Men usually go for the sure thing with a gun that's so fast and accurate they won't feel their departure.

Women tend *not* to shoot themselves. It's very messy.

Doctors have categories of suicide attempts.

There's one classification known as a "suicidal gesture" implying it wasn't "serious."

To my friends in the mental health community and the many therapists I have seen, all suicide *"efforts"* or *"gestures"* that leave us alive are still *serious*.

If you want to kill yourself, there's a big problem, period – full stop. You shouldn't live in so much psychic pain and despair that the only reasonable solution is killing yourself.

There's a part of me that believes suicide is, *in part*, a reflection of the defects in western society, but that's another conversation…

My diagnosis? Atypical clinical depression. In other words, a depressive episode could often be *triggered* by an event or a person. Stay away from the triggers and for me the triggers were/are everywhere. But if I was brutally honest, the biggest trigger was Tina. One of the most profound symptoms of my depression is insomnia, and this pervasive sensation of functioning while on the verge of drowning. Since I don't swim, anxiety sets in.

Years later I found an apt definition of character disordered people in M. Scott Peck's book, *The Road Less Traveled*. He said that character disordered people make "disastrous parents, blissfully unaware that they often treat their children with vicious destructiveness. It is said that neurotics make themselves miserable; *those with character disorders make everyone else miserable. Chief among the people character disordered parents make miserable is their child."*

Joint therapy for Tina and me was highly recommended. She regarded therapy as a gross invasion of privacy and considered it a deceptive practice. Therapy was a trick because, *"They make you solve the problems. That's psychology. They can't tell me anything. What does a psychiatrist know about my life? I'm not going to let anybody tell me what to do! I'm a professional woman."* She would only go to a therapist because of me, the sick one. I had shamed the family with my "foolishness of suicide" bringing disgrace. When I returned to Bennington, I was instructed to continue therapy. Tina's response was, "Therapy's too expensive. We can't afford that." This from a woman who owned among other things at the time, a white mink pantsuit, custom made.

Tina's refusal to cooperate in any meaningful way was predictable but still hurtful. She was hoping there would be something she could buy that would take care of the problem, new clothes, a trip, something!

I had to unlearn everything she had done to me and would continue to do until she died. It wasn't easy and to this day I have lapses. A lot of the damage is permanent.

I, who've been held at gunpoint in a foreign country, have given "direction" to Jesse Jackson, endured the high pitch of working for the late Senator Edward Kennedy, watched and studied the movie *Gladiator* more times than I'll admit to, and know the fear of being in a country about to explode, with all that this implies, with all the reading and understanding, I still have no defenses against the madness of my mother. Easier and safer to look in the eye of a young soldier, who doesn't speak or understand English, while he holds a rifle with a bayonet that he's itching to use against an American journalist.

In the first draft of this book, back in the eighties, I wrote that I could hardly recall when I didn't suffer from depression. *"Those very early days down South with Papa live at the horizon of my memory. I often walk towards that horizon, my heart aching from something that refuses words. I walk slowly at first, then quickly, hoping to arrive at that thin, distant line off-shore before it slips even farther from my reach. Resting on the imperceptible line where sky meets earth, I know the blissful absence of hurt. The only peace I achieve is by standing still and accepting that for now that bliss can only be embraced through death. After all, said theologian and writer, Tossiter W. Raymond, 'Life is eternal, and love is immortal and death is only a horizon; and a horizon is nothing save the limit of our sight.'* That is still the case.

A Word About Braunwyne

An Ancient Act of Recognition, Indissoluble

If you subscribe to reincarnation and past lives, and believe we're accompanied into each life with the same group of people playing different roles that allow us to learn whatever lessons we need to complete or to help us in some way to get to the next level of wisdom and understanding, or to save a life, lend a helping hand, teach a life lesson, or simply pass and wink an eye at one another while we stroll down the halls of eternity, you may understand the significance of Braunwyne in my life. If you don't subscribe to any of this, that's okay. All you need to know is she's an essential part of my life – *is* not was.

Her distinctive voice and dry, sardonic sense of humor could get me through just about anything. She was so creative and so gifted. She had written a story for a class and the Professor wrote that her work reminded him of Dostoyevsky's *Notes From The Underground*. She loved the natural world, and I needed the natural world for my sanity.

Sometimes we'd just sit and gossip on Common's lawn, with the white clapboard dorms surrounding us like a necklace of square beads with windows and doors. We'd sit chortling like two old women who'd seen it all. Not too long ago I read something from the website, Brain Pickings, and found myself thinking, "God, if Braunwyne were here, we could talk about this. She would understand." What I read was the following in part:

Mother's Madness

"We are in the habit of imagining our lives to be linear, a long march from birth to death in which we mass our powers, only to surrender them again, all the while slowly losing our youthful beauty. This is a brutal untruth. Life meanders like a path through the woods. We have seasons when we flourish and seasons when the leaves fall from us, revealing our bare bones. Given time, they grow again."

Imagine having someone you could discuss this with as easily as you talked about last night's dinner and why someone we knew in our dorm felt green Jello was superior to all others! There wasn't much we couldn't talk about. Politics and the faults of the Republican Party were constant subjects. We shared eye rolls about our young rich peers who fluttered around campus mistakenly thinking they were speaking some secret language.

We joked about retiring to some mythological resting home I called, "Shady Acres," and sitting on the porch, rocking back and forth, reviewing history and the politics of this country. It was implicit, we were supposed to grow old together. But there was another plan, and we ran out of time.

In 2005, she called the Friday before Thanksgiving and said, "Pryor, I've got some heavy news."

"What's wrong?" I asked. Maybe one of her kids got in trouble or her parents were sick.

"I've been diagnosed with pancreatic cancer."

"I'll book a flight and come out tomorrow," I said. I didn't have to think about that. It was a reflex. She was in crisis. I had to be with her.

"I haven't told my family yet. Maybe right after Thanksgiving."

"Friday. I'll come Friday."

"Friday's good," she said.

"I'll tell Strong, but I won't dawdle…" That was the last thing I said to her. I had to call Betsy or Strong. (We referred to each other usually by our last names.) Betsy would want to know. We had all been residents of the same dorm, Leigh House, at Bennington. Maybe Betsy and I could go out together and visit Braunwyne, say good-bye, tell her we loved her, ask her what we could do for her children.

Monday, I found a message from her sister on my answering machine asking me to call her back. I was with another friend and said, "This can't be good. Why is her sister calling?" My stomach felt like a block of ice. I knew. I felt it. Braunwyne was gone.

He said, "Stop thinking the worst."

Braunwyne had died over the weekend. I wanted to scream. I was asked to write and read a eulogy for Braunwyne's memorial service, something her children could keep. I printed the eulogy, one for her daughter and another for her son. Over the years, Braunwyne had sent me photos of her children as they grew up. I selected two and rushed to the framing store I used with two copies of the eulogy. I asked what it would cost to frame each one. I don't remember what he said. What I remember is hearing Braunwyne's voice all but shouting, "Pryor that's too much!" It caught me off-guard. I made up some excuse and told the clerk to simply mat the eulogies and photos. I told the clerk that it was probably best to let the kids select the framing. What else could I say? I had heard Braunwyne?!

There was so much I told her children and so much more I didn't have time to tell them. I did break down while reading the eulogy. I had never cried before in public. I remember her children trying to console me. I was determined to get through it.

They had to know that their mother helped save my life; that "she is one of a few who knew all of me…"; that "I found comfort, safety, joy, and camaraderie in the shelter of our friendship"; that "we are not offered guarantees [according to Oriah Mountain Dreamer] 'What we are offered is knowledge of life and ourselves, and if we are awake, glimpses of the wisdom held in the story our life is telling the world.' Our story, your mother's and mine, had to do with friendship."

With complete certainty, I told her children, "Your mother and I will meet again and pick up right where we left off. The air will be clean. The sky will be clear, the water pure. We'll find that porch and she'll tell me wondrous things. Until then, please know that for as long as I'm here, you will always hold a special place in my heart."

That eulogy is folded into quarters. It's in my date book and goes everywhere I go.

Chapter Thirty-Two

A Sidebar About Depression: It's a Disease

Depression is a disease, not an attitude. It consumes me one bite at a time, as if my entire being were a plate of food served for its satisfaction. It chews me slowly and carefully, working steadily towards my weakest, most vulnerable organ, my heart. Somehow, I manage on most days, but not always. I often want to scream at all those so called, well-adjusted people, who tell us, "Snap out of it!" and I say, "Don't begin to think *you know* what it's like to suffer from depression." Andrew Solomon says in his book on the topic, "...depression is a pain so severe as to be immemorial." He couldn't be more correct. Depression is old as time and holds the potential of being fatal.

My mother's abuse and lunacy comprise the essence of my depression. I was into my forties before I learned I was probably predisposed to depression. It ran amuck through Harry's family. Tina had no clue and when I pointed it out, her response was, "Oh shit."

There are so many lingering cultural myths that say Black people don't commit suicide and by inference, Black folks don't have mental health problems. These are lies, evil fantasies, delusions negating our humanity. Today, as I write this in 2022, I want to believe, based on more Black folks coming forward to talk about their pain, we are on our way to shedding our cultural shame about focusing on mental health.

However, in the first draft of this book decades ago, I found a quote from an African-American woman who was being interviewed for a book about Black women and depression. She said, "Depression? I don't think they were talking about us. That is not a luxury we can afford." The author tells readers that many people found humor in this possibility of Black women being depressed. "Don't get me wrong," another woman said, *"It's just that when Black women start going on Prozac, you know the whole world is falling apart."*

Every significant Black person in my life has made a conscious decision to avoid self-examination, to do what an older Black friend of mine calls, "the deep work." They have no interest in understanding why they do what they do. We, as a people, in the twenty-first century with Trump's version of Conservative madness rearing its head, can no longer side-step the big questions. Where does the public pathology of racism end and your private pathology begin? Where did Tina fit in this American convergence of injustice and personal defect?

With all that, there's another cultural legend that doesn't serve Black women. This should not be "news" to the enlightened and aware women among us. It's the one about *the strong Black woman.* We've become so damned good fighting oppression, suppressing our own pain and ignoring dysfunction that bell hooks says in *Rock My Soul,* as a consequence, *"the emotional neglect of Black children has almost become the accepted norm."*

Because we have a tradition of doing things we detest to survive doesn't mean our hearts escape being wounded. Blood pours out from all the wrong places, requiring regular social, cultural, political, religious cauterization to keep us alive. We have become so proficient at camouflaging the scar tissue and shielding open wounds, disregarding core truths, and placing so much value in appearances as dictated by white America, it's a wonder any Black women are sane. This was true for Mama, true for Tina, and true for me. It's a miracle we weren't crazier.

When I was at Bennington, suicide among young people was a problem few wanted to acknowledge. The gasps caught in your throat, and we all understood whether we admitted it or not, that the monster, suicide, was on campus. Now, in the early decades of the 21st century it's completely surfaced. Maybe the specifics are different, but the core, that place where suicide settles in and begins to feed and seduce you with its benefits, is the same.

Suicide, my constant companion, is sponsored by depression. So, *every day* I must fight it, look it in the eye, and stand my ground. If I succumb to suicide, it won't be from something big. I can cope with the big things. *It'll be from something small*: the tone in someone's voice, a misunderstanding, someone will say the wrong thing at the wrong time, a rejection on a day when I'm too tired, a stretch of cloudy weather, my car breaks down, a disappointment of any kind. These small things are everywhere. You get tired, and that too is a by-product of depression. Some days you simply can't move, and I often wonder if one day I'll wake up and just be too tired to continue and vanish like a wisp of smoke.

I look for people who've been to that place where suicide settles in, those who know the topography intimately. *No amateurs!* Anne Sexton and Sylvia Plath knew that place, so did Elizabeth Bishop. I had another good friend at Bennington who knew that place. We need each other for sustenance and validation. The specifics don't matter.

Chapter Thirty-Three

An Embarrassment of Riches

Sometimes you can have too much to tell, but there're a few more things you should know.

I returned to Bennington driving a new car, a Triumph GT6, turquoise blue with tan leather seats. It was a fastback. This was Tina's prescription for my suicide attempt, a car, paid for in cash. Nothing's simple. Tina and I had to see a therapist because she refused to let me drive the car. When asked why by the therapist, without missing a beat she told him, "Well, she might get in an accident." I can't remember how many sessions it took for her to loosen her grip on the Triumph, her fear, and me, but eventually she caved in. I think she knew that I was going to drive that car regardless.

Somewhere during my sophomore year, Bennington stopped being "the cage" and became home. This wasn't an exclusive experience. There were quite a few of us who began to feel that way. How did we know? We stopped leaving for the weekend. By our senior year we were gripped by deep ambivalence. We wanted to "get out of this place" versus "we can't leave. What the hell are we gonna do?" It dawned on us, rather dramatically, that few of us of us were fit for traditional employment. Bennington didn't prepare you for a job back then. It prepared you to change the world, or at least a little piece of it! Remember, Bennington taught you how to think and process information. We left with an interesting skill set, regardless of what we majored in.

If you were Black, there were some moments that prepared you for the "real world" unlike any course could ever do.

Bennington was a little petri dish of racism, classism, and what's now known as micro-aggressions. This is still the case. Too many white people, students, and professors alike, were stupefied by your mere presence. You either received wide-eyed looks or were victimized with what Black people call "stupid questions." It's particularly annoying because people of color in this country must learn the culture and "ways" of white people if we want to survive. White people have the privilege of not knowing, something they do very well, and have no awareness they're ignorant. It's been safe for them to be oblivious, or ignorant. It's what allowed the father of a white friend at Bennington to ask me, "Do they have a good scholarship program here?" When I told him I didn't know, the confusion and bewilderment on his face defies articulation to this day. This same friend invited me and a few other friends to her parent's summer place in some exclusive enclave in Florida only to discover that I couldn't come because they didn't allow Black people unless they're domestic workers… Only one friend said, "I don't know…if Pryor can't come… maybe we shouldn't go." It's hard to forget that. But I encouraged them to go without me. Have a good time. *That was me setting them up. I wanted to see who would take a firm stand regardless.* It didn't happen during that era of peace and love. And yes, segregation had been outlawed but so what? A few years ago, I learned that a white student at Bennington had named their pet mouse, (maybe it was a rat or hamster), Nigger, and couldn't figure out why a Black friend was upset.

I was a cultural conundrum in the Bennington constellation of over achievers, black and white. I was then and I think I still am. My sophomore year saw an "explosion of Black students." I think there were six [Black students] admitted that year. It was a very big deal.

I managed to do a good job staying away from the Riverdale house as much as possible and spending more time with the Gaynors. When I did go to the Riverdale house, I did my best to ignore Tina and Harry and focus on Mama and Papa. Graduating was paramount and graduating on time was absolutely mandated from Mama and Papa. What that meant was I had to take extra courses to make up for the spring semester I missed. I did.

Art majors had a unique load to carry. If you wrote a thesis, you knew if you were going in the right direction from your professors and thesis advisor. They were there every step of the way. Surprises were few and far between. But art majors? Your work for the Senior Show wasn't reviewed until a few weeks before graduation. It's such a subjective pursuit. There was always the possibility that your work would be rejected, and you wouldn't graduate. That rarely happened, but once was enough. You were a basket case until your work was chosen for the Senior Show.

If that wasn't enough, Tina called to tell me Harry was coming to graduation. In the calmest voice I could muster, I said, "If he comes, I won't be here."

Silence. "You wouldn't," she almost whispered.

"Try me," I said. Tina hung up. Harry didn't come. But she did bring an entourage. She didn't count on the Gaynors showing up. That threw her off her game. Blackie came and, Esther, another friend of Tina's who gave me a worn metaphysical book, and whose brother-in-law was the Ambassador from Guyana.

"This is for you sweetheart. I've been waiting all your life to give this to you."

I thanked Esther and carefully packed the book among my things later. Tina was watching me like a hawk. I could feel her discomfort, so I knew the book was important. It would be years before I read it.

Tina came to graduation prepared to party. I was horrified. All of us who belonged to the Crazy Mothers Club had spent too much time anticipating how our parents would either embarrass us or push us to the brink of suicide... again. Tina brought a magnum bottle of champagne for one of my art teachers, Pat Adams. She gave me shelter at her home for a short while. Pat was and still is, at age 94, one of my idols, one woman who made me think it was possible to be creative, live a fulfilling life on your own terms, even if it wasn't perfect. This is the teacher whose work was shown at the Zabriske Gallery.

Graduation was a two-day affair. I just wanted it over. We received our diplomas Saturday morning. Papa looked at it and said, "Well, I paid for this..." I have no idea where the diploma is! All that was important to the Lawrence family was I was now the third-generation college educated, Tuskegee, Spelman (and Columbia University for Tina's graduate work) and now Bennington College for the baby born with a veil over her face who came into the world "already owning herself." I was the child Papa worked for and accumulated property for, so I could securely "indulge in these increased wants of art and music."

Chapter Thirty-Four

"It's late September, and I really should be back in school..." *

The months following graduation felt like I had been pushed off a tall building, falling straight to the bottom, with no idea of what or where the bottom was, much less how I would land. I wasn't allowed to work during any summer. Remember, growing up, I wasn't allowed to cook. I wasn't allowed to iron. I didn't know how to do the laundry. At Bennington, I'd throw all my clothes in the washer, set the temperature on cold and pray! We could send out our sheets and anything that had to be dry cleaned.

I didn't know how to find a job, much less what I would do, and no one offered any help or guidance. I didn't know how to ask. I didn't know if asking was "allowed." I was a studio art major at Bennington focusing on painting and architecture. The only one who had any regard for that was Papa. As far as Tina was concerned, *I* was a huge waste. Her best advice? "Do whatever you want."

I loved architecture, loved designing buildings and residences, but had no capacity for calculus or geometry! Decades later I would spend a summer at the Harvard Grad School of Design taking a semester in studio architecture crammed into six weeks. I hoped to get it out of my system. It didn't work. When it was all over, the instructor wrote, "Janis has a huge contribution to make to the lived environment." Realizing years later what could have been and how content I would've been broke my heart. I comforted myself by saying, *"In another life, Janis. Another life."*

Mother's Madness

I caved into family opposition and gave up the theatre. I would always hate myself for that, allowing their belittlement and denigration to all but paralyze me. To this day I refuse to talk about it in depth. But I could always write, regardless of what my freshman literature professor told me. He said I had no talent whatsoever. He died an untimely death. I wasn't sorry at all.

Living was becoming a bigger mystery with each passing day. Fieldston Road felt increasingly like a tomb with little to no air. One thing was certain, I had to get out of that house. The problem was I had no idea how to make any of my talents and skills translate for the "real world." Early fall after graduation Tina began to ask, "Aren't you going to find a job?"

"Doing what?" I asked. This is the same woman who told me to do whatever I wanted to do. All I could hear in my mind and endlessly on the radio was Rod Stewart singing, *"It's late September and I really should be back in school."* *

Tina had nothing useful to suggest. She continued to drink. Depression raced up and down Fieldston Road trying to find me. Mama and Papa wanted me to stay in the house until I got married, something Mama advised me to never do. If I didn't get married, I guessed I would stay in the house forever. Maybe Mama, Papa, and I could go home then. That was my fantasy.

I moved out and stayed with some friends in Manhattan on the Upper West Side. I loved it there. Mama, Papa, and Tina went nuts. Tina sent someone to "get me." It was enraging. In the short time I was gone, Tina found a housekeeper. She was a sweet, hardworking woman who looked nowhere near her real age. Carrie became part of the household. She showed up bright and early, every day, rain, or shine.

I asked Tina how she could afford a housekeeper since she

was always complaining about money. Tina looked at me and said, "Carrie's a gift from the board president."

"What? What do you mean she was a gift? What is this, some new version of slavery?!"

"Why do you ask so many questions?"

"How do you give someone to another person?" I could sense that Carrie was going to be vulnerable to Tina's madness. She was very dark-skinned.

I had to get out of New York City. I can't remember who I talked to at Bennington. It was probably 'Becca Stickney, our own version of Katherine Hepburn. She was our beacon, our true north star. She was one of a kind and I think my class was the last class she admitted as Director of Admissions. She went on as Assistant to the President. Bennington was her life, and it's no exaggeration to say she was a legend during our time. One of the conversations I had with her resulted in an offer to come back and work in the Admissions Office with Jean "Short" Aldrich, who was the new Director of Admissions. I was happy to return. Yes, go back "to your school". That was the perfect solution for Tina, Mama, and Papa.

After returning to Bennington and working a year in the Admissions Office, I knew this was wrong for me. So, I headed to Boston where there was a Bennington community of recent graduates including a close friend from the Crazy Mothers Club. 'Becca also had an apartment on Beacon Street in Back Bay. What more could I ask for? Mama, Papa, and Tina were crushed for different reasons. Once again, I defied their expectations in the worst way. From their perspective, I refused to do what they wanted. I couldn't be controlled.

Maggie May Performed by Rod Stewart

Many Words About A Quick Trip To Europe

Class is a complicated reality. It shapes your expectations, your assumptions, your behavior, and the choices you make. It's reflected in the way you talk, the way you think, what you wear and how you wear it. Too often it's invisible to those trying to acquire class and irrelevant to those who've had it for generations.

So off to Europe I went with my friend, Fee, from Junior High along with my expectations, assumptions, behavior, choices, and everything else that created class difference. Europe was also another way to avoid Riverdale.

But there was a third companion, hidden from Fee, clear as gin to Sylvia Plath, Anne Sexton, and me, to anybody whose day job was to keep suicide at arms' length.

Fee and I landed in London, groggy and grumpy. We saw all the usual things, including the changing of the guard at Buckingham Palace. Soon I understood where Beacon Hill came from. Where the "New" in England came from. And I was reminded of the "gift" I was born with when I looked across the street at the palace and realized it was the early 19th century.

I could tell by the clothing people wore and the horse drawn carriages. A woman dressed in black from head to toe scurried down the street with a basket in her hand. It couldn't have been more than a minute and then she and the 19th century were gone. Back to the present.

Fee and I found a restaurant called, The Great American Disaster. The only place in London, at the time, that had a decent hamburger! If I saw another Wimpy's hamburger, I didn't know what I'd do!

I bought my first Pentax Camera, and visited Esther's sister who was married to the Ambassador of British Guyana. (She was the sister of the woman who gave me the metaphysical book for graduation.) What a terrific place she lived in! I was comfortable! I could breathe. We went grocery shopping. The chauffeur pushed the cart while she dropped food in it. He had to be ready to catch anything fragile. Oh my!

Fee was very frugal. I didn't have to be. I wanted trustworthy bathrooms and clean sheets on the bed. But I yielded to her constant search for cheap hotels, rooms, whatever! That was a mistake. We parted ways. She never forgot that! But we remained close friends until the day she died.

I found a wonderful hostel. Signed in. Had a great room to myself, with a huge window, no screen, and then Tina called about money. I woke up one morning and my companion appeared, so calm, so patient. I realized my breathing was shallow. The window looked like a portal of relief. I had a strong impulse to jump.

I packed and flew back to New York that day, leaving my companion doubled over in laughter. I fastened my seat belt. The plane tiptoed down the runway. Then it picked up speed. The hum of the engines increased with no thought to our comfort. I looked up and there was my companion, so calm, so patient, waiting for another opportunity. I never told Fee.

Chapter Thirty-Five

The "Short" Story About The Seventies: Conflicting Realities

No one prepared me to become a self-supporting adult. I pieced together some essentials, but that was it.

What I knew was *I got bored very easily*. Nine to five wasn't in my DNA. The fact that I accomplished anything in the traditional world of work is nothing short of a miracle. I rarely got paid a decent wage, maybe twice, but that was it. Another miracle? I didn't have to depend on my paltry salaries to support myself.

My annual salary for my first job (at First National Bank of Boston) was $6,500.00. When I told Mama, Papa, and Tina they were shocked.

Tina said, "What are you supposed to do with that? You can't live on that!"

I could, just not the way I was accustomed to, and the way they insisted I live. Checks from New York arrived, and money dysfunction settled in. It was an insidious disorder that frequently paralyzed me with panic attacks. I found ways to control it, but I would never be free of it.

Oh, the mistakes I made! This business of learning through your mistakes had very little appeal to me. The biggest mistake I made was thinking Tina wouldn't try to collect one day through manipulation. Nothing is free, not even if it's your own money.

I remember hearing some folks of color wondering how "all these white kids are living with these 'pay nothing jobs or internship positions.' How were they surviving in their upscale apartments?" I'll tell you how. Trust funds, checks from home, and "just send the bills to Dad" or some perverse combination. I fell into that last category. It was a blessing and a curse.

Those checks from New York were what allowed me to create what others now call "a well-lived life", of which material items were a small part from my perspective. When I heard that or used the phrase my companion and I smiled. We knew how much I paid for this well lived life that so many people would find impressive and exciting.

I didn't know much about Boston other than it appeared to be a "nice little town" when I visited in the late sixties. This was before Copley Place was built, before women wore fur coats in the dead of winter as if they were simple overcoats the way they did in Manhattan. This was way before the "new Boston" development on the harbor took place, and before anybody could conceive of Boston becoming a "majority-minority" city. Bonwit Teller was housed in an elegant building that was once a museum. Ken's at Copley's was the only place open late where you could get decent food. The Pewter Pot and Jordan's Department Store had wonderful, if not legendary blueberry muffins! Filene's was in its prime. Bookstores were everywhere in Cambridge! This had to be heaven.

Rumor hath it Boston streets were former cow-paths! The only order to the streets existed in the alphabetized cluster of streets from Arlington through Gloucester in Back Bay. That was it. I learned to drive in Manhattan where the streets were laid out on a grid: streets crossed avenues, traffic lights were synchronized, and drivers were fierce. You took no prisoners! If you lasted driving in Boston for a month or so, you were unfit to drive anywhere else! It seemed like everybody driving in Boston

Mother's Madness

was lost. People backed down one-way streets, made U-turns with no warning. It was insane!

I found an apartment on Beacon Hill with a garage. It was right across from the State House. I stayed there for four years, during which time I had to learn how to take care of myself. I learned to cook by reading Julia Child's cookbooks. I found a dry-cleaner and drug store at the bottom of Beacon Hill on Charles Street, a gas station, and a supermarket. I remembered how Papa taught me to balance my checkbook and I was very good at it. The apartment next to mine housed a troubled little family, a couple, and their grown son, who called me Warrior Princess Pryor. Across the hall was another Black woman. Hallelujah. We became friendly and down the hall was June Rinker. June was kind and wonderful. We became friends. Her brother also lived in the building. Cancer took her too soon from this life. I was shattered. This loss was practice for all that followed.

I knew very little about finding work. So, what do I do? Look for a job in one of the most boring institutions on the face of the earth for someone whose natural predilections were rooted in the arts. The problem was (and still is) when I got bored, I got in trouble, emotionally. I felt trapped, and like a caged animal there was no telling what I would do.

Somehow, I managed to survive the world of banking for two years. It was excruciating! There was one payoff, valuable only to me. I worked in Trusts and Estates in the bulging "pregnant" First National Bank of Boston office building in Boston's financial district. I discovered a fair amount about wills, trust accounts, and estate planning. There really are no accidents. The bank experience happened for a very good reason that would reveal itself to me in 1980. At the very least, I gained some insights into those statements Papa got with the heading, *in trust for*, with my name after *for*. But I would later learn there were so many gaps leaving loopholes just big enough for Tina to slip through and use to her advantage with lies that were so outrageous... And she would tell these lies over and over until she had everyone believing them except me.

Bussing erupted and Boston was beside itself. It was national news. I could see folks in the South, Black and white, laughing their pants off! Finally, the Yankees are getting their comeuppance! It was a nightmare for Boston.

One morning while dressing for work I heard a radio ad for a position as Legislative Aide for the Massachusetts Legislative Black Caucus. I wasn't sure what a Legislative Aide did, but I knew I could do it! All I had to do was walk across the street for the interview in the big building with the golden dome, the State House. I did and I got the job! Hallelujah! I was free from the financial district.

My first day as Legislative Aide for the Caucus is burned in my memory by Ted Landsmark. He was a professional African American man, dressed in a three-piece suit, briefcase in hand, attacked on City Hall Plaza by three young white men with *the tip of an American flagpole*. It was 1976, America's Bicentennial. A photographer from the Boston Herald happened to be there and shot the photo of this incident that would garner a Pulitzer Prize. That was my baptism by fire. Welcome to Boston politics, an advanced course in the human condition.

The nightly news showed footage of white people throwing rocks at buses carrying Black kids to school in Southie. One of those people would become Mayor of Boston. Where was I?! Nowhere near Mississippi! Welcome to Boston, the cradle of liberty, a city balkanized by race, class, and ethnicity, a city with a small class of Black brahmins who convinced themselves nothing like "this" could ever happen in Boston, and if it did it certainly wouldn't involve them. I received an astonishing education working for the Caucus. A year after I started, I was promoted to Administrative Aide.

Two significant things happened to me during the bussing crisis in Boston. A white man spit at me as I walked down Park Street, past the Paulist Center. I dodged the phlegm. He glared at me. I kept walking. That never happened to me in Gulfport. I had to come all the way to Boston for that experience. I didn't tell Mama, Papa, and certainly not Tina. They would've arrived, with a mover, to get me out of Boston.

One day I decided to park across the street in the State House parking lot because I was going in my building and coming right back out. Why drive into the garage? I parked close to the corner. If I looked to my right, I could see down Bowdoin Street to the corner of Beacon Street. I was just about to get out and run to my building when out of the corner of my eye I saw a group of four young white men, perhaps they were in their late teens. A chill ran down my spine. I wondered if I would be able to get to the entrance of my building before they were close enough to "do something" to me. I wasn't sure, but I knew my presence would provoke them. Someone who looked like me wasn't supposed to be on Beacon Hill as a resident, and I didn't look, walk, or talk like anybody's maid. I was afraid. There was nowhere in Boston that was safe for Black people. That was the exact moment I decided to move "across the river" to Cambridge for my own safety.

Massive nosebleeds returned before I moved to Cambridge. Blood gushing from my left nostril led me to call 'Becca. Her apartment was a few blocks down at 180 Beacon Street. I asked if she could drive me to Mass Eye and Ear. She said no. 'Becca was getting in bed and instructed me to get a cab. I stood there, in shock. With blood running down my shirt, I, a Black woman in Boston during bussing, getting in a cab with a white driver... What were the chances he'd resent my presence in the "wrong neighborhood" and "get lost" driving less than ten blocks to Mass Eye and Ear, a part of Mass General Hospital, and do God knows what to me as I tried to manage the blood rushing out of my nose? I remembered the warnings from Mama about taking white cabs down home, and Tina's terror at the thought of me getting into a cab with two white men in New York. Maybe I was overreacting. Maybe not, but I decided to stay inside, pack my nose with cotton, and go to the hospital in the light of day. 'Becca called the next morning to see if I went to the hospital. I told her no. She was shocked, but she was white. She had no idea what I had to consider to stay safe. I never asked her to do anything for me again. The legendary 'Becca Stickney of Bennington had let me down.

The seventies took me from banking on Federal Street to the State House, to my first professional job on a political campaign to the NBC affiliate, WBZ-TV and Radio, to the People's Republic of China and back to the NBC affiliate. I became an action junkie, working in worlds that Tina read about in the newspaper. She was shocked and intimidated. I was out of her control, again.

She was appalled I took a job with the Black Caucus. She thought they would be jealous and "mistreat" me, talk down to me, ask me to do inappropriate things or embarrass me in front of white colleagues or other elected officials. Whenever we did talk now, her first question was, "What did they say to you?" She also wanted to know *how* they said anything. She wanted to know every comma, period, and question mark.

"You'll upset them," she said.

"What do you mean?"

"You got more than they do. They'll resent you."

Every time I talked with her I got a headache. Our relationship had drifted into the murky waters of siblings. She was the twisted sister who relinquished her role as mother for the second time. Tina was now my big sister-advisor-mentor. That wouldn't last.

A few weeks after this conversation one of the Black State Representatives, Ray Jordan from Springfield, MA, sat next to me during a meeting. He glanced at my left hand. I was wearing an aquamarine ring with four stones arranged to configure a diamond shape. He kept looking at my hand.

Finally, he asked me quietly, "Are you rich?"

I thought he had lost his mind. I looked at him and said, "No. Why do you ask?"

"The ring, what is it?" he asked. "A diamond?"

"Oh no," I replied. "It's aquamarine."

He nodded and said, "Oh…" I was a little uncomfortable after that and thought about what Tina had said.

She wasn't all wrong about the Caucus and how they would perform professionally. They did drive me crazy with frustration and disappointment. While I worked with two of the most extraordinary politicians and public servants of that divisive era in Boston, State Representatives Doris Bunte and Mel King, it wasn't enough to keep me there.

I left the Caucus and worked for the Secretary of State, Paul Guzzi. He was a decent man, and Tina was relieved until I told her about my immediate supervisor, a white woman who appeared to resent my appointment by the Secretary. There was no sisterhood between the two of us. It reached the point of no return when she expected me to drive to her town, pick her up along with another colleague, and drive them to Maine for a meeting. I told her I wasn't going to do that. After all, she had a car and at that point she was much more familiar with metro Boston and the New England coast than I was. She was shocked when I refused to pick them up. Tina and Mama would've beaten me within an inch of my life had I done otherwise. When I related this incident to them during one of my infrequent visits to Riverdale, Tina's first comment was, "How come she can't drive? You ain't nobody's servant!"

Mama's comment? "Oh no. No."

Papa shook his head from side to side, looked solemnly at me and said, "You don't have to do those things." It was Papa who instructed me to never take a job you can't afford to leave. What a privilege that was. He made it possible.

Working for the Massachusetts Black Caucus and Paul Guzzi constituted the preamble to a world of work that terrified Tina. She was afraid she couldn't hold onto the spotlight. While I was learning about soul murder, Adult Children of Alcoholics (or ACOAs) and personality disorders, Paul Guzzi announced he was going to run for the U.S. Senate against incumbent Edward Brooke. At the time, Edward Brooke was the only Black U.S. Senator elected since the turn of the century. I resigned from Paul Guzzi's office and went to work on the Brooke Campaign. This overshadowed Tina. She had to find a way to maintain control, hold the spotlight and recognition. In the process, she underestimated me.

Chapter Thirty-Six

The Seventies: Part Two

Something else happened during the seventies. A body of work was released about adult children of alcoholics (ACOAs) led by the late Janet G. Woititz. She was the one who put into words what I'd been trying to do most of my life, guessing at what normal was, because I had no idea! That was just one characteristic of ACOAs. We also tend to jump around from job to job. Don't know how to deal with anything unless it's a crisis. Some of us can't finish anything, have no follow through, tend to be hypervigilant, become action junkies. We judge ourselves harshly and can't have fun. Our sense of responsibility is "overdeveloped". It's easier for us to be concerned with others rather than ourselves. I spent the seventies examining the depths of this dysfunction, it's impact on children, how it shaped their adulthood, where I fit and didn't fit. I was still an information junkie.

I remember one evening while walking to North Bennington, I happened to glance in the dining room window of a private home. I remember watching the people for a minute, wondering what they were doing, asking myself what that felt like to sit and talk and enjoy dinner with *your family*. Was this something that happened in other homes? The only normal experiences I had were with the Gaynors. I considered them special not ordinary.

A friend of mine had taken a workshop specifically designed for adult daughters of alcoholics. She insisted I sign up for the next workshop. I did. It was jaw dropping! The role of denial in alcoholic households is huge, not to mention how appearances factored in. You had to keep up a good front. All the roles children embraced in alcoholic homes often to divert attention made me weak. This information along with an incredibly patient therapist, the late Susan Martin of Lexington and then Concord, MA, helped me understand (again) that while I was damaged from living with two alcoholics, I wasn't crazy. Growing up in a household with alcoholic parents had a price attached to it. In my case, a high price was exacted that almost resulted in my death and may still do that.

Keep everything sealed tightly. The last thing I wanted was somebody knowing the reality of my life. *Any lie was better than the totality of my truth.* I couldn't answer simple questions about my family, much less about myself. Those verbal talents I honed at Bennington came in very handy.

There was another doctor, Alice Miller, who wrote two brilliant books that opened me up to the complexity of this dysfunction, *Prisoners of Childhood,* later released as *The Drama of the Gifted Child,* and *The Body Never Lies, The Lingering Effects of Hurtful Parenting.* The genius of Alice Miller exposed the depth and breath, of "abuse." It isn't confined to physical or sexual violations, but *includes psychological abuse perpetrated by one or both parents on their child.* This is usually revealed by an event, or the onset of depression too often caused by suppressed rage and pain "as a result of subconscious childhood trauma that was not resolved emotionally." Miller pointed the finger of responsibility for this trauma at the parents, thereby shattering that rule so many of us learned, honor thy mother and father. She didn't have to worry about me blindly following that rule. Tina and Harry weren't suited for parenthood. I knew that the minute I met her and saw him when I was a child.

The general public is familiar with the best seller, *The Road Less Traveled*, by M. Scott Peck. He wrote another less well-known book, *People of The Lie*, that drew a portrait of Tina with such accuracy I was left motionless after reading it. He said, "I have learned nothing in twenty years that would suggest that evil people can be rapidly influenced by any other means than raw power." I felt like I dodged a bullet. And I had, at least for a few years.

Never having been diagnosed, Tina probably had a personality disorder that made her the least able to parent. Listening to Tina, she'd have you believing that *nothing was ever her fault*. She was *never* there for me and rarely for anybody else. She was always right and *never* wrong, *never* responsible for anything. It was Tina's way or no way. She wanted me to be an extension of her because Tina had to be the center of attention. It was mandatory for any semblance of sanity to be maintained in her world, not mine.

Dr. Leonard Shengold, clinical professor of psychiatry at the New York University School of Medicine, coined the term *soul murder*, in his book of the same name. The murderers often succeeded in killing the souls of their children. What jumped out for me was his description of depriving a child of his or her own identity and ability to experience joy in life. This was Shengold's definition of committing soul murder. It's *"the perpetuation of brutal or subtle acts against children that result in their emotional bondage to the abuser and, finally, in their psychic and spiritual annihilation.* Not every child survives this psychic onslaught from a parent, *especially if it was the mother."* When I first read this, I remember thinking, "Not this kid. Tina's had her day." Little did I know what it would take to bring Tina down, much less to survive this woman.

There's no medication to treat this kind of complicated lunacy that I know of, although the pharmaceutical industry keeps trying. Antidepressants were not enough for me. I had to find something else in addition to keep from going stark, raving nuts – and I did. It was and still is information and knowledge. I needed to understand what had happened and what was still happening as much as I needed antidepressants and food. If you're looking for how I felt and how I reacted, this is it. I was driven to understand. My survival depended on that, along with dissociating myself from Tina as much as possible. Otherwise, I was going to go crazy again. This too is who I am. Loving books and the craft of acting had many benefits.

Some therapists ask, "What's your complaint?" I've never known how to answer that. My first response has always been, "She's crazy! I can't live with a crazy person. I don't care if she is my mother. She's going to kill me." But I did some deeper thinking. One of the problems was I had lost respect for her. She placed no value on anything I valued. She was intelligent yet at the same time stupid, arrogant, self-centered. She had to be the center of attention. My loss of respect for her rested on a bed of contempt. Tina endangered so many people, starting with her immediate family and extending to her kingdom at the school. It was and still is hard to survive this. Today I tell my therapist(s), "Your job is to help keep me alive because I don't want to live. Tell me why I should."

But there was an additional remedy, my American cocker spaniels, four of them, followed by two King Charles Cavalier Spaniels, and now one frisky Cavapoo, soon to be joined by another. They get me out of bed every morning, are responsible for my erratic physical fitness and somewhat worrying mental health. They were there when no one else was. They keep my anger in check and they're the real reason I'm still alive. My first spaniel, Prince, nicknamed by my friends as the "Cary Grant of dogs," saved me from driving into the back of a MAC truck. I was driving to New York, tired and depressed, and I nodded off. Prince started barking in my ear. I came to and I was not more than eight to ten feet from the back of the truck. I started pumping the brakes to slow down so we wouldn't fly through the windshield. Prince stopped barking. He decided to give up the back seat, and sit next to me as a passenger, just in case. I started taking a series of deep breaths to calm down. I was wide awake for the rest of the drive, thanking Prince profusely.

I've shared my life with seven spaniels. All of them were and are amazing teachers, companions, and protectors. There's not a pill in the world that can save your life or warn you about people, much less wag its tail and lick your face. Beware if I'm without a canine companion. After I wrote the first version of this, a friend and associate read it and complained about "...the dogs. We don't want to hear about the dogs," she said. Well, hear this. They saved my life on more than one occasion and, again, *were there when no one else was.* As for that friend and associate? We rarely talk anymore. It's better for both of us.

Herbert H. Gravitz and Julie D. Bowden wrote, *Recovery: A Guide for Adult Children of Alcoholics.* I underlined the following, "*A child who is not allowed to talk about the alcoholism in their family begins to think there is something wrong with him or her. They feel confused, sick, scared, bad or crazy. No one may talk about what is going on to anyone else... to break this rule is to court disaster...*"

Woititz said in *Adult Children of Alcoholics*, "If both your parents were alcoholics, life was even less predictable, except they took turns getting worse. Being home was like being in hell. That nervous, angry feeling in the air... Yet there was no way to get away from it, no place to hide, and you wondered, 'Will it ever end?' *...you couldn't let the rest of the world know what was going on in your home. Who would believe you anyway?"* And there was Betsy McAllister Groves, who wrote in *Children Who See Too Much, Lessons From The Child Witness to Violence Project*, *"We know that when young children witness an extremely scary event, their outlook on the world and on their place in it changes dramatically, and that this shift in worldview affects their behavior."* Imagine if I didn't have the Gaynors and my grandparents.

Chapter Thirty-Seven

TINA!

While I stumbled through the seventies, Tina soared. On May 22, 1975 Tina's school was named after her. She invited me to the dedication ceremonies of the "Leontine L. Pryor Day Care Center." I declined. Tina had been ruling as Director ever since May 22, 1952. Many people would think about leaving after twenty-three years in the same job. Not Tina. She had plans. I threw a monkey-wrench into her vision of perfection created solely for public consumption.

The seventies were horrific times for the "capitol of New England." The news footage from Boston triggered images in my mind of Bull Connor, Black people down south being attacked by dogs and apprehended with high power fire hoses, as they protested with knowledge of "strange fruit" hanging from limbs of trees scattered all through the south. Here I was, in what a local journalist, Al Lupo, called "liberty's chosen home." Home for whom? Boston was feeling more and more like "up-south Alabama."

The Charles River that separated Boston from Cambridge was more than a geographic distinction. Cambridge is a philosophical, social, cultural, economic alternative. Cambridge was and is a state of mind! It was nicknamed the People's Republic of Cambridge for some good left-wing, liberal-progressive, highly academic reasons, primarily but not exclusively, Harvard and MIT.

Tina came to Boston to convince me not to move to Cambridge. Looking aimlessly around my apartment, she asked, "How will you move? It costs so much money to move and

Mother's Madness

where will you move? You said something about Cambridge? Where is that? Do they have stores there? How will you find a place? Do you need more money? I don't want you to worry about anything. We can get along somehow. You know your grandfather is getting weaker, Janis."

I felt a headache coming on and suggested we go to what was then Dunfey's Parker House for lunch. Tina looked around the hotel, searching for something to criticize. Once we were seated, she leaned over to me and whispered, "Look at that bowl of cracked ice sitting right over there."

I knew exactly what she saw before looking. Cracked ice was Tina's code for very wrinkled white women. "Tina, I'm not going to look," I said quietly.

"Look, look! She's right over there," Tina said looking to my right.

I didn't look because I was afraid I'd burst out laughing. Thankfully, I heard a mildly, booming voice saying, "Hey…how ya' hittin' em!" I looked up and right in front of me was Jerry Dunfey. His family owned the Parker House. The Dunfeys were Democratic supporters and activists. They did more than write checks. I had gotten to know Jerry when I worked with the Black Caucus. He belonged to my "decent people club." He's a good man. I introduced Jerry to Tina, and they chatted a few minutes before he left.

Tina looked at me and asked, "Who was that?!"

"His family owns the Parker House and several other hotels," I said.

"Really! And you know *him*? He's so handsome," she said almost gleefully!

"Politics, Tina. You get to know a lot of people when you work in politics."

"I guess so… Well, you'll definitely need to keep your wardrobe updated. What kind of stores do they have up here anyway?"

Among other things, Tina was a provincial New Yorker. Nothing of any good existed outside of New York City. It would be seventeen years before she returned to visit me in Cambridge.

During the last few years of the seventies, her behavior became more disturbing to me. Before I moved to Cambridge, I spent the weekend with a college friend in Maine. I told Mama, Papa, and Tina that I would be away that weekend. When I returned from Maine, Tony, the building attendant who supervised the garage and acted as an informal doorman, concierge, and protector, greeted me when I drove in. He asked if I would be stopping by the lobby to pick up my mail, and I said yes. When I did, he walked over to me and said quietly, "The police were here to search your apartment."

"What?!!" I was stunned. I stared at Tony for a few seconds and asked, "Why? What did they want?"

"I'm not sure, but they said they were checking… Looking for evidence of foul play," he said while looking at me with great concern.

"Were they from the local precinct?"

"Yeah, the one down by Government Center. Maybe you better call 'em."

I called and found out Tina had reported I was missing. I assured the police that everything was okay. I hung up and called Tina. I told her I was back and waited for her to say something. She continued to make small talk. I interrupted her.

"Why did you call the police? They came over here and searched my apartment!"

She was silent.

"Tina! Did you hear me?"

"Yeah," she said sheepishly. Tina, the little girl with the high-pitched voice appeared. "I thought maybe something had happened…"

"You don't remember that I told you I was going to Maine this weekend?" I asked.

"I don't know. I guess I forgot."

Tina wanted to find out anything about my personal life. I decided when I was a child, I would never tell her anything. She would find a way to denigrate me, regardless. Tina would tell me she told Mama everything when she was growing up. I asked her why.

"Because she's my mother."

I didn't believe her. If she'd done that, marrying Harry wouldn't have shocked Mama. I knew that the more information I disclosed to Tina, the more endangered I became. *What irony*, I thought. I treated Tina the way most Black women would treat "nosey white women" who want to "get in your business."

Tina had no real interest in *getting to know me*, nor what was important to me, nor what I did, unless it was going to enhance her standing. I became some kind of fantasy in her head that she created according to her needs. I was an investment that had to be maintained. Tina could then tell a story about how she was critical to my achievements. If it hadn't been for her… The reason I ended up working for all these *"famous people"* was because of her.

Chapter Thirty-Eight

My Grandfather Left

I went to China in the late seventies, promising myself if Tina didn't tell me Papa died while I was gone, I would find a way to kill her slowly and painfully. Papa's health was deteriorating rapidly. He finally quit working when he was 88.

Tina kept drinking. I couldn't figure out how she was functioning at all. When she drank, her disposition often became mean. But sometimes, Tina the Little Girl, would appear, drink in one hand, high-pitched voice, usually one leg crossed over the other, swinging that leg back and forth. The image was unsettling. It was out of place. She was a grown woman not a child! When sober, she was hostile, aloof, argumentative, and unreceptive at best. From time to time, I had the feeling that underneath the hostility was an impenetrable amount of fear. I knew she was afraid of dead people and ghosts, but there had to be something more. Of course, if she was in public, she was charming, gracious, sweet, and sincere as a three-dollar bill! People fell for it.

I couldn't stand being in the same room, much less the same house with her. She made me choose between my sanity and being with Papa during his last months. If I lost it because of her while visiting him, I knew I would kill her.

The last real visit I had with my grandfather was a month or so before he died. He was propped up in bed with pillows. Motioning for me to come closer, I saw he was holding a blue velvet box in his hand.

"I want you to have this."

I knew he was giving me something because he sensed he would die soon. I employed "Janis logic." If I didn't take the box, he wouldn't die. He placed the box in my hand. When I opened it, I found one of the most unusual pieces of jewelry I've come to own, an oval turquoise stone set in gold. I'd never seen anything like it. I wear it on the second finger of my right hand.

One of the last conversations we had, months before he was bedridden, focused on Ted Kennedy challenging Jimmy Carter for the Democratic nomination for President. Papa thought it was a dumb move for Kennedy. When I mentioned the possibility of working on Kennedy's campaign, Papa shook his head.

I was surprised. We were in the living room and the news was on. I didn't know what to say. After a minute or two, I said, "But Papa, even if he loses, he'll still be Senator and I live in Massachusetts! So, I win regardless."

Papa smiled.

When Papa died, it was the beginning of twenty years of hell. Everything I had gone through was nothing like what I would face. I was not ready. It's hard when your mother becomes your active enemy. At least there would be no more subterfuge.

Chapter Thirty-Nine

1980

The LORD is my shepherd; I shall not want.

He maketh me to lie down in green pastures: he leadeth me beside still waters.

He restoreth my soul: he leadeth me in the paths of righteousness for his name's sake.

Yea, though I walk through the valley of the shadow of death, I fear no evil: for thou art with me; thy rod and thy staff they comfort me.

Thou preparest a table before me in the presence of mine enemies: thou anointest my head with oil; my cup runneth over.

Surely goodness and mercy shall follow me all the days of my life: and I will dwell in the house of the LORD forever.

This was Papa's favorite psalm. He helped me memorize this, along with the Lord's Prayer before I started going to Sunday School as a child. For someone who stopped going to church after Uncle George died, he knew a lot about the Bible, prayer, generosity, humility, and patience. I was well into my adult years before I realized how much of this I had absorbed. And I would need every bit of it with the war against Tina.

Chapter Forty

They Die

Papa died in January of 1980. Mama died in October of 1989. I have no desire to relive, remember, or re-feel any of this, but their passing is important to every life they touched, especially to their daughter and granddaughter.

Tina had Terry call me with the news. I had just gotten in. It was late, close to 8 or 9 PM. "Uncle Will passed," Terry said slowly. I had the feeling he had practiced saying that before he called. I hung up, dropped to my knees, and bent over suppressing the need to scream.

I heard that question from childhood. "What are you going to do when your Daddy dies?"

"I'll die too," I remember saying. Bent over, I realized that was still what I wanted to do. If I could've destroyed the building I lived in at the time, all of Harvard Square that was a few blocks away, and blow up everything in sight, I would've done that. But I couldn't. So, I stood up, looked around my bedroom and packed. I had to call the Kennedy campaign and let them know. I couldn't take off too many days.

I flew home numb. I kept asking Papa, "Why did you leave me here?" I'm told this is the natural order of things. I didn't give a damn about the natural order of things. I felt disemboweled, abandoned, frantic and in danger without Papa. The threat was his daughter, Tina, my mother who betrayed me!

Homesickness erupted the minute the wheels touched the runway at the Gulfport-Biloxi Airport. As the jet-way was being connected to the plane, I felt the heat that had a touch of humidity. Memories, the tactile reality of the warm, damp air,

Terry driving us home where roosters often crowed in the early morning while growing up, the noises of our childhood, Black southern accents laced with more sounds than words, pine trees, pecan trees, seeped to the surface of my consciousness. During that drive, I didn't want to return to Cambridge. I remembered telling Terry's mother, when I was still a child, how much I hated New York and never wanted to live there. I was home now, and I didn't know why I couldn't stay.

Terry was talking to me, and I snapped out of, it. The wake would be held early evening at Hall's Funeral Home, a business established by my Godmother and her husband long before I was born. I looked at my watch and realized early evening was roughly in an hour and a half.

Tina had called and ordered me to wear the mink coat she gave me.

"It's going to be too warm," I told her.

"Well, throw it over your arm. That way, people can see it." She paused for a moment and the with all the authority of a military officer, roared over the phone, "I mean for you to wear it, Janis."

"Tina, I'm not doing that. It doesn't make any sense," I said. January in Gulfport was not like January in Manhattan or Boston. What would I look like with a mink coat?! What kind of nonsense is that? But I knew exactly what kind of nonsense it was. It was more "Tina Think." She could address the fashion issues of going to a funeral. She wanted to impress people, but she couldn't tell me Papa had died. She left that to Terry.

What I remember is finding Harry sitting on the porch, not a smile on his face. He looked at me and mumbled, "Hey." I barely acknowledged him and walked in the living room.

Aunt Ophelia, Aunt Alberta, and Aunt Ella Floyd were there. After exchanging some solemn greetings and a few hugs, I asked, "Where's Tina?" And they said, "In the kitchen," one right after the other like water spilling down rocks. I left my bags in the living room, walked through the dining room to the kitchen, and stood in the doorway. I can feel what I saw as if it was happening right now. The smothering sensation of humidity. No windows were open, only the front door and the back door. The heat from the overhead lights made me tense. Stagnant air. I wondered if I was going to pass out.

Tina was seated at the kitchen table surrounded by a half-dozen men, most of whom were her cousins. I see J.W.'s face, bronze colored and shining from the heat and humidity. Romeo, Terry's father, Papa's nephew, Aunt Emma's son, chocolate colored cheek bones chiseled and high, the most distinctive feature on his face, curly black hair that was dark as tar. Cousin Ed, Mama's nephew leaned against the stove, so quiet, so dignified. There was still no air circulating. Everything was at a standstill, except for the movement and sound of liquor being poured into glasses, and the motionless air disturbed by Tina's laughter.

She looked up and saw me. With a wide, empty smile she said, "C'mon in." Her voice was high-pitched, echoing the needs and wants of a child, that little girl persona that often tiptoed out when she drank.

J.W. looked at me with another smile that said, "Nothin' I can do about this."

And Romeo, Terry's father? "Hey baby. How you doing?"

Cousin Ed, who played golf with a passion that transcended segregated golf courses in Jackson, gave me a soft smile, "Baby, how you doing?" Every time he visited Mama, I always wondered what he did or what he said or what or who he knew that made the white men of Jackson, Mississippi let him play golf on "their" course.

Another voice asked, "You made it all right? You didn't have no trouble, did you?"

"No sir. No trouble. Terry picked me up."

"Aw'ight," said a voice with a face I couldn't identify.

As I turned to leave, I said, "Somebody please open some windows."

"The baby said open some windows. I guess we ought to open some windows." It was Tina's voice caught somewhere between delight and lunacy. I expected her to jump up and twirl around after she said that. Thankfully, she didn't.

When Papa died, what still stands out after all these years is Tina. The limousines came to the house to drive us to the church. It was a block away! Terry was running from one limo to another. I had no idea what he was doing. Mama was helped into the first limousine. Dementia had established itself to the point that she was really confused about what was going on, but had enough clarity to know, "William's dead." It was the first time I saw her cry.

Tina was escorted to the limousine by five men. She wore a white pantsuit, one of many she owned, and a perfectly coiffed ash blonde wig. She kept looking up at them, helpless, lost, fearful. It was as if she was the only one grieving. These same five men had to help her down the aisle of the church. Where was Harry? I have no memory of him being at the church.

The service was led by a minister who never met Papa. All the minister knew was Papa laid the cornerstone of the church and he was a Lawrence. Papa was "the" Lawrence. The block we lived on was the Lawrences' block, Houston and Ella-Floyd

Lawrence, Emma Lawrence Williams, and William and Josephine Lawrence.

I flew back to Boston that evening arriving close to midnight and continued working the next day on the Kennedy Campaign, never missing a beat. Several days later I had to drive down to Riverdale to get things moving on Papa's will.

It was early afternoon when I arrived. I told Tina, "We've got to deal with Papa's will."

She glared at me with nothing short of hate. "Well, I be dog gone. That's all you can think about, isn't it? You little red bitch! The money! Always the money!"

I used every ounce of energy to remain calm. "Tina, it's about the law. He has a will. Everything goes to Mama but there's a policy for you and for me…"

She cut me off. "How do you know all this?"

"Because I've seen the will, Tina. I have a copy of it right here."

"How come you got a copy?" And then she snatched the will from my hand with the swiftness of a snake's bite. She quickly read the first two pages. "He made you executor?! Ain't that a blip! I'll take this!" Tina turned and stomped out of the living room. I never saw the will again.

She strutted past the living room and into the kitchen later that day. Flowered housecoat falling sloppily around her body, anklet socks and satin slippers. Her thinning hair was twisted and wrapped slickly around her head, cigarette and a half glass of scotch in her left hand. Saying out loud, to no one in particular, "I can be Daddy. I'm strong. I can be in charge." She walked back and forth repeating this delusional mantra three or four times. It scared me. She seemed dissociated and I wondered if she was talking to someone, or something only seen by her.

The possibility of her stepping in Papa's shoes and "being Daddy" was somewhere between slim and none, more evidence of her lunacy.

She looked at me and said, "He was *my* father. He did so much. I can be Daddy. I'm going to do what he did. Daddy was unbelievable. I never disagreed with him. I couldn't. He was the strength of the entire Lawrence family. Is that why Aunt Ophelia calls me? Because Daddy was the foundation of the family? Maybe that's why."

There was a lot I could've said but chose not to. I never took my eyes off her. At that moment, I felt she could do anything. Knots formed in my stomach. Tina believed she could be the kind of person her parents, especially Papa, would be proud of. All she had to do was emulate him, defy the odds. That's what Papa did. He broke the rule that governs Black lives. The rule dictated that to be successful in America, one must not be Black, or any other color that wasn't white, but he was successful. The census records a friend of mine researched recorded him as a "mulatto", able to read and write, owner of his home in the early part of the twentieth century. That made him dangerous as far as white people were concerned.

Every Saturday afternoon for almost a year, Tina called me, sobbing. *"Do you know what happened on Saturday? Do you know what day this is?! My father died. He died just about this time. Did you know that?"*

"I know, Tina."

"He was my father."

She called me on Papa's birthday and asked, "Do you know what day this is?"

"It's Papa's birthday," I replied.

"Oh, so you remember, little lady! I made sure they put flowers on the grave today. *He's my father.*"

A year of these calls led me to say with some trepidation, "You need some help, Tina. Something's wrong."

"What do you mean? My Daddy died," she said.

"Your grief... there's something wrong."

"I don't need no Goddamned help from anybody! I have to take care of my mother. You have to be taken care of, this house, the property down home, the property in Jersey! I'm fine!" The bitterness of the sneer her mouth takes when you challenge her was palpable. I was in trouble.

Several months went by and I heard nothing about Papa's will, but those checks kept coming. Finally, I confronted Tina and she exploded. Only parts of sentences and phrases remain burned in my memory. "You ain't getting nothin'! Don't you talk to me like that! Who do you think you are? *I'm in charge now.* I'll make sure you never see those documents. There're no documents! Never."

Mama was becoming more and more confused. Yet she had enough clarity to scare Tina into complying with Papa's wishes regarding me. Suddenly, a flurry of bank signature cards arrived in the mail, with instructions to sign in various places.

I called and asked Tina, "What are you doing? Why do you want me to sign these?"

"I'm settin' up some accounts for you," Tina said tersely.

"What kind of accounts? What happened to the trusts?"

"God dammit! Just sign the cards," she screeched. "I mean for you to sign those cards and put 'em in the mail to me!"

The tone of her voice caused my breathing to become shallow. All the fight went out of me, but a thought landed in my mind from God knows where. The thought was very direct, *"This woman has got to be stopped."*

What could she be doing? And what could be wrong with her setting up accounts for me? At least the money was still there and as long as Mama was alive, Tina wouldn't do anything too outrageous. At that exact moment, I felt the walls closing in around me. My head started to hurt. I knew there was something bad going on and no matter what I did, Tina would do what she wanted. I had to remember Tina cared nothing for the truth.

While restructuring our finances, she also stripped Papa's garden. I came down to Riverdale another weekend and looked out my bedroom window and up the gently sloping hill where Papa had his garden and saw nothing but barren land. I asked Tina what happened. She looked at me blankly and said, "I had somebody come here and kill all the grass and all that other mess out there."

"You did what? You killed Papa's garden?"

Tina looked at me as if I had grown another head. "What is wrong with *you*? So, I killed the garden." She turned around and walked away from me.

A Caveat

Tina's Shenanigans

With all of Tina's financial shenanigans, I developed attitudes about money that were and are highly inappropriate if you live in a cut-throat capitalist society. The lack or presence of money has a different impact on me. Money became a powerful moral marker in my world. What some people would do to grab a dollar or make a deal; how they would use it and for what told me volumes about someone's integrity or how they viewed you, their priorities, their sense of compassion. Money often becomes a mirror of someone's soul. It's the third rail in most relationships.

Decency is lacking among many people not to mention generosity. You add race and things get sticky. Money Monsters appear in a variety of disguises. Look what slavery wrought. Why do you think we have such a hard time paying people a living wage? Slavery taught white people they could get just about everything "for free".

Greed is another disguise. Greed is a virus in this country because not many of us know how much is "enough". Enough is usually "more". I watch all this from a social, cultural, political stance, and then Tina's shenanigans enter the picture. She was desperate. Money equaled power to her and power was the ability to control. I have unexpected, brooding responses to money. People find it either startling or stupid. Mama and Papa would understand. They're the only ones I'm comfortable with regarding the subject of money. Nobody else.

Chapter Forty-One

1985 and 1989

By 1985, Mama was bedridden, unable to do much of anything for herself. Mama had never been sick during my life until Papa died. Watching her slip away was shattering. She was gone, but still here. She didn't know anyone anymore. Sometimes she would smile hopefully at me and hold my hand. The last time she visited me in Cambridge a few years earlier, she asked me while taking off her coat, "Whose little girl, are you?"

Mama would have moments of clarity, moments, not hours. I called Tina and told her she had to be there before the plane landed to meet Mama, that she couldn't let Mama travel alone anymore.

"Why not?" Tina asked as if you had insulted her.

"Mama is sick, Tina. The flight attendant had to lead her off the plane. She told me Mama seemed confused. You can't let her fly alone anymore."

"Mama's not sick. Why are you always telling me what to do?"

"I'm worried about your judgment, Tina! My God! What is wrong with you? So help me God, I don't want to hear about you not being there to meet her. If anything happens…"

"Mama's not sick…"

There had been signs. Some were amusing like the time Mama thought her underwear was a hat. Some were mortifying like the time she left a gas burner on. A few years before she became bedridden, Mama and Tina had gone down home to see about the house and take care of some business. When they returned to New York, Mama found a policeman while Tina was

Mother's Madness

gathering the luggage. Mama told the officer while pointing to Tina, "...that woman stole all my money." Tina had a lot of explaining to do. There was more truth than confusion in what Mama said. Papa was lucid almost to the very end, balancing his checkbook, reading the newspapers, watching television. I couldn't bear watching Mama die, one thought at a time.

Tina's mantra was, "Mama's got to get well."

I lost it one time when I was visiting and said, "Tina, Mama's not going to get well."

Tina glared at me from the side of her eyes and said, *"Oh yes she is. Mama's gon' get well. Yes, she is."*

Tina hired two full time nurses to care for Mama. One was a wonderful woman recommended by Dr. Gaynor. Her name was Gloria. She was from Jamaica. She had a thick, melodic Jamaican accent and worked during the day. Gloria was tall with short jet-black curly hair and skin as smooth as chocolate syrup. Tina adored her.

The night nurse was also from the West Indies, Aclema. She didn't get the same adulation from Tina. I thought it was because Aclema was heavy and, while she was light-skinned, Tina had nothing but contempt for overweight people. But after several months, I realized that wasn't it. Aclema saw another side of Tina that was revealed only during the evenings and late night.

When I was at the house for the weekend, Aclema joined me in the living room one night. The eleven o'clock news was in progress.

Harry was upstairs. I rarely saw him when I came. Every now and then he'd come downstairs and sit in what was Papa's chair in the living room. I seethed but not so much that I couldn't see

Harry didn't look well. I assumed the drinking was catching up with him.

One Friday afternoon on another visit, I walked into Mama's bedroom to let her know I was there, hoping she would register my presence. A hospital bed had been rented for her, and she was propped up with three or four pillows. At first, I didn't register what was lined up against the guardrails of her bed. Tina had a big smile on her face. One of the nurses put lipstick on Mama and did her hair in a series of small knots. Mama would've hated that.

"Doesn't she look pretty?" Tina asked.

Tina's smile sent out a strange vibration and I started to feel queasy and slightly dizzy. Gradually I began to focus on what was in Mama's bed. There were dolls and stuffed animals everywhere! Mama was surrounded by them.

"Where did all these dolls come from, Tina?"

Tina's smile grew wider. "I got them for Mama to play with. Aren't they pretty?"

I looked at Gloria, who smiled sheepishly and dropped her head. I wanted to back out of the room slowly and drive back to Cambridge with Prince, as fast as I could. I kept thinking about a quote from the anthropologist, Ashley Montagu, regarding family as "an institution for the purpose of perpetuating mental illness."

In August of 1989, I received a call from Gloria. I remember it because she called on my birthday. Whispering, she begged me to come down. Something was really wrong with Tina.

"Gloria, why don't you call Dr. Gaynor. He's right around the corner."

"No, no Miss Janis. Your mother would kill me! She won't let me."

"Call 911 then! *What do you mean she won't let you?*"

"You know how Miss Tina is. You're the only one who can get her to the hospital."

I remember hanging up, putting my head in my hands, and saying, "God give me strength…" Within an hour, Prince and I were headed to Riverdale, roughly a three-hour drive. It gave me time to fortify myself and wonder, *"What the hell is Harry doing? Why can't he talk to her, or have they stopped talking to each other?!"* Anything was possible.

Prince and I pulled into the driveway. The minute I opened the car door, the late August heat hit me full blast like an oven set on high. Prince jumped out, shook himself, and started to pull me towards the front door while I struggled with my bag and his, containing his food, bottled water, and food bowls, treats including Chewys. The front door was open, but the screen was locked. I rang the bell.

Tina materialized from the far end of the hall. Mama would've called her, "an ol' haint*." At best, Tina looked ghostly. She couldn't keep her balance and kept falling against the right side of the hall wall. As soon as she touched it, she took her left arm and pushed herself away and upright. This was repeated several times before she reached the screen door. Her hair appeared as a wispy nest of brown and gray strands. She wore her quilted robe, anklet socks and those satin slippers. It had to be in the nineties!

"I'm okay. I'll be aw' right. Don't worry about me… I'm okay. C'mon. C'mon…" Tina said this, two or three times before she got to the door. She could barely unlock it, and when she did, she weakly pushed it open towards me and turned around.

Prince charged in. Tina stumbled into the living room, the nearest wall or door catching her each time she began to fall. She dropped like a rock onto the couch. Somehow, she picked up a lit cigarette in an ashtray on the coffee table. With Prince now at my heels, I went to see how mama was. It was hard to tell if she was asleep or unconscious. I looked at Gloria and asked, "How's she doing?"

"Oh… some days are better than others. Today she ate good. She's sleeping now. She fell asleep just before you got here. Miss Janis, Tina's not good."

"What the hell is going on here, Gloria?"

Gloria looked at me, helpless. She didn't know where her loyalties were at that moment. Tina was very good to her.

I walked to the kitchen and filled Prince's bowl with fresh, cold water and set it down in his space before going to the living room. Tina was still on the couch, her face shining due to perspiration. The windows were closed. She was wrapped in that quilted robe, one arm around her waist, the other hand still managed that lit cigarette as if it were a weapon. She looked up at me and said, in that small, little girl voice, "Hi! Did you see mama?"

"Yes." I looked into Tina's eyes. They were yellow and unfocused. "Tina, you've got to go to the hospital. Carrie and I are going to help you get ready. I'm going to call Dr. Gaynor's office and let him know we're going to the emergency room."

"I can't go. He's on vacation."

"There will be someone covering for him."

"I don't want to go," she said, bewildered by the possibility.

I sat on the coffee table so I was eye level with her. Her skin was sallow, her eyes looking worse by the minute, and she appeared drugged. "Listen to me. I don't know what's wrong with you, but whatever it is, it's bad. You need to go to the hospital. I'm calling an ambulance."

"Oh no! Oh no! Not going in an ambulance," she weakly declared.

We spent almost a half hour "discussing" this and I finally said, "I'm taking you to the hospital *now*. Forget the ambulance."

"No, I'm cold," Tina said.

"Tina, it's over ninety degrees outside. It's got to be ninety degrees in here," I said.

"It is? I'm so cold," she muttered. "So cold."

Tina sat there and stared into space. It scared me. Was she dying right before my eyes?

It took Carrie, who always went beyond the call of duty as our housekeeper, and me, forty minutes to get Tina into my car before I could drive to Montefiore Hospital. Carrie and I didn't say a word. We arrived at the emergency entrance. Carrie helped Tina out of the car and into a wheelchair. After I parked my car, I registered Tina's name at the admitting desk. Then, we waited. Tina's head suddenly dropped. Drool slid out of her mouth. It appeared as if she lost consciousness. I ran up to the desk and told the nurse what happened. Instantly, two nurses appeared along with a nurse's aide, and they wheeled Tina into an examining area. Carrie and I were told to wait outside. We sat and waited for what felt like days before a doctor came out to talk with me.

"How long has she been drinking?" the doctor asked.

I sat up and thought about it before answering. "I'm not sure. I don't live here anymore, so I don't know exactly what she's been doing."

The doctor looked down at his chart and then looked at me. He took a deep breath and said, "This is the worst case of alcohol poisoning I've seen." He told us she was suffering from *severe* alcohol poisoning, kidney failure, malnutrition, dehydration, and that possibly, she had suffered a small stroke. When the doctor finished going through this medical litany, he said to me, "It's a good thing you got her in here. Another day and she would've been dead." He paused and repeated, "Never seen such a severe case of alcohol poisoning…never…"

It was late evening when Carrie and I drove back to the house. I had never heard of alcohol poisoning. How much does one have to drink to become poisoned by alcohol?

Harry was seated in Papa's chair. He looked at me and asked, "Where is she?"

"In the hospital," I said. "She's going to be there for a while." If that constituted a conversation, then that was our first and last one. He walked upstairs, bumping into a wall as he made his way out. I didn't want to know what was wrong with him. He didn't seem drunk, but what did I know? I felt like I was in a house of horrors. Prince and I went for a walk.

When I returned, I was still grappling with the enormity of alcohol poisoning. I wondered just how much liquor was in the house. I searched Tina and Harry's floor. In addition to the magnum bottles of liquor openly displayed like trophies, I found bottles in closets, behind books, in the kitchen behind dry goods, in shoeboxes, behind furniture and numerous bottles neatly placed in vacant cavities of furniture frames. When I found the 67th bottle, I stopped counting.

Late that night, Aclema, came to talk with me as I watched the eleven o'clock news. Prince was curled up next to me. He lifted his head to watch her until she sat down in a chair next to the couch.

"How's your mother, Miss Janis?"

"Not good," I replied. "Aclema, what's going on here?"

"Your mother very sick. Gloria don't see what I see. Mrs. Pryor drink heavily. She stay up all night watching me and drink."

"What do you mean?"

"*I mean she stay up all night watching me watch your granmama,* and drink and then somehow pull herself together and go to work the next morning. I never seen nothin' like it... I don't know where she gets her strength from. But it was the pills..."

"What pills?"

"Her doctor prescribed valium, you know, to help stop the dee-tees. He tell her to stop drinking, but she kept on drinking with those valiums. She don't listen to the doctor. *She do what she want to do.* She don't eat nothing, maybe peanut butter. She just keep going, you know. Drink, drink, drink... You can't go like that."

"She drank while taking valium?"

"Listen to me, your mother should be dead, Miss Janis. Some nights, I be sittin' with your granmama, and I hear *thump*, like something falling. So, I rush out here, you know? Mrs. Pryor, on the floor! Fallen! Only God keep her from hitting her head on the corner of that coffee table."

"Why didn't you call the doctor?"

"Oh no, no, no! Your mother already fired me twice!" Aclema laughed a little. "I don't want to lose this job. We call you. We figure only you could handle her." Aclema smoothed out her uniform and looked at me as she stood up. "I just thought you should know what's really going on. Nobody else tell you."

"Thank you, Aclema." I didn't know what to do, scream, cry, pack up my things and leave with Prince in the middle of the night, but I didn't. Prince and I were trapped by my conscience and everything Mama and Papa taught me.

Tina stayed in the hospital for over three weeks. She was a difficult patient. Since Dr. Gaynor was on vacation, she was subjected to several other doctors. She hated all of them and despised the social worker assigned to her case. Any questions the social worker asked about finances, family, support, Tina refused to answer. She threw things at doctors, glasses, bowls, flowers, whatever she could get her hands on. She cursed at them and tried to escape whether she was in bed or seated in a chair wearing nothing but pajamas and her robe. One evening, clutching the wall for balance, she was found all but crawling towards an Exit. She couldn't walk down the stairs. She would've fallen at least one or two flights. A nurse found her a few feet from the Exit. Eventually, Tina had to be restrained in bed and whenever she sat in a chair.

Chapter Forty-Two

No Good Deed Goes Unpunished

I walked in her hospital room as she was squirming out of the restraints. Her eyes had a feral quality. They were slightly glazed, bobbing around, her mouth in a tangled sneer, and her body still twisting its way out of those restraints. Now I understood why some patients were drugged motionless. I happened to catch the eye of one of the nurses as she was repositioning and securing Tina in her chair.

The nurse said to me, "Mrs. Pryor can be difficult…"

I wanted to say, *you don't know the half of it*. Instead, I said, "I understand."

The other nurse looked up at me and said, "Are you her daughter?"

"Yes."

"You look a lot like her," the nurse said. Well, that wasn't really true. Tina and I have different chins, different facial structures, and differently shaped heads. Her eyes are light, mine are dark, and our noses are shaped differently. I have high cheekbones. Hers are not pronounced. Her hair had been reddish-brown for as long as I knew her, what Black people called "sandy". My hair was still black. Those who draw would see these differences. But there was still a resemblance we share. It's that same arrangement of features when seen in a certain light, an expression, a moment when the muscles in my face may tighten or loosen, and there she is. Tina gradually emerges from beneath the features people have come to recognize as me. Those were the moments of resemblance. I hated them.

Eventually, Tina calmed down, but not before sneering at one of the nurses again. The social worker, a bright-eyed woman, who looked painfully young, walked in while I was there. Fortunately, she was Black, brown-skinned with shoulder length, straightened hair. She was also small. Tina might show her some kindness.

Tina was in a room with three other women. She wanted a private room. Her bed was next to a window and the windowsill had enough flowers from her colleagues and associates to be mistaken for a florist or a funeral home! The social worker introduced herself to me and eyed all the flowers. I looked into her eyes and knew she didn't have a chance with Tina.

"So, Mrs. Pryor, I understand you're an educator," the young woman said brightly. Her enthusiasm was distressing. I wanted to warn her.

Tina, assuming the demeanor of royalty said, "That's right."

"Well, it would be wonderful if you did some volunteer work," the Social Worker said.

I saw the look on Tina's face, and I shut my eyes for a minute, thinking, "*Oh God...*"

"Volunteer?" Tina snapped. "I *don't* volunteer," Tina said.

The social worker asked with a smile, "You wouldn't? Why not? You have so much to contribute!"

"I don't volunteer." The conversation was over.

On another visit, Tina's Administrative Assistant was at the hospital. She had worked with Tina for almost twenty years, always the loyal employee, the confidant, and Tina's eyes and ears at the school. This woman got on my nerves. She was soft spoken, saccharine, and as far as I was concerned, dumb as dirt. *But she wasn't. It was a front.* I had heard that no one liked her at the school. They couldn't figure out what she and Tina had on each other that tied them so closely together.

Tina had designated the Assistant to be my "guardian". If anything, ever happened to Tina, she would step in and take care of things, pay bills, pay my bills, take care of the house, etc. As far as I was concerned this woman wasn't playing with a full deck on the best of days. She was playing with a deck unique only to her. As Terry would tell me later, the Assistant was the daughter that Tina wanted. What I witnessed during her visit with Tina made me realize I had grossly underestimated this woman in the worst way.

I walked in and she was standing next to Tina's bed with a large, loose-leaf binder checkbook that I had never seen. Tina was telling her to whom to make out the checks.

Upon finishing, Tina ordered, "Now, sign my name."

I watched this woman *perfectly forge* Tina's name on several checks. I could tell this wasn't unusual. I wondered what else was going on. I must have been looking at her with an incredulous gaze, and she felt it. She slowly turned to me and smiled. I never saw that checkbook again.

Although Tina wanted her to "take care of things" I was paying the household bills, along with the nurses' salaries from two accounts. I didn't know what to expect. Were we really broke? Had Mama's medical expenses drained us dry, financially? That would make sense. Thinking about this made me fearful while Prince and I returned to Cambridge. Both checkbooks were joint accounts with Tina's name first, mine was second. So, was this what the signature cards were for, at least two of them? What about the others?

Tina kept very accurate and complete financial records. Every checkbook was balanced. There were notations and receipts. If there was any information missing, it was because she didn't want you to know. I was amazed, but not half as amazed when I looked at the balances in the two joint accounts. There were three other account statements that came in while she was hospitalized, which I also took. Two were trust account statements for me.

I opened the statements. The balances in my trust accounts were so far from what I had been led to believe by Tina, that the figures left me light-headed. There was a lot of money, more than most Black folks would ever see, and enough to impress most white people. I thought I was hallucinating. But where were the trust documents? What had she done with them? Could I assume they were in a safe deposit box, or hidden in a shoebox or a paper bag? Did she really destroy them?

A rush of past conversations about money, the lack of it, why my financial needs always became a way to manipulate me, the frustration, the slow drip, drip, drip from the IRS because I had no significant deductions, and Tina's insistence that there was not enough money for me to buy, at least, a condo. All of this conjured up painful, humiliating, angry memories. Why was all of this a secret?

What else was hidden in closets, hollowed out books, safe deposit boxes or underneath mattresses? I felt the swell of blood begin to expand in my nose and I was afraid of a huge nosebleed erupting. Prince was curled up at my feet and I started to deliberately breathe slowly. It was the only thing I knew to do that might calm me down. Thankfully, Harry was upstairs or out. I didn't care. I was grateful he wasn't around me.

One of the accounts were specifically designated for the nurses' salaries. I let out a big sigh of what, relief? It didn't feel like relief. It felt like I had dodged a bullet. Why didn't Tina just tell me this?

For three weeks, Prince and I traveled back and forth between Cambridge and Riverdale. On the fourth week I decided to stay put in Cambridge. I was tired and worn out. Tina was physically improving but the doctors were not ready to release her.

It was late morning, and I was sitting in my study, making out checks to the nurses when the phone rang. It was Tina.

"Where are my checkbooks?" she demanded.

"I have them, Tina."

"You better send them back here right away or I'll have you arrested!"

"What?"

"What are you doing with those check books anyway?"

"What am I doing? I'm paying the household bills! Where are you, Tina?"

"I'm home! I left that damned hospital. *I'm well,*" she triumphantly declared!

"Really?" I asked sarcastically.

"Who told you to take those checkbooks, anyway?!"

"What are you talking about? You were near death. Do you understand that? Somebody had to keep the house running."

"And you thought *you* could do it? I want you to send those damned checkbooks back! Or get in that damned car and drive 'em back down here. *What are you doing? Stealing money?!!*" She was screaming so loudly that I had to hold the phone away from my ear for a few minutes and then I interrupted her.

"Why are you doing this to me? What is it? Where does all this come from?" I asked.

"*I don't want you to have anything that's why! Now dammit, send me all those books back, and I mean it, or I'll have you arrested!*"

"Tina, I'm going to hang up now." I mailed the checkbooks and the statements back to her that day.

Chapter Forty-Three

Mama Dies

Mama died in mid-October of 1989, roughly four weeks after Tina was released from the hospital. I flew down home for another funeral, arriving the night before the service. It was the first time I had seen the house since Tina had "renovated" it. Her renovations were more like exercises in design terrorism. Instead of the open expanse of the front screened porch where light and air flowed in, now there was a tight, airless room with two narrow barred windows. She closed the fireplace in the living room and built a back porch that was also enclosed with fake wood paneling. Years later I discovered it wasn't fake wood paneling, but Contact Paper glued to the frame of the porch. There was no drywall, no insulation. She added a second bathroom with no windows using the same dark brown "wood" paneling that was another version of Contact Paper. In a short amount of time the "wood paneling" in the bathroom would warp and peel from the moisture and humidity. Tina had carpet on what would've been the wood floors of the front and back porches. She also had one of the windows in the back bedroom sealed. The house was an airless box. I wanted to scream.

When I got home and opened the front porch door, I found Harry sitting in semi-darkness. He looked at me, nodded and said, "Hey." I nodded back and kept walking.

The minute I walked into the living room, I gasped. I stopped and mumbled out loud. "Oh my God. They're here." I could feel Mama and Papa's presence like a warm breeze coming up 31st Avenue from the Gulf of Mexico. I didn't need to see them. Feeling them was all I needed. I walked past some people in the living room, through the dining room and into the kitchen. Tina was leaning against the sink with a drink in her hand surrounded by the same men who were there when Papa died. Tina had a big smile on her face. Her skin shining with perspiration from the humidity and the overhead kitchen light. Her wig was off, and her hair was pulled tightly back in a small knot. She wore one of those anonymous cotton housecoats.

Lifting her glass up in the air when she saw me, I was greeted with, "Here's the baby!" The slur in her voice told me she'd had more than one or two drinks. (A year later, I would witness her putting teaspoons of sugar in a glass of white wine.)

I thought to myself, *"This is the woman who just recovered from alcohol poisoning."* I watched her knock back one drink after the other. Common sense told me she wasn't going to last long. I left the kitchen to get dressed for the wake at my Godmother's funeral home.

I managed to get home an hour before it began. Terry and I walked to the funeral home both of us muttering about Tina's drinking, her behavior.

There was an open casket. Seeing Mama motionless was a gut punch. Living without Mama and Papa terrified me. I sat down and let Terry have a moment with Mama. Within minutes, Tina made her grand entrance. She had to be escorted in and physically supported by two of her cousins. The look on her face was the definition of trepidation. Death terrified Tina. I don't know what she did with her grief, but I knew she wouldn't collapse. She would get that white suit dirty. She kept her eyes on me as she was led to the casket. What did she think I was going to do?

The wake concluded, and eventually everybody left. I walked back to the house and went to bed. I was in the front bedroom where I slept as a child. Tina had placed a plastic cover on the mattress. It made a crinkling noise every time you moved. I tried to open one of the windows, but it was nailed shut, as were the others. I tossed and turned trying to get comfortable, trying to ignore the sound of the plastic mattress cover. I wanted to scream. Would I spend the rest of my life swallowing my screams? Finally, I stopped and became still. My childhood at home ran past my memory. I remembered how Mama would leave the bedroom door open some nights when she was still watching television, allowing me to watch also from bed. I remembered how Papa would stand in the doorway and help me with my prayers. I remembered how I'd wake up in the morning and overhear Mama talking to someone from the front porch. Every now and then someone would ask, "How's the baby?" And Mama would laugh and say, "Oh, she's still laying up in the bed." More laughter would follow.

I tried to suppress my grief. I didn't want to think about how much I hurt. What was going to happen? What would Tina do now? Mama's gone and Tina was free to treat me anyway she wanted and do God knows what with the money my grandparents left me.

At that moment, I felt the corner of the mattress by my left foot sink slightly. The sound of the mattress cover made a small noise from the same area. I opened my eyes after a few seconds and lifted myself up on my elbows. Seated at the foot of the bed in an almost imperceptible yellow-white light was Mama. Seated in an upholstered chair in the corner across from the foot of the bed was Papa, smoking his pipe, and bathed in the same yellow-whitish light that almost sparkled. Mama had that contented, "Don't worry now," look on her face. Papa sat there with a look I had seen hundreds of times, confident, soothing, peaceful, powerful. Both looked younger, but not enough that I didn't recognize them. As much as I wanted to go with them, they let me know I had to stay. Papa's face and Mama's hand reaching towards me were the last things I remembered before falling asleep.

The next morning, the minister, a heavy-set, dark-skinned man came by the house to lead us in prayer. Tina wore another white pantsuit, another blonde wig, and lots of gold jewelry. Once again, I left the mink in Cambridge, incurring her wrath. I stood in the living room wearing a black suit while the minister was saying a prayer. When the prayer was finished, the limo pulled up to take us to church. Again, I felt silly being driven to the church that was a block away. And again, Terry was running back and forth from car to car. I had less of an idea what he was doing now than when he ran from car to car during Papa's funeral!

Tina and I sat in the back seat of the limo in silence. I don't remember where Harry was. So long as he wasn't in the limo with me, I was fine. Lost in thought with having seen Mama and Papa, I was somewhat consoled and smiled to myself. I don't know who designed the service, but it was clear from the piss poor sermon that the minister knew one thing about William Lawrence and his family. They gave money to the church. The only thing the service got right was a hymn Papa loved, *Precious Lord, Take My Hand*. I wanted the Lord to take the minister's hand and lead him somewhere else.

After the service, Tina, and I got to the cemetery first, following the hearse that carried Mama's casket. Tina had a brick mini mausoleum built for Mama and Papa. Tina announced,

"No dirt shall fall on their faces, *ever. These are my parents, my mother and father.*" She had Papa's coffin exhumed and placed in the mausoleum. It was unsightly. People wondered what the hell it was! This rectangular, red brick structure was the only one in the cemetery. There were still two spaces left in the Lawrence plot. One is mine.

As everyone else arrived, I watched Tina showing off the mausoleum like it was an expensive car. I wondered what Mama and Papa had learned from raising their children. What mistakes had they made that they were determined not to make with me? Would I ever know?

One thing I knew as the day closed was, I was in trouble. With Mama and Papa gone, there was no telling what Tina would do. Little did I know what she had already done.

Chapter Forty-Four

Tina's Revenge

Within a year, Tina held me hostage financially. What she hadn't already done, she would finish and successfully cripple me for life. Sometimes it becomes too late to undo things. The longer my grandparents were dead, the more dysfunctional I became regarding money and taking care of myself. I managed to stumble along for seventeen years before crashing because of all this. And who knew? I don't think anyone did.

Looking back, Tina was masterful. After Mama passed, I went to Riverdale with the intent of initiating the protocol of settling her estate. I knew it would be complicated. Obviously, I had a lapse. Did I forget what Tina did when Papa died? What made me think Tina was going to "play nice"? She was quite crazy. What was I thinking?

Prince and I walked into the house and instantly you could feel the tension in the air. After getting settled, Prince and I walked into the living room and waited for Tina. She came bouncing down the stairs and briskly walked in, cigarette in one hand, legal sized papers in the other. Without looking at me, she shoved the papers in my face and said, "Here's your grandmother's will." I examined the document. It didn't take long. I had seen Mama's original will.

"What is this, Tina? This is not Mama's will. This is some 'do it yourself' kit! What are you trying to pull here?"

"Oh, this is your grandmother's will! It's signed and everything," Tina said confidently.

Mama's signature was barely legible. You could tell her hand had been shaking when she tried to sign it. The witnesses listed were people I didn't know, but most disturbing was the date on the will, a week before she died. Everything was now left in Tina's control, including real estate and money.

I looked at Tina. "You're not getting away with this."

"Get away with what?" she asked in her high-pitched, girlish voice.

"This will not hold up in court, Tina."

"What do you mean? Of course, it will."

"We'll see."

"What are you going to do?"

"First, I'm going to find a lawyer and we'll take it from there."

"You *can't* find a lawyer. What kind of lawyer would you find? *Who's behind all this?*" Tina's eyes were wide beyond measurement. Her mouth tightened and there was not one cigarette for her to grab.

What she didn't know was one of the nurses told me, that after Mama signed the "new will" Tina marched through the house laughing and saying out loud, "I got the house and the property now! The little red bitch will have nothing!"

Chapter Forty-Five

Lawyers, Money, and Books

I did find a lawyer. He told me it was doubtful Mama's will would hold up in court. He wanted to know if Mama had been in sound mind when she signed the will. I told him no. Just having to admit that, out loud, felt like someone had placed bricks on my chest! Of course, going to court would make it public. He suggested that Tina and I come to his office and see if we could "work something out." When I told her, she was astounded and refused until I told her that otherwise we would have to go to court, and *it would be public.* I could almost hear the wheels spinning in her head. She didn't want anybody to know anything.

A few weeks later, we headed downtown to lower Park Avenue to the lawyer's office. As we rode up the elevator, Tina said, "This lawyer's expensive. He'll want money."

"Well yeah," I said. "Of course."

Tina muttered, "Makin' money!" She hated paying people for their services. When presented with a bill she thought she was being taken advantage of, especially if it was for something intangible. Paying a lawyer or a doctor was not like paying for a mink coat. She was tense and avoided looking directly at me.

Watching her as we rode up, I thought, *"If looks could kill, the entire island of Manhattan would be pulverized by now!"*

When she walked into the lawyer's office, her demeanor completely changed. She became, Tina the Sweet, the Bewildered, the "there's got to be some terrible misunderstanding here. I only want the best for my daughter." That's exactly what she told the lawyer. Before the meeting was over, *he was her lawyer*. She secured his services to draw up her will. My interests became a forgotten item on the agenda. I was simply "over- reacting."

The lawyer extracted a promise from her that she had to carry out the "prime directive" that had been stated in the original wills of my grandparents. I should get copies of any and all documents, including the original trust instruments. I knew they existed because I had seen them! Those accounts were to be turned over to me, along with any and all funds from insurance policies where I was named sole beneficiary. Property divided equally in New York, Mississippi and New Jersey. My housing was covered with funds from one account, dedicated especially for that purpose.

It was the threat of going to court, of our "business" being made public that frightened Tina and she agreed to everything, while telling the lawyer, "All I want to do is make sure Janis has everything." She agreed to send me monthly checks to "spare me" the bureaucracy of dealing with banks... All I wanted was *what was left to me*, no more, no less, and as little to do with Tina as possible. We returned to Riverdale in silence. Deep down I knew holy hell was about to be unleashed on me. Tina's word meant nothing, and she rarely listened to anyone, much less a white, Park Avenue lawyer. All those promises she made in his office – useless.

The lawyer's impact on Tina all but dissolved within a few months. I insisted that we go to a family mediator, otherwise we go to court. The mediator's interaction resulted in Tina forking over a thirty thousand dollar check she had been "keeping for me." As for the rest of it? She swore there was nothing, but she would send those checks that came from "nothing" every month. She adhered to the promises as long as it was convenient for her. After that, it was back to the money games of hide and seek with Tina in control.

She had a variety of excuses and problems when it came to my money. The easiest was delay, she forgot, she got mixed up, the banks don't listen to her, and so on. When I questioned her, she suddenly became confused, bewildered. She didn't understand what had happened. Why weren't the checks coming from the bank instead of her? She didn't mail the check is what happened because she closed some of my accounts.

Sometimes I wondered how I would buy groceries. Bills didn't get paid on time. My credit rating plummeted, and I stopped opening the mail, including financial statements. I would freeze regarding any money issue I couldn't readily figure out or pay with whatever slim salary I was making in the face of rising costs. Often, I'd get to the point where I couldn't add or subtract or if I did, I kept coming up with preposterous sums! A check would bounce, and I would collapse into what felt like a storm of rage and fears. There were times I was left hanging, twisting in the wind of financial uncertainty. If I called and told her I needed groceries, something "tangible", she would drag out her repertoire of compassionate responses.

"Oh no. Poor little ol' thing. I can't have you go hungry. I'll send something up tomorrow."

"Do a wire transfer, Tina."

"What's that?"

"Call the bank. They'll do it for you," I said.

"I have my own bank now. I closed those other accounts Daddy set up for you. I'm saving that for you, when you grow up or get married, you'll have a little nest egg."

I was almost forty. When did she think I would grow up? And what if I never got married? That was something she refused to

Mother's Madness

imagine. When she died, roughly twenty years later, I discovered I had more money than I thought.

Every now and then she'd do something disturbing. She sent me a check made out on her school account. I called and asked her why she was doing this?

Yelling at me, she said, "What do you care where the damned check comes from?!"

"Send me a personal check. Send me a check from the trust. I can't take a school check."

"You don't know what you're talking about! You ask too many damned questions. This is my school! If you want the damned money, the only way you'll get it now is through that check. I'm not writing another check! You're always telling me what to do. I'm not a child."

My head was pounding. "Look, I'm just..." She cut me off.

"Get off the Goddamned phone and cash the check!" She slammed the phone down.

I spent days longing for help and not knowing who to go to. Anxiety attacks became a constant companion. I developed a spastic colon. Migraines increased. You can't get rich trying to save the world. Politicians may get rich, but not activists and rarely did their campaign aides pocket big money. Yet, it was one of the few occupations that didn't bore me to dangerous distraction. I sent the check back. I kept hearing the word, "wrong" dance across my mind. I don't know how I got through that month, but I did. Eventually, I would send all the bills I couldn't pay in a manila envelope to Fieldston Road.

Tina's management of my finances fell somewhere between mysterious and ludicrous. She seemed to make up rules with little to no regard for the consequences or the law! When I explained that the IRS was taxing me heavily because I had no significant deductions, she gave me the following instructions. Looking me straight in the eye she said, "Lie."

Nausea filled my entire being. It would be wiser for me to throw myself in front of a firing squad, say a few prayers, and yell, "Anytime you're ready!" I was not about to lie to the IRS. It was the IRS that got Al Capone.

What do you do when your mother betrays you and becomes your most formidable and dangerous enemy? I didn't know how to fight that. All I knew was each time we had any kind of conversation, I felt like I was watching a dangerous storm creeping towards her. The sky darkened. Winds picked up and she became engulfed in nature's revenge while I ducked for cover.

Tina became a Money Monster, still ordering me to go to the best stores to buy the best clothes and send her the bill. Furs and jewels kept coming that I never chose nor wanted. I could refuse and get verbally browbeaten and viciously attacked. There was no peace, no middle ground. But she did make me an offering, to end the conflict.

"You can have all of your money if you'll just move back home with me," she said sweetly. "No more problems."

I paused and then said, "I don't need it that badly. I'm not coming back to New York." And there was no way I was living under the same roof with her.

"You're draining me dry," she said. "You're going to be the cause of my downfall. You need to help me from going broke." It was as if someone or something had flipped a switch in her. Where did this come from?

I never said whatever she wanted me to say. Her response? "People are going to talk about you."

I wanted to say, "People are already talking about me!"

Her verbal abuse escalated after that. Every time she lit into me, I made her pay in the only way that mattered in her world. I purchased something royally expensive. But what drove her nuts were the books I'd buy. She couldn't understand how I could spend so much money on books, nor why. This is how I punished her. Stupid but satisfying.

When Tina left graduate school, she believed she knew it all. There was nothing else for her to learn. Any changes or advancements that came along in her field she felt no need to understand nor follow. As she often said, "What could they tell me? What's in a book?"

Books nurtured me. I read the way starving people eat a good meal. I love the smell of a new book, the touch of freshly printed pages, the sound of new pages being turned, and old pages being revisited. It's a thrill to hold a new book, especially a hardcover. I look at books as efforts to illuminate and solve life's puzzles, to shed light on the human condition. If I had to suffer, at least I would be informed! I would spend money on books before I'd pay utility bills! Remember, at the time, I lived in what was, book heaven, Cambridge, Massachusetts.

Tina thought my values were twisted and that constituted stupidity. All this reading, what purpose did it serve? As for painting, drawing, architecture, those interests of mine continued to frighten her until the day she died. One day I saw her sitting on her bed cutting out two pieces of material, one orange, one yellow. I asked, "What are you doing?"

She pointed to a magazine that had an Ellsworth Kelly painting and said, "I'm making one of those. I can do that." I didn't bother to explain who Ellsworth Kelly was, nor why his work is significant. And I certainly didn't tell her how offensive I thought her "project" was.

Tina was not curious about anything unless it presented an opportunity for her to shine. The only thing she believed she knew and understood was money. Power was a close second. Nothing else mattered.

One year, she wanted me to meet a new money manager she had found. Prince and I drove to Riverdale to meet this man. Introductions were made and he started to ramble about what my portfolio should be. I thought he was crazy. Did he understand what kind of work I did? Where did he see this money coming from? What did Tina tell him? I let this silliness go on for roughly fifteen minutes and explained to him my reality. When he left, Tina marched through the house, laughing loudly declaring, "That's right, destroy all the men."

An Addendum

Tina's Reflections in 1997

I was determined to figure out who this woman was. However, talking with her felt like I was being gutted. I asked her to write down her thoughts or responses to my questions and send them to me. I deluded myself into thinking that having her write her responses would elicit more thorough and insightful answers. In mid-August of 1997, I asked her to write about losing Mama and Papa. It took her roughly two months to respond. This is what she wrote.

"*10.12.97*

Janis,

The death of Mama and Papa was devastating. I will never get over it. They were such special people even though they controlled my life to a great part after I became an adult. I accepted it and it made a better person out of me. Yes, I have a lot of their traits, particularly Mama.

When you were growing up, I knew very little – nothing about parenting. Today I would tell you to tend to your business and just have those little guys* up there. Sometimes you don't know how to speak to me. Just silent. Disgusting. Yes disgusting.

Greatest challenge with you – it would take ten pages to write such. Just bear in mind that we are living over our budget and every day it becomes increasingly worse to meet the medical needs.

Women's movement – I could have the same job as a man – providing it was not too physical.

Civil Rights Movement – that came I believe under L. Johnson, President. The BASTARDS are still doing the same thing. Just cover it up. I had to work that much harder. I will always hate how they treated my parents and me.

One thing, you are so brilliant. When they open their mouths, you are read. You do it so much you forget that you are talking to me. I like to hear you talk about what you said to someone or what you are going to do. For the life of me, I can't remember what you said two hours later. Getting forgetful. What kind of life did I want? Just what I got except for this illness.

My marriage was ok for a middle-income family.

All I know is that I love you very much and sorry my illness is going to take me away so soon. But I will always be with you in spirit.

Tina"

I asked her to tell me more about the devastation of Mama and Papa's deaths. Papa was 90 when he died, Mama, 94. Tina told me, "I'm blaming her passing on me. Did I have enough nurses? Did I do enough? Every day I ask myself this. I can be walking down a grocery aisle, and something will come over me, and I wonder, she wasn't supposed to die!"

"Tina, Mama was 94," I said.

"No, no! I haven't ever been able to accept death. I hold onto things. Why did my mother have to go? She died from ... her heart stopped beating. What does death mean? Death. You're gone. You won't be back."

Chapter Forty-Six

He Died...Finally

Shortly after Mama died, Terry returned to New York and lived with Tina and Harry. Tina offered Terry a job at her school, doing what I don't know. But a computer was involved that Terry was never taught to use. He would earn more at Tina's school than he ever would down home. Terry could save his money and send it home, a time-honored tradition. But he didn't always do that. In 1989, Terry was what I called a "legitimate grown up" at the age of 35. He was married to a solid, good, hard-working woman, Mary. They had two sons, Ted, and Mark. Terry had responsibilities and working in New York would help him fulfill his obligations theoretically.

Of course, Tina had conditions. Terry could have no friends from Tina's school. She didn't want any of those people "in her business". Terry wasn't allowed to go out...until he was interrogated by Tina. Mary wasn't permitted to visit Terry in New York. Why? Mary was too dark. Tina wasn't wild about his kids wanting to visit their father either, but she could tolerate them better than Mary. When they did visit, Tina threw a fit when they were playing basketball across the street with a neighbor's son. Why? "They don't want those black niggers over there. They have a [white] daughter. I made them come away from over there. They could watch television." Why did Terry tolerate this? Money talks.

Eventually Harry was hospitalized. Tina called and told me to come down and go see him. I refused. A few years earlier, Harry had been hospitalized and Tina browbeat me into visiting him. I got to the hospital, he looked at me and said, "Hey..." He turned to the man in the bed next to him and said, in the flattest tone I've ever heard from any living being, "...my daughter." That was it. I left within minutes.

Now, a few years later, Harry was hospitalized again, and Tina was asking me, "What do you mean you're not going to see him? He's your father!"

"Look, I've never had a real conversation with this man in my life!"

"So, you've never had a conversation with your father... So?"

"Listen up," I said firmly. "I'm not setting foot in that hospital. I did that once. I'm not doing it again."

"You have to go! He's your father!"

"I don't have to do anything, Tina."

Silence on the end of the phone. I hung up. Within weeks, Harry died. Terry told me about the funeral because I did not attend. It sounded like an extravaganza, limousines, a band, a sit-down meal or as Tina described it, "the whole nine yards."

A year or so later, she would have Harry's body exhumed so it could be placed in a mausoleum that she purchased in Westchester for what seemed like an outrageous amount of money to me, ten thousand dollars. She called to let me know that she made sure there was enough room for me also. I told her that was a waste of money. Just the thought of being buried with them made my skin crawl.

Terry told me later about the relationship he began to forge with Harry before he died. Terry realized he was an asset to Tina. He could help take care of Harry, who had become legally blind and was no longer able to drive. Terry became his driver. He would take Harry to the doctor, to be with friends in Harlem, to get his hair cut, to play the Numbers or to pick up his winnings. During those drives, the two of them "started gettin' kind of close per se... he kinda started talkin' a little bit," Terry said. "When he had won big, he gave me two or three hundred dollars and said, 'Don't tell Tina. I want you to go ahead and spend it on yourself,' Terry said.

I was amazed and curious that Harry talked to anybody without threatening to kill them! "That's interesting," I said. "What else did he say?"

"He appreciated me being here and helping out and all like that." Terry stopped a minute and then continued. "He said something, but you may not believe this."

"Go ahead," I urged. My curiosity was growing. "Terry, he never talked to me, so I don't know!"

"He caught me off-guard. He really hated he didn't know you better. And I hope I'm sayin' this right... to whereas he hoped that you didn't turn out like your mother!" Terry laughed nervously.

Roughly seven years after his death, Tina told me all Harry's sisters and cousins had diabetes. She mentioned this as if it was an item on a grocery list. She didn't know there was a hereditary component to diabetes just like she didn't know the hereditary predisposition to alcoholism and depression. I started to wonder if I represented some kind of genetic trade off. Was I spared from diabetes and alcoholism but cursed with depression instead?

Terry thought Harry went into a diabetic coma due to an accidental overdose of insulin. He had become forgetful. Terry had given him a shave earlier in the day along with his insulin shot. Maybe Harry forgot and gave himself another injection.

"When the ambulance got to the house, I told them what had took place up to that time. He started feelin' sick. Tina couldn't wake him up... something like that. They took him to the hospital, and he never returned to the house," Terry said.

"How was Tina during all of this?" I asked.

A sly grin sneaked onto Terry's face. "Well," he began, "She said, 'My Harry is gone.' She didn't really break down. You never know about Tina. I've seen her at other funerals. You know... those tears pop up and *you know they're not for real! You know she didn't care nothin' about that person.* Ten minutes later, talk about 'em like a dog! I mean, the whole nine yards! Like at Aunt Ophelia's funeral. She got up there and said, 'This is a poem that Janis wrote. And I'm readin' it for her.' Girl..." Terry exclaimed.

"What?! I never wrote a poem for Aunt Ophelia's funeral."

Laughing, Terry said, "I was sayin' to myself, 'Tina, hurry up and get from up there!' She copied the poem from someplace or made it up! It didn't rhyme! *But you wrote it!* You sent that to Aunt Ophelia. Oh girl, I thought you knew about that! If I'm lyin' I'm not sittin' here right now! She was on the pulpit reading this poem! You know how you just bite your teeth or your lip when you're supposed to be cryin'? That's what she did. And had to stop a couple of times! She should've won the Academy Award!"

The next time I heard anything substantive about Harry from Tina was in October 1997. There were too many gaps I wanted filled in. *"I miss Harry so much. Very lonely without him, even though I dominated him a lot. He apparently liked it because he grew up without a mother. She died at childbirth. His father died when he was quite young and he was shifted from one relative to another, but he made it!"* This contradicted her earlier statement made years before that implied Harry's father died when Harry was an adult.

She told me she was going out with a married man before she met Harry. "Robert was my boyfriend before I was married. He's still in touch with me. I met him when I was teaching in Virginia." Robert followed Tina to New York City when she was studying at Columbia University. During that time, she had another boyfriend from her freshman year in college, John, from Washington, D.C. "We were going to get married when he came out of the service, but I was too wild. When John came back, I was in New York City. He came to see me the same day Robert was there. It was sort of sad."

"John said, 'Close your eyes. I got a surprise for you.' It was an engagement ring, but I was already engaged to Bob. John slapped me when I told him. Robert asked him [John] to leave. He was mad. Robert never divorced his wife. He told me he had a friend that just came out of the service. We were invited up to Yonkers to this friend's house. That's where I met Harry. Harry took me out every weekend. Saturday night he took me to the Apollo theatre. He took me everywhere!" She was aglow with the memory.

I listened intently to this story of the whirlwind romance. It wasn't the story she told in the past. I remember her telling me how handsome Harry was and how impressed she had been with him. This version of the story had them meeting in a bar. Another man had been bothering her and Harry intervened. Harry threatened to flush his head down a toilet if he didn't stop making a nuisance of himself. Tina was very impressed with that, and she and Harry started to date.

Harry told Tina that Robert wasn't going to marry her. "He's not going to get divorced." Tina inhaled on her cigarette and told me, "I went home, woke him up, and told him I never wanted to see him. I'm through with you for life!"

I thought about the implications of what she said. Two people living together today is not a big deal. Back then, in the 1940s? And how did she fall for the line that Robert was going to divorce his wife? Didn't everybody know that the likelihood of that was somewhere between slim and none?!

Harry and Tina were married on December 19th or the 21st. She couldn't remember. They were married at the Justice of the Peace. "I could read the vows faster than the minister! I called Mama. Why? Tell Mama everything. That's my Mama. Papa said Harry sounded like a nice guy and to bring him home." The truth was they were married in 1946 in New Jersey.

By now, Tina was telling me how much Mama liked Harry, and how he and her cousin, Ed, got along so well. "We'd come home for Christmas and vacation time. We didn't have any money. Mama would take Harry crabbin'. The red bugs would bite me." As I listened, I kept hearing Mama's version of this. She told me Tina sent her a telegram, followed by a letter with a photo of Harry. Mama took one look at the photo and cried.

Tina was painting a rosy picture. Very little of it was true. I blurted out, "What the hell happened?"

Tina became pensive, almost childlike. "Things started to go bad when we all lived together. I had no say. And I wasn't going to hurt my mother's feelings. Mother would tell me everything about how Daddy's sisters ignored her. They had lots of girlfriends for Daddy, but they admired Mama. She had strength. She would stand up to them and his sisters would tell Daddy to do whatever. Papa would give things he had given to Mama to his mother. Papa was the only one who really accomplished anything though." Tina began to ramble as if she were somewhere else. "Uncle Dan got tuberculosis." (Tina's grandfather, my great grandfather, took Uncle Dan to Tucson,

Arizona for this tuberculosis.) I knew the white folks liked us. They liked Mama, my Daddy. We'd get nice gifts from them… and jobs. We could get jobs."

I sat there wondering, "*So what was it? White folks were good to you, or they treated you badly?*" The contradictions were crazy making!

"Roughly a year later, I asked why she chose to live with her parents after she married. Straightening up in her chair, she said, "*My parents wanted to be near me, near Tina!*"

Sorting out the truth in a mine field of Tina's lies frightened me because I began to realize she didn't know what the truth was. Did she know what a fact was and its relationship to the truth? It began to sink in how readily she could make up things to suit her needs.

The call from Detective DeGatano was roughly a year away.

Chapter Forty-Seven

Up the Mass Pike

After Harry's death, Tina started visiting me in Cambridge, frequently. In the beginning she had someone drive her and Terry from New York. One of Harry's last purchases was a large, dark brown, Mercedes with tan leather seats, a gold frame for the vanity license plate, and every option you could order. The car drew attention. It was ostentatious and easily mistaken for a drug dealer's car. The police did pull them over once when she let Terry drive her somewhere. He took a wrong turn. Within seconds, police cars surrounded them, and Terry was questioned. Tina told me, "I simply looked out the window while all this was going on and smoked a cigarette…"

You would've thought that car was the Ark of the Covenant the way Tina regarded it. Right after Harry died, she didn't trust Terry to drive it even though he had driven Harry to the doctor, the barbershop and any other place he wanted to go in the Mercedes. She found a middle-aged, rather unsophisticated Black man, Carl, "the driver", who had some connection to Tina's best (and probably only) friend, Ruth. Carl thought Tina was white. That's how he described her to his girlfriend, Pam, that I came to regard as an angel. Pam took one look at Tina and knew better! The angel would save my sanity later.

Tina instituted a protocol around her visits. There was a procession from the sidewalk to my place, down a narrow brick path. I could look out a first-floor window or stand at the front door and watch them. Tina would lead. Terry followed carrying things. One time he brought two small televisions. Last in the procession was the driver, Carl, usually with his mouth half open, wide eyed, and looking very skeptical.

The first time Tina visited she stood and slowly looked around, unsmiling. It was a free-standing duplex unit, with a loft like area on the second floor where my office, bedroom, bathroom, and washer-dryer were located. The first floor had all the usual spaces, a living room, dining area, kitchen with pantry, second bathroom and a room that served as my library and guest room. Her eyes finally rested on the fireplace. She asked, "Is that a live fireplace?"

"Yes," I said.

She looked at the two large windows in the living room before walking over to the sliding glass doors to the deck and back yard. Her head oscillated from left to right and back before she spoke. The driver and Terry stood absolutely still.

Fixating on the yard she looked at me and said, "I guess you plant…what? Flowers out there?"

The second time she came, it was a similar drill. Only then, she escorted the driver upstairs and said to him, "Look, she has a computer!"

I could see him from the first floor looking at some framed photos I had. He pointed to a small cluster of them and asked Tina, "How come she's got these photos here? What's she doing with these people?"

Tina looked at him, indignant and said, "She worked for them!"

"Them" at the time was Ed Brooke, Ted Kennedy, and Jesse Jackson. There were two famous speeches that EMK (Edward Kennedy) had made. They were printed and signed by the Senator. I had them framed. The driver looked at Tina and asked, "She did? That looks like Kennedy's signature. He signed it?"

Every trip was punctuated with unwanted gifts. One trip produced bags of Ivory soap, six cans of Lysol Spray, and boxes of plastic garbage bags. Once we went to Crate and Barrel and she bought me a new couch for the guest room. We'd go to Bread and Circus, now known as Whole Foods, and buy more food than any one person could eat in weeks! She wanted to know if the owner of my condo unit wanted to sell it. He didn't. This had to be one of the few times anyone said no to her, except for me! She bought me a new car, more jewelry, new coats, and a variety of items from Saks.

I had been one of the original customers at the Fifth Avenue Club, a private shopping service for customers. Tina insisted I needed new clothes. Off to Saks we went. Tina was overwhelmed and delighted. One of the club employees said to me, "I've never seen you so tense." By that time, I had been coming to the Fifth Avenue Club over a decade.

The Fifth Avenue Club was like an elegant apartment right inside of Saks. Faye was my person at the club. I loved her. I was always in good hands with Faye and over the years we became friends. There was a bit of Mama in Faye. She made sure my clothing was altered, that shoes were brought up from the retail floor. Anything you were considering, it was right there. And they would serve you tea or coffee, even go out and get you something. You had a private dressing room with a triple mirror for the seamstress to alter your clothes, a lovely couch to sit on and more breathing room than you could ever imagine if you tried on clothes in the equivalent of a "stall" out on the floor. You walked through the French Doors of the club, and you were in another world. *I never worried about anyone following me around to see if I was going to steal anything!* That was not an experience I endured in *any* store I shopped. All Tina ever wanted to do was shop, and anything was better than enduring the brittle silence between us.

Given her constant smoking, I never let her stay at my place. Terry could stay. She checked in at the Charles Hotel and that was her base. I was standing in the lobby waiting for her on one occasion. Her entrance had to be staged by MGM! Ash blonde wig perfectly coiffed and shining, diamonds aglow, with the white mink coat draped over her shoulders. Each shoulder flowed back and forth in synchronized motions so specific you would've thought her movements had been choreographed.

Looking at the coat and cream-colored pantsuit, I said quietly, "Tina, people don't really dress like this in Cambridge."

Her mouth parted slightly, and she asked, "Why not? The women don't look like nothin' up here anyway. They let their hair go gray." She gave me the once over and I waited.

"Don't you have anything better to wear than jeans and a sweater?"

"Tina, this is Cambridge. When in Rome…" She looked so out of place. Heads did turn.

Once I recruited a friend to help me endure her visit. It was an election year and during brunch Tina announced she would be voting for the Conservative candidate, Pat Buchanan. "After all," she stated provocatively, "he's simply saying what all the rest of 'em are thinking." Then she looked up at the ceiling and blinked her eyes very deliberately with flirtatious, self-centered overtones.

Tina never let me forget how cruel she could be. Another friend of mine she met was seriously overweight. A few weeks later, Tina asked about her, which was unusual. I told Tina she was fine.

"Oh really," Tina exclaimed.

"Yeah, she's fine."

"Is she still fat?" Tina asked.

How do you answer that kind of question-statement-accusation-judgment in an honorable way, or any way at all? I paused and then said, "Always a kind word, Tina. Always a kind word."

"Shut up," she said.

I adjusted to Tina's visits and prepared myself for anything when she arrived. The trip that set off an alarm was during the spring in the early 90s. As she waddled down the brick path in a salmon-colored pantsuit, I tried to hide my shock. I thought I was hallucinating until I saw the look in Terry's eyes. He was walking behind her looking straight at me. Tina had bloated into a tiny stuffed animal! She looked like one of those obese people she hated. I had never seen her anywhere near being fat. She managed to walk in, cigarette in hand. It didn't matter how many times I told her there was no smoking in my place. I had to repeat it and endure her look of disdain.

"Tina, when did you gain all this weight?"

"I don't know. Gettin' fat!" She giggled and shrugged her shoulders.

"Have you been to the doctor?" I couldn't help staring at her.

"No, what can the doctor do? They don't know nothin' anyway."

Eventually, she did go to the doctor. She kept having pains in her lower abdomen. Shortly after, she called and told me she was going into the hospital for surgery.

"What kind of surgery?" I asked.

"They have to take out a itty-bitty tumor... that's all."

"A *little* tumor?! What kind of little tumor?"

"It's nothin', Janis. It'll be one, two, three. In and out."

"So, this is an outpatient procedure? You won't have to stay in the hospital?"

"Why the hell do you ask so many damned questions? I told you this is not a big deal!"

But it was a big deal. I also knew I wouldn't get any more information from her that either made sense or was close to the truth. And, if I did, what could I do? Go down there and be a target for her madness?

J.W. came up from Alabama for the surgery. He and Terry waited at the hospital. She was operated on in 1993. I found out years later that her doctor had given her six months to live. Tina lived six *years*.

The doctors found tumors everywhere. Her doctor was a gynecological oncologist with a reputation of being very competent and highly regarded. She was also a cancer survivor. Unfortunately, she had the warmth and bedside manner of a sledgehammer. Tina had been diagnosed with ovarian cancer. She never told me. What she did tell me a few days after the surgery was everything was fine. "They got everything. The only things that's left are itsy-bitsy Rice Crispies. That's all. I'll take some chemo, and everything will be fine." Rice Crispies?!

Shortly after her surgery, Terry started making passing references to a dispute regarding her school. There was some kind of inquiry being launched. Terry didn't quite understand what was going on at first. Tina dismissed it. She told Terry, "This'll blow over. It's just some mess from downtown." The mess from downtown had a name, Rudolph Giuliani, the newly elected Republican Mayor, determined to root out corruption and clean up New York City. That storm cloud I would often see regarding Tina, was looking darker and approaching the shore of her life with increasing speed.

Chapter Forty-Eight

"Traditionally Conflicting Constituencies"

By this time in my work-life, I was regarded as a political operative, someone just below the radar who wasn't interested in the spotlight. I had a long list of politicians and activists I had worked for and with, along with a respectable tenure in television winning a few awards and nominations to prove it. I had stopped working traditional nine to five jobs many years before. It was a blessing of privilege that made that possible, but it also created some awkward moments with Black associates in Boston. The idea of a Black person not having to work a nine to five job put me in a different category. They were puzzled by me, and suspicious. Not so with white friends, but some white bosses I had before I left that nine to five madness, especially those who had come from the working class, thought I was a "kept woman." How else would I have such nice clothes?

I had started to work with Boston's Ten Point Coalition in the early nineties as their political and media consultant. I worked for them almost seven years. Ten Point was a faith-based coalition of Black clergy who decided to actively confront the issues of gang violence and youth homicide. Gang violence involving young Black men and women was a way of life. Boston was in crisis. These young people were being killed wholesale. A turning point was reached when some gang members barged into a service for another gang member and doing the unthinkable. Gun shots inside the sanctuary of a church. That incident is etched into Boston's history and adapted years later in a cable drama-series about Boston in the nineties. I remember watching the scene and feeling slightly ill. Oh, the details and nuances the writers and producers missed, the shock, violation, and depth of the impact was missed or deliberately omitted. But the essence of that incident was nailed! That was probably all that was needed.

My job was to make Ten Point a viable political entity. Their success became nationally known as the Boston Miracle. The real miracle was not the unprecedented drop in gang violence and youth homicide. (One year the youth homicide rate fell to zero.) *The miracle was the methodology that led to the drop in gang violence and youth homicide.* It arose from convening what I coined as "traditionally conflicting constituencies" to solve historically defined and widely believed insurmountable problems through dialogue under the guidance of a collective form of leadership with the police, educators, gang members, fellow clergy, city officials, etc., all the stakeholders. *That* was the genius of Boston's Ten Point Coalition.

It was an all the time job with phone conferences at midnight too often and phone calls as early as 5:30 AM. I talked with politicians. I did media training and produced videos. I wrote statements, did damage control, and ran more interference than they will ever know. Went to LA with them while Disney wined and dined all of us, hoping to get their permission to do a movie about them. * They said no so back to Boston we went. As another colleague of mine said, "…it's like herding cats!" It was worse.

This was the time I received the call from Detective DeGatano. Tina denied the seriousness of what was going on. Bits and pieces of information about "the men at the school" started to come from Terry.

With each trip to Cambridge, Tina looked worse and worse. She was beginning to physically vanish, like a slow fade in the movies, while insisting she was well. By now she hated her oncologist. Tina's hostility grew in part from the way her doctor spoke to her. Tina told me she asked her doctor, "Who do you think you're talking to?!" With all of this going on, she still found time to berate me for working with Ten Point.

"What the hell you doing working for those nigger ministers? All they want is your money. You don't have a bit of sense!"

Bits and pieces of information grew from a trickle to a rush of stupefying reports from Terry. I heard myself say the following.

"Will you tell her this is not an episode of *Law and Order*! She's got to get *a lawyer, a criminal lawyer...* The house has been under surveillance?! What do mean, Carrie's involved? How could she be involved? ...the Board President? This isn't *The Godfather*! This is real life, Terry! *What do you mean she still had dead people on the board?* You mean she never replaced them? Are you serious? ...You realize this isn't going to end well..."

To this day, I can still hear Terry telling me, "I told Tina nobody was going to jail for her!"

And then the police came. One evening, shortly after Tina and Terry got home, Tina received a call saying the police were at the school taking documents and file cabinets. Tina and Terry rushed back. According to Terry, upon arrival there was at least one police van outside the school as officers rolled out file cabinets. Police were searching Tina's office. She was outraged. As she began to protest, she was served with a restraining order. She was no longer allowed to set foot in the school, her school! Terry told me one of the detectives found a file in her desk labeled, "Janis Pryor."

The detective asked, "Who's Janis Pryor?"

"She's my daughter," Tina stated.

"Why are you keeping a file on her?" he asked.

"I like to keep tabs on her." I never found out what was in that file just like I never found out what happened to the life insurance policy she took out on me.

Tina continued to tell me that all of this would blow over and I should mind my own business. My primary concern by then was avoiding an appearance before the Grand Jury. I didn't know what to expect when the time came for the phone conference with the Assistant District Attorney, DeGatano, and my lawyer. I had found a lawyer through a good friend who had been Lt. Governor. The deal was, I would answer their questions on the phone, and I wouldn't be subpoenaed. I could avoid going before the Grand Jury.

The A.D.A wanted to know about Carrie. "In what capacity did I know her and for how long?"

I was puzzled. Why was Carrie an issue? I told them I knew her in the capacity of our housekeeper. She had been our housekeeper for a very long time, twenty years or so.

"Where did she live? Did she stay with us?"

"No! She didn't live with us." She had an apartment near Tina's school. Why were they asking where Carrie lived? This was making less and less sense to me.

"Have you ever worked at your mother's school?" This was the second time they asked.

"No!" And then I remembered that work-term I spent there when I was in college. I told them about that.

DeGatano said, "No, more recently."

"No!"

They thanked me and I hung up relieved but quite mystified.

Terry was interrogated at the police station. They wanted to know what he did at the school. What was his relationship to Tina? They had some information on Terry that I had never known about, and they used it for leverage. Apparently, Terry had spent a short time in prison! Why and/or how did he end up in prison? Something to do with taking the fall for a union official down home, who did some creative bookkeeping, according to Tina.

Terry was "advised" by the police in New York, to live somewhere else, to put some distance between himself and Tina. He moved out. Tina was shocked and felt betrayed. She would tell me that she kicked Terry out for betraying her. All I could hear was Terry's voice trying to tell Tina no one was going to jail for her. That included Terry. Eventually, Terry went back home, leaving Tina alone. I told her a few years before that if she didn't stop treating people like pond scum and pushing them away, she was going to end up alone. Now she was alone.

Before Terry left, he called to let me know Tina had announced she was getting married.

"To whom?" I exclaimed.

"She said it was an old boyfriend from her college days," Terry said.

"Are you serious?"

"She hadn't told you yet?"

"Oh, why tell me?!" Tina and I talked shortly after this conversation. I let her go on and then said, "You're getting married, I hear." Silence.

Tina giggled for a minute. "It was a joke, that's all."

"A joke?"

"I wanted to see what people would say."

Chapter Forty-Nine

Reality

I would never know the complete reality of Tina's "situation" but enough was revealed that was both affirming and jaw dropping. As the charges against Tina piled up, I asked Pam, the angel, if she thought Tina ever recognized her role in all this. Pam laughed and said, "I was waiting for that question. When she became very ill, she used to sit and talk and ask me things. In her mind, she had not done anything. And she felt that she had favor in the courtroom because they would never let her sit out in the courtroom. She would come in. She'd sit at the defense table and the nice judge would say, 'Mrs. Pryor, would you like some tea? Come into my chambers.' They knew she wasn't well. They felt the pressure of the trial would be too much for her."

Rarely did Tina understand what was going on, Pam stated. Tina relied heavily on Pam to tell her what some of the charges and the rulings meant. Tina received conditional discharge and would probably have to pay some restitution. I never found how much nor where the money came from, but I had some thoughts.

"You see," Pam said, "the whole thing with conditional discharge is that word 'discharge'. You tend to think discharge means it's going away after you do restitution and whatever. But with conditional discharge, you have a criminal record that stays with you for life. In Tina's mind, it meant it all went away. She never saw her actions as anything criminal. She never saw herself as misappropriating funds."

This belief allowed Tina to write a letter to Mayor Giuliani and ask, "Why, your Honor, does an acting agency, feel obligated to stick their fingers into funds raised by the original agency. Why?"

I had a hard time believing she was that insane. What was she thinking? Bits and pieces were revealed, not all of them but enough to leave me motionless with the realization that my first impression of Tina at the age of five or six was right. All those people inside her were false personas that she would trot out to serve her needs, to fool people, and to kid herself when needed.

The reality about Carrie? Tina was paying Carrie from school funds. Carrie was a Teacher's Aide as far as the city was concerned, not Leontine Pryor's housekeeper, or as the Daily News reported, her "maid." That's why the District Attorney's office had the Riverdale house under surveillance. They knew when Carrie arrived and departed. They knew where she cashed her checks and how often. Tina's defense? She had paid for Mama's nurses from her own funds, and she produced the cancelled checks to prove it. What the D.A. wanted to know was how Carrie was being paid. Tina kept producing the cancelled checks for the nurses.

The reality about Tina's health? She was not cured. Weight kept falling from her body like autumn leaves from trees. Her skin was pale, almost gray. When I looked into her eyes, I saw an embittered soul who was flirting with evil. I had no idea then that she had embraced evil, but I would find out. And that's the precise word. Evil.

I asked her how she reconciled all the charges and accusations with being Christian? She told me with great confidence the following.

"The Bible says they cut your left hand off, you cut their right hand off! That's what the Bible says. You don't know about that do you?"

"No, I don't." Although thoughts about the Inquisition, and the Salem Witch Trials ran through my head. A partnership with evil demands intelligence, a kind of sinister "wokeness." You don't accidentally "hook up" with Satan.

All this information and commentary came from my decision to interview her. That, plus what I was hearing from Terry about the next-door neighbor, "Peggy", a young woman Tina hired as a teacher at the school. Hiring Peggy was a stupid move. Peggy was very, very smart.

Chapter Fifty

What Peggy Told Me

"This is a woman who was very intelligent. In the conversations I had, Tina knew so much about children, about early childhood education, things that teachers needed in the classroom, she knew. The lighting, the equipment, the measurements, the chairs! The kids were never harmed. It's interesting, the cleanest day-care center I've ever seen. The best of food, but they were hurt in other ways. Not having professionals work with the kids who really needed it… That's what was taken away from these kids. She gave these kids everything on the outside. Everything on the outside looks fantastic. But there's no interaction, none whatsoever!"

Terry said, "She never went into the classroom and sat down with the kids and say, 'Oh read this to me.' Or 'What do you think about this?' Never! Because, like you said, she could tell you right off the bat, square footage…"

Peggy added, "We would walk into the room and the kids would run to us and hold us for dear life. I mean, we'd sit down and roll on the floor with them, play games with them. Tina walks into the room. Did you ever see one kid run to her? Kids have an instant reaction when they feel safe and warm and they want to run and hug and touch somebody or play… [Janis], there's so much I want to tell you."

I thought about the scandal, the hard facts, and the charges. There were so many aspects. One example, the Parent's Association Account. The last balance Terry saw was roughly $42,000. What would parents do with that kind of money, and where did it come from?

Peggy and Terry tried to explain Tina's mathematics. "Raffle tickets. Whoever sold the most tickets… these tickets were sold in a book of ten. Every ticket or coupon was worth fifty cents and every book was worth ten dollars. If every kid sold five books, you're talking about fifty dollars, and if your average class had forty students… Multiply that!"

Two grand per classroom, multiplied by four or five classrooms, gives you eight to ten thousand dollars per year. After several years, forty thousand dollars didn't seem to be so far-fetched.

Terry said that there was a school bus contract dispute.

I asked, "What bus?"

"The bus that used to be parked out front," he said.

I did remember a very large, maroon van that Terry drove Tina back and forth to work. "So," I asked, "what's the story with the bus?"

Both Terry and Peggy groaned and said almost simultaneously, "Oh girl! The money!"

Terry tried to unravel the bus story. "The Board of Education pays the school x,y,z dollars for each kid. We had an agreement with this bus company, whereas Tina went out and got this bus company. She will pay them what she wants to pay them. A new contract was issued, and the bus company found out what the Board of Education had done. The Board of Ed decided to deal with the bus companies *directly*. So, they put in a bid, but Tina told them to put in a bid and say, 'We want this company.' Well, her and the owner of the bus company got into it, so the bus company decided to keep all the money, whereas…"

My head was spinning. "Was she hoping to get a kickback?" I asked.

"Probably," Peggy said. "Under New York state law, any school that services kids or children with special needs who have to be picked up and driven to school, cannot own the bus company that transports the children. However, the way Tina had set it up was that she owned the school bus. Tina gave her bus company a different name. And she had a bus from a legitimate company, and they had their own driver. But this company was only getting the amount she told them they would get or that she gave them."

"And she was pocketing the difference?"

"And she was pocketing the difference." Peggy said. "The employees were so afraid because they would see Leontine Pryor Day Care School. They thought Tina owned the school. Tina never owned the school. It was the Agency for Child Development. They just named it after her, but people thought that this was her school."

"Therefore, she can do anything she wants," I said.

Anything she wanted included refusing to hire qualified teachers. I couldn't understand why she wouldn't hire the very best candidates she could find. There was the Banks School, her alma mater where she did graduate work (Columbia University), so much to draw from and rely upon. Yet Tina's school was filled with unlicensed and unqualified teachers.

"The reason she didn't want to hire professionals is because she would have to pay them a salary. When any agency or organization came to do the auditing, you can always explain to them that you're on the verge of hiring. But because you couldn't find anyone just yet, you have these people in there. When I was taken out of the classroom, my license was still being used as a teacher in the classroom. After I left the school, my license was still being used. Where was I? I wasn't there!"

"So, she had people impersonating people?"

"Sure, that happened."

Terry added, "Or, you wasn't there because…"

Peggy finished his sentence with, "You were sick that day!"

With some wonder in her voice, Peggy said, "Boy, could she control! Most of the people she hired… She had many things over them. One thing was intelligence. A sharp woman. She would turn it on, and a lot of these people were not the brightest, so when they worked there, they felt they had nowhere else to go, and they took whatever they could even if it meant being bawled out every day. They were yelled at, screamed at, belittled… She would mistreat people so horribly, so miserably. Terry can tell you! One of the loveliest women I met while there… She came from a household where the husband was an alcoholic. He would beat her, and both 'the Assistant' and Tina knew that, and they would use that against her. They would laugh at her, belittle her. Sometimes her husband would come to pick her up and in front of everyone they would say, 'There goes your drunken husband. He's out there picking you up.' They would start rumors that this woman was having an affair with another staff member, which was untrue. They made her work like a dog, like a slave. This woman could not even use a sick day. They wouldn't allow her to go to the doctor! 'After five you go to the doctor.' The woman told them that her doctor wouldn't see her after five and they said, 'That's your problem!' That's how they treated this woman who felt she couldn't go anywhere."

All I could think about at that moment was Tina telling me, "People respect you if you have power." Was this Tina's idea of power?

I asked Peggy, "What about things like staff meetings?" I asked.

"Staff meetings never happened! Well, maybe once a year. Any school board has a UFT member, a union person. So, if you want to find out how many sick days, benefits and so forth… Well, you know who our school rep was? The custodian! He worked the night shift, so no one ever got to see him! And people just accepted that. And the board members who were listed? Dead people! Fictious people that didn't exist! There was the board President, a retired police officer or detective!"

"It was interesting since he was the President. If any employee ever… didn't do what they're expected to do, they were called into Tina's office and then they're facing this big guy who also knows a lot of police… So, whom could they go to complain? Tina? The union rep who worked at night? Who were they going to?"

"So, Tina tried to intimidate them?"

"Right," Peggy said. "These people were afraid. The Board President was Black. Most of the employees were Black. A lot of people are afraid of the police. Statistics say that the chances are if there's a white person or a Black person, maybe they'll arrest the Black person before a white person."

Over the years, as Tina's school grew, more services were provided. It was on the cutting edge of delivering the most innovative teaching and instruction for pre-school special ed children. At one time the city provided a psychologist, a dance therapist, and a speech therapist. The few times I heard Tina refer to these innovative services it was always in a derogatory fashion. The more I heard, the more exasperated I became. Why do all this when it's just as easy to do the right thing? Given Tina's intelligence, her credentials, the precedent she set and her drive, she could excel at it. I had a growing feeling that she was striking out at somebody or something that only she knew about. I kept thinking this was her way to conquer white people, but there had to be more to it. As her rage grew, the more desperate and preposterous her actions became. There was something dangerous going on, something dark. I could feel it. In a short amount of time, I would find out. I would understand why a cold mist of fear was beginning to seize me.

Chapter Fifty-One

Reality 2.0

It was months before Tina let go of the fantasy that this investigation would blow over. By 1996 she decided she was being persecuted. She used her illness, her pride, her accomplishments, and the loyalty she had secured over the years from parents and teachers as her primary defenses, but never race, not yet. When Reverend Al Sharpton began to make inquiries, and word got back to her that Reverend Calvin Butts of the Abyssinia Baptist Church in Harlem were concerned, Tina refused their help. She told me, "I don't want this to be a racial thing with people marching up and down the sidewalks." What she did do was try to bribe the judge presiding over her trial with a box of candy. She was infuriated when the candy didn't produce the desired results: have all the charges dropped and return "her school".

She had her lawyer believing, according to Terry, that she had been done in, abused by the system, and wrongly accused by two vindictive staff members at her school. This image fit nicely with the other fairy tale she had begun to promote after Harry's death. She started to describe herself as a "poor wida' woman, left to fend for herself in a cruel world." Tina, the poor widow woman, usually appeared when she didn't want to pay full price for an item or thought she was being overcharged for something!

An elaborate web of lies and delusions began to form. So much so that I finally called her lawyer. I introduced myself and told him that I knew he couldn't discuss Tina's case with me. "All I want you to do is listen. If you don't, you're going to walk into court and get blindsided. You can confirm what I'm telling you with our cousin, Terry." I told him what I had heard and what I knew about Tina. When I finished, he was silent for a moment and then said, "I've defended members of the mob who've been more cooperative than your mother."

As the months spilled into years, I heard things about court appearances and restitution from everybody but Tina. She and Carrie were arraigned in court one evening. The Judge told Tina she would have to come up with $10,000 right then or along with Carrie, spend the night in Rikers. She made a call and "magically" the money appeared. Carrie was on the verge of a nervous breakdown. The most humiliating event came when Tina's name was taken off the school building.

On March 13, 1996, a three-and-a half-page press release was issued from the Bronx Office of the District Attorney, Robert T. Johnson. The release read in part, *"Bronx District Attorney Robert T. Johnson today announced that the 75-year-old founder and Executive Director of a city and state funded day care center and three other people, including a former New York City police detective [board president] have been charged with embezzling more than a quarter of a million dollars over a ten-year period."*

"The grand jury has indicted 75-year-old Leontine Pryor on 2 counts of Grand Larceny in the 2nd degree, 1 count each of Grand larceny in the 3rd and 4th degrees, 34 counts of Falsifying business records in the 1st degree, 53 counts of Offering a false instrument for filing in the 1st degree and 67 counts of Criminal possession of a forged instrument in the 3rd degree.

It is alleged that Pryor arranged to have co-defendant Carrie M., placed on the day care center's payroll as a teacher's aide, although "M" actually served as Pryor's personal housekeeper. "M" has been charged with 1 count of Grand larceny in the 2nd degree.

Pryor's Administrative Director ...54 year old "X" has been indicted on 2 counts of Grand larceny in the 2nd degree, 1 count of Grand larceny in the 3rd and 4th degrees, 38 counts of Falsifying business records in the 1st degree, 21 counts of Offering a false instrument for filing in the 1st degree, and 51 counts of Criminal Possession of a forged instrument in the 3rd degree.

Pryor and "X" are also charged with falsely claiming that their daughters were employed at the center as teacher's aides and therefore entitled to coverage under the center's insurance policy...

The grand jury has also indicted "Y", 57, President of the Board of Directors of the Parkchester Bronxdale Day Care Association...

The defendants are facing a maximum sentence of 3 to 15 years imprisonment if convicted of the most serious charge of Grand larceny in the 2nd degree."

And it went on. I didn't discover this document and others until a year after Tina died. It was the first clear accounting I found that laid out all the charges. It's still hard for me to believe that Tina didn't understand what was happening.

I also found a child's drawing illustrating their distress and puzzlement over Tina's removal and a handwritten draft of a press release responding to charges. (I didn't recognize the handwriting and assumed a parent must have written it. But much of the phraseology is pure Tina.) The following are excerpts from this release.

Agency for Child Development/Human Resource Administration has assigned a Board of Directors that does not reflect our children and community. The population in the neighborhood is Hispanic and

African American. What we are requesting is not racial. It is basically practical.

...staff members are being dismissed and replaced by "others." Those remaining are being placed under unusual probationary periods and report to work ill. Because they are afraid of being fired. What an outrage, don't you think so?

The school is so beautiful. It looks or looked like a child castle. With sturdy colorful furniture. Quality food and the menus designed to meet the cultural background of the children and the Welcome Mat.

There is an aroma of racial discrimination permeating this area... What else could it be? First shifting and removing the original name, a la J. Edgar Hoover Justice Dept. Building still exists. However, there had to be a good reason why the name was there in the first place...

I found among her papers, a copy of a handwritten letter to the Bronx District Attorney, Robert Johnson. It was dated, March 1999. The following are excerpts from the two-page letter.

"Honorable Robert Johnson.

We continue to see your ongoing strength and professionalism and we are most proud of you.

I am Leontine Pryor, the director accused of taking an aide home to be my maid or caring for my mother. Very strange. My attorney refused to let me testify, did not know why until it was pointed out that the other attorney was formerly under training from Commissioner Scorpetta – that we would be back to work in a couple of weeks.

Boards are composed of community people, teachers, housewives, church people __illegible__ parents. Look at the boards:
- *a) Shield of David, lasted a half-day (not of the community)*
- *b) Leake and Watts, lasted two months.*
- *c) Birch Society (who has a CEO) presently functioning, cutting staff, removing furniture...disgusting when one of*

their directors stated she was afraid of Negroes – she was removed immediately.

The real issue is not told, because they do not know. I wrote the Vatican and personally spoke to the Pope's Secretariat. I was given permission to share with you and the judge – who was indeed a jewel and the Assistant D.A. A child __illegible__ was suffering from an overdose of drugs coupled with administration of a half tablet of Ridlin. Your honor, this is not all. Cancer of the Brain and misuse of bathroom evacuation. I bought the child and mother to my home – I did not see anything wrong with that. I toilet trained him, gradually cut the half to a quarter Ridlin. His head was becoming larger and larger until surgery had to be administered. So, the weekly visits to my home had to be canceled. I could not save the mother.

I don't have a family – all have died – only a little daughter.

Your honor, thanks for reading this. We understand you have an addition to your family, enjoy and God bless."

I found several passages in documents Tina had written describing the court. One read, "A bit about the court, it was a professional setting. I was given a chair with arms on the side and a glass of water, and the first day, a menu. I had the honor of going to the Judge's conference room several months later. A gentleman if there ever was and so was the lovely assistant D.A."

Chapter Fifty-Two

The End Was Coming

As this crisis swelled to a scandal fit for the tabloids, Tina called and told me she had written the Pope about her "situation." I remained silent. She wanted to know how to formally address the Pope. She also started going to confession. Was she Catholic? Had she converted? Not that I knew of. Tina also wrote Hillary Clinton. On one of her trips down home, she sat next to the rhythm and blues, pop singer, the late Isaac Hayes. She convinced him to sit on the board of her new school that she was forming. Her next step was ordering me to research the possibility of getting grants from the federal government to establish a new school. I refused.

"Look up that dot com... That's where it is," she kept telling me. I kept ignoring her.

During all this, her illness intensified. She called once to say that someone had stolen "her money." How much? Twenty thousand dollars. I tried to figure out the who, what, when, where, and why. Twenty thousand dollars was still a lot of money.

The money was in a file at her school in the form of a proposal. Someone had called and read passages to her. She recognized her own writing and knew they would submit the proposal and get twenty thousand dollars that belonged to her. She was inconsolable. She asked over and over why anyone would do that to her. She emphatically stated it was her money! There was a pause, and then she blurted out, befuddled and accusatory, "I got my writing from you!" Confusion and delusion were the new substitutes for facts and reality.

The sicker Tina became, the more uneasy I became. It had nothing to do with anticipating impending grief. I felt, with increasing urgency, that I needed to put some psychic space between us. Something was unfolding that I couldn't verbalize. *What I wanted to do was run. I couldn't shake the feeling I was in danger.* I was about to learn that *evil is real*. It's alive and active. As cousin Mary Frances, Mama's niece, told me, "Satan's busy."

One late Cambridge Saturday afternoon in early spring, I was sitting in my favorite rocking chair in the living room, slowly rocking back and forth while reading when I got the distinct impression Mama and Papa were standing behind me. I became still. My spaniels were sound asleep, and I heard Papa's voice. "Tell Tina to take stock. It's time to take stock." I don't know how long this went on. When their presence left, I leaned back and closed my eyes. Tina? Taking stock? I doubted that would happen, but I reported this message to Tina the next time she came to Cambridge.

With her little girl voice, she said, "Really?" Her eyes darted about the living room. Her shoulders hunched up as she continued to look.

She finally sat down, and I asked her what she had fun doing when she was growing up.

"I had fun doing the things you're not supposed to do." She stopped for a moment and then told me a story from her college days. "You had to sign out on Saturday if you were going downtown. I'd tell them I was going to shop, when in fact I went to a bar. We would sit there talkin', smokin', cuttin' up! The Dean would check these places though and we would have to pack into the bathroom. I began to like it more when I lived off campus."

"I liked to have a good time, go out!" Her voice was triumphant. "Each student had a chore when at Spelman. I had the responsibility of sweeping in front of the house," she said referring to her dormitory. "I was not accustomed to sweeping, so I wrote Mama and told her I had to sweep. Mama wrote a letter back telling them she didn't send her daughter to school to sweep." Tina howled with laughter.

"I didn't like Spelman. I didn't want to unpack my trunk, but I had no choice."

Tina resented being told what to do so she plotted revenge against the dorm supervisor. The bathroom was right above the dorm supervisor's suite. Tina turned the bathtub water on and walked away. The water ran into the dorm supervisor's suite.

As for church? Tina said, "It was a social gathering place. You had nothing else but the church. Your friends were there. We ran the junior part of the church. We were given a quarter to put in church. We'd keep the money and buy candy! We knew the old people... a old lady would go back and tell Papa what I did. Daddy read that lady! *He told her, 'Leave my daughter alone!' Mr. Lawrence cussed her out! Not gon' do that to me!*"

I asked her, "What about God, Tina? Where did God come in?"

"I learned about God in Sunday School. There was always a bible open in the household. Now, I just seem to depend on it so much. I believe there is a God and if more than one person prays or asks, it will come to pass. He will act in time. He will answer all your prayers. Ask for forgiveness. I've gotten everything I've asked for."

"What are you requesting now?" I asked.

"Life, and spare me from cancer. I was a pretty sick wench when it was over. Always God is there. I don't get out of bed without praying."

"Do you have any questions for God?"

"I have requests," she said. Her eyes were never still. "I don't want anyone to hurt you after I'm gone, and don't let the family take over!"

I had no idea who she was referring to. I was and am the last of my grandfather's line.

Her eyes narrowed and she looked at me. *"My will is your bible! Give nothin' to nobody!* Just keep me here as long as you can and don't let me suffer." She lit a cigarette and inhaled. I ignored that. "I just want you to take care of my jewelry. My two-thousand-dollar necklace. My five-thousand-dollar ring in the box..."

Tina kept subjecting herself to more chemotherapy. It had gotten to the point where her oncologist started talking to her about "quality of life" issues and whether the treatment, at this point, was really helping. Tina continued with the chemotherapy. It was a nightmare, more hair loss, more weight loss. She became weaker and weaker, but she kept going.

We were living in a dual reality comprised of Tina's illness and the investigation. The longer the investigation went on the less I knew. Had it not been for Terry and later, Peggy, I would have known nothing. I asked Terry if Tina understood how I could be impacted by this scandal.

Terry said, "Yeah, I told her."

"Well, what did she say?"

"She said they don't get New York papers up here."

I told Tina this is Cambridge, Massachusetts. We get papers from around the damned world up here. I can't be a bigger story than my boss. I let go of any thought of returning to mainstream politics. I want to say Tina didn't understand any of that. The truth was, *she didn't want to understand.* It was too bothersome.

Tina flew to Cambridge in July of 1997, but not without "kvetching" about the expense of coming. Once she arrived at my place, she stalled for as long as possible, trying to play with my spaniels, arguing with me about her smoking and objecting because I still wouldn't let her smoke in the house. She would stand and look out the living room windows into my backyard. It was punctuated with hostas of monstrous proportions. One was located at the base of a huge oak tree that covered the entire roof of the condo. It was easy to think you were in the woods of Vermont or New Hampshire, not four to five blocks from Harvard Square!

"Yard's so pretty," Tina mumbled.

We had been doing these interviews for a few months. I told her I was writing a book about her. Her first concern was I might not write "nice things" about her. I told her I was writing the truth as I knew it. She didn't know what to say. But it was a book *about her* and that's all that mattered. This was the woman who signed autographs at a PBS reception when an edited version of my three one-hour documentaries on Jesse Jackson were being shown on the PBS network, nationwide. Someone thought it was cute.

This was our third or fourth talk where I asked questions and she answered, or at least tried to. Eventually she resigned herself to the unpleasant task of talking. As she sat down, she bent over in pain. She closed her eyes tightly. You thought she was going to throw up at any minute. Her face screamed agony, as she whispered, "I'll be aw' right. I got some pills in my bag." I searched inside her bag and found a bottle of prescription pills. I gave her a glass of water and waited for her to take them.

She looked up at me and said, "The pain is so bad. I get so cold." It was July.

I revisited the question of why she chose to live with Mama and Papa after she married. Straightening up in the chair, she said, "My parents wanted to be *near me, near Tina!*" Now she only talked about the good things. She never mentioned Harry being drunk and violent. She didn't mention the fights and she didn't mention how she swore at Mama, calling her a bitch, while Harry referred to Mama after drinking as Tina's "damned Mammy!" Every time I heard him say that something in me shattered. Remembering this still makes me sick to my stomach and disgusted with Tina.

She leaped to my elementary school years. "You were in school... *You were so defiant.* So many questions! I remember you told Jack Benson to shut up. I had so many encounters with your elementary school principal."

"About me? Because of my defiance?" I didn't remember any of that. What I remembered were the consistent comments from my teachers about how quiet I was in class, withdrawn, but I always asked good questions.

"Oh! *Your principal underestimated my position in life.* So, I volunteered for everything. You graduated from elementary school and were chosen to give the salutary address. You wrote it. You always seemed to be in that environment you know, with white people. You were in the elementary school play... You were the bunny rabbit. The principal wanted to know if *I knew how to make the suit*! I told him what my credentials were. 'We don't get paid as much as you do, yet. But my credentials are just as good as yours.' He said, 'Oh yeah. That's right, you're the director of that little nursery school.' *I had three encounters with him where I had to let him know who I was!"*

(Tina never volunteered for anything. It would've interfered with her work. *I was ordered to never volunteer for anything.* We "volunteered" enough through slavery. Sitting in my brain, was the other me, muttering what I wouldn't say out loud. *"What the hell is she talking about? A salutary address?* The dictionary says "salutary is an adjective. Promoting or intended to promote an improvement or beneficial effect: a salutary warning. Promoting or intended to promote health."

I asked Tina if she thought this exchange had to do with race? She ignored the question and fast forwarded to the present babbling curses under her breath. I concluded that this scandal that erupted in the nineties, was not an isolated incident generated by a momentary lapse on Tina's part, or some disastrous personal or professional crisis generated by racism, but the logical outcome of behavior that began in her childhood. Race, in Tina's case, exacerbated an existing flaw. This scandal or something like it was inevitable.

Tina continued talking. She focused on the investigations that led to her losing the school. She was all over the place.

Bewildered, she said, "We can't really understand why you wanted *your name* on this building," referring to "her school". She looked at me and said, "We know you're going to give us a hard time." Was she referring to someone in law enforcement or someone else? "I'd take them all the way through the school. I would never say white. Perhaps people of another race get away with things, *but I have to do more.* Another investigator was sent to evaluate the program. The state Social Service Department...

It was out of the ordinary to do that without prior warning unless your school has received some complaints…"

My mind was doing back-flips as I listened. At times, I felt like I was struggling to pick up dropped stitches on a knitting project.

"I had the parents' support. They wanted to take out a small business loan to build additional stories to the school," she said.

"Who were your friends, Tina, during all this?"

"I had six white friends… and that's too many to have! Two were personal friends."

"How do you define a personal friend?" I asked.

"If I needed a dollar, I could ask them." She began to list names, seemingly oblivious to my questions and presence. "Connie Barron's daughter sent a letter to the state education department to say I padded the attendance sheet. Jane, Tom, Mrs. Black's daughter… I was betrayed. And then Terry."

"What did Terry do?"

"I was told he stole money, backup cash, contributions from parents and vendors." Tina paused and asked, "Why do people do this?"

Chapter Fifty-Three

Not Yet

Tina grew sicker but I was beginning to think she would never die. I had friends whose parents were passing away. Some contracted cancer and died in a relatively short time. My beloved American cocker spaniel, Prince, died at 16 years old. I was heartbroken and enraged. I had never felt a loss like that. Murphy, his parti-spaniel brother, and I grieved and grieved. I couldn't understand why Prince had to die and Tina was still alive, tormenting everyone.

The rational part of my mind struggled for equal time. I knew *one day* Tina would die. And then what? Things like wills, trust funds, deeds to property popped back in my head. What was Tina doing about all this, especially the property? I knew there were certain tax advantages regarding properties depending on how you left your assets. Did Tina keep the lawyer we went to see several years before? Who knew? Who would she tell? Certainly not me. I eventually asked her. She told me she had it figured out. I was frightened. She dropped the lawyer we had seen. I convinced her to see someone who specialized in estate law. I scared her by reminding her of the IRS, inheritance taxes, *assets owned on date of death,* and anything else that was still in my mind from that first job working in Trust and Estates at what was First National Bank of Boston.

Losing money motivated her to hire the attorney who helped Harry years before he died with some other matter. Drawing up Tina's new will had to be an experience because she refused to tell the lawyer much about her assets. The first version had her Assistant receiving a hundred thousand dollars. The Assistant

Mother's Madness

was identified as her trusted friend and companion. How did I know? Tina threw a copy of that will in the back seat of the car. Terry found it and showed it to me.

Of course, when the going got rough the trusted friend, companion, and assistant, was nowhere to be found. She rarely came to see Tina when the cancer confined her first to the house and then to a hospital bed. The assistant said she was following her lawyer's advice to put some distance between her and Tina. The distance resulted in the assistant relocating South, to one of the Carolinas. Tina eventually changed her will and made the assistant and J.W. the co-executors, a stroke of utter madness. J.W. protested. It was all in vain. Tina ignored his wishes.

As long as Tina could string a sentence together, I was going to try to ferret out as much information from her as humanly possible. She was dangerously upset with the Assistant District Attorney assigned to her case. Tina said, "That ADA didn't know how I'd taken it. She would've given up! Watch her because she's going to do something." There was a far-off look in Tina's eyes. She paused and muttered, "Was it racially motivated? Yes," and Tina looked at me, then turned and stared back into space stating, "Federal and state by-laws..." She became silent. *Everything became unnaturally still.* After several seconds she spoke.

"I'll be most proud of this discrimination suit," she said.

This was the first time I'd heard about a discrimination suit. I didn't know if I was too tired or simply frightened, but I changed the subject. "What about your other roles in life, Tina?" Maybe she would say something about being a daughter, a wife, a mother! What follows is her reaction. She took a deep breath before starting.

"I didn't do a lot with parents. Dr. Abrams is the school psychologist. She weighs over 250 pounds. Interacting with parents is too hard because parents are resentful. They're on dope. I'd be afraid they might hurt you, but they wouldn't slap a white lady! I'd rather not deal with parents one on one. I can threaten teachers. I had all minority teachers with the exception of a few. The white ones pass the exams. *Us* can't pass 'em. I tell 'em, if you don't get it now, you never will. *White folks rarely helped Black folks unless you were so good, so good, you had something they wanted, and I had something they wanted! You can impress people with your power.*"

She never looked at me while saying this. I had the impression she was still speaking to someone else. I cleared my throat and that brought her back to the here and now.

"Tina, what do you want people to say about you when you're gone?"

"That she fought to the bitter end and still hadn't completed all the work she wanted done."

"You know some people think that relationships are what life is about," I said. "It's the impact you have on others. I was talking to a friend about how we wanted to be remembered... and I said I wanted to be remembered as a good friend who tried to care for those she loved."

"Really!?" Tina's eyes widened. They started to look everywhere but at me. Her eyebrows raised.

"What are your goals now?" I asked.

"My goals? Get on that boat and go to the Panama Canal, and go to Switzerland!"

It was hard for me to concentrate on what Tina was saying and not saying. This was the first time I'd heard her say anything about the Panama Canal. But she had mentioned Switzerland many years ago. It intrigued her.

Tina kept declaring that she was well. Herbal remedies were embraced. She kept referring to something called, "Noni". Noni was going to cure her. She proceeded to list all things she was doing. "I'm doing the exercises," she proclaimed, and then moved both her arms up and down, twice, to demonstrate her exercises. She couldn't understand why she wasn't getting better. Exasperated, frustrated, she blurted out, "I'm eating the leafy, green vegetables...!" She pronounced it as if it were spelled, veg/geh/tab/bulls. The rest of her diet consisted of peanut butter, oatmeal, and toast. *What kept her living was her fear of dying.* Her thinking grew dull from all the painkillers she was taking. Tina popped Percocet's like candy! Her judgment made her dangerous to herself and others, and there was not one thing that could be done about it. She was still "competent" and there's no law against being bitter.

I leaned forward and quietly asked her, "What happened at work? What went wrong?" I wasn't sure she heard me, but she eventually responded.

"All those people... I just wish I had an invisible car so I could crush 'em!" She extended her hands and made tight, squeezing, motions with her hands. "Just squish 'em like little pieces of tomatoes!" Her mouth twisted.

At that moment, the tone in her voice made me think of a story somebody told me about one of her trips to Gulfport. The passengers were standing to exit the plane. Tina had flown first class. She heard a male voice make a racial slur towards her. She was the only Black person seated in first class. Turning to glare at him, she said, "If I had a gun, I'd blow you away!" The flight attendants heard that and called airport security. No one went anywhere until security and the local police escorted Tina off the plane. I'm assuming she talked her way out of it. What was she thinking, a Black woman, threatening to kill a white man in the deepest, darkest, part of the South? Where was her judgment? That could've turned out very differently for her, regardless of her high yellow skin.

What would it have taken for Tina to be happy in America? What does happiness look like for a well-educated, well to do Black woman who looked "damn near white" in this country? It would take courage and introspective thinking to know oneself. You'd have to be sober also. For Tina, specifically? She would have to be crowned Queen (perhaps of the universe) and be *rich beyond any known standard*. Tina was interested in *money and power*, not in accruing wealth and influence. Everyone would have to obey her. White people would have to vanish, or she would have to actually be white with limitless power. Love, friendship, compassion, kindness, and selflessness would not play big roles.

A Caveat

Signs and Omens

The investigations and all that went with it vanished. That's what Tina wanted me to think. By late 1997, early '98, she stopped answering my questions. Cancer was claiming her body. Visiting nurses were recommended, but Tina insisted that she was "well," that nothing was wrong. Given her denial there was very little I could do in a straightforward manner. I had to find ways to do things without Tina knowing. Were bills being paid? How much was her treatment costing? Where was the money coming from? Had she "borrowed" from one of the mysterious accounts left for me? I had a fantasy that as she became sicker, she would want to make things right. I was wrong. She became more difficult, more embittered, and on one occasion, more incoherent. Regardless, I circled back to advocating for visiting nurses to supervise her care.

"Tina, you need nursing care," I said. And then it began.

"And who is Janis Pryor? Don't say that to me! I have to be somebody. Don't talk to me that way. And then he didn't come back, and I can see his head and feet. He's so tall," she said.

My stomach turned to ice, but I let her continue.

"My program has been on TV. Make sure you have plenty of water for the baby in the car," she said referring to Murphy, my spaniel.

Looking off into space she continued. "I found out something. You'll find out late in life… This weakness will invariably leave now. This lady who's in…oh God…charge, the visiting nurse service. She said, 'I'm sending the nurse out tomorrow morning and she will observe for four or five hours, the nurse's aide. You know, the whole twenty yards! Okay, I'll accept that. I'll accept that."

"Did you agree, Tina, to let them come?" I asked hoping for a breakthrough.

"The visiting nurse will come and supervise, wash all your legs... She's a very dark Afro-American. Mrs. X came by. She said, 'You've got some heavy medical bills.' The bitch! I lay there and thought, let it be, let it be."

"So, the lady will wash me and then she'll clean out the refrigerator. Clean out anything that's not edible. You understand. This medication is extremely expensive. It comes in threes. This is called medication for an appetite," Tina said pointing to a bottle of medicine beside her. "I don't know... lots of calls from... I don't know. They are so anxious..."

She seemed to be in some kind of stupor, but she continued. "This new chemo is in five divisions. I take it five days a week. They are so anxious that I finish this... because of the potency! Living to me is very important!"

"That doctor," Tina began, referring to her oncologist, "she's just so overbearing... but in a nice way. She said, 'We don't have any children.' I told her I didn't know that! Hold it! Hold it! It's not as big! Like something you would see on TV! Up and down, up and down! I'll be forgetful. So, I'll have a pad and paper. I'm going to get this money."

I listened, growing more troubled with each sentence she uttered. I let her talk because I didn't know what else to do!

"I have to give you some money. It has to be drawn. The Federal government... okay, okay! Instead of letting the Federal government steal it... Who was the President before Clinton? I'll come up there and look around," she said referring to Cambridge.

"I can't stand these little charges! All these little charges come draining on you. This is my responsibility. You should be comfortable and move on. I have a large sum of money from the Director's Association. What I'm going to do now is stretch out on this little red couch and then around eleven o'clock I'm going to call him from the back and we're going to make some hot cocoa and soft eggs. They had a robot coming by the door and she's there."

"So, I'll convene my boyfriend! The lawyer! There's that detailed sheet of directions and I think I'll put maybe some more... All you have to do is call upstate to the mausoleum. *It's very exquisite!* Watch them niggers. Thank them all very much and that's it! Get rid of 'em!"

"I sat on the side of that hospital bed and turned over and to the left side of the door, and there was a soldier standing at the door. Standing erect. Let me close my eyes. To the right, a lady was standing. Her hair was snow white and she looked directly at me. Wait! I'm talking to you just then and I thought I visualized someone coming over to you, to get some candy. I attributed it to two things..."

Barely breathing and trying to follow her, I asked Tina, "What did these people look like?"

"Female. I'll fix her ass, so she won't get back on the phone! She ain't gon' call me! I received a catalogue. I get this letter. No prayer is necessary. Now, shut up! It's so interesting to read. You should see it," she said in a matter-of-fact tone.

"The people will come here, you know. Be very positive with them. They won't let anyone take advantage of your mother. He wants to know if Terry is coming and I went through the roof," she exclaimed while lighting a cigarette. "I'm sick on the stomach." Taking a drag, she continued with, "The same ritual with him! Just tell them! I tell them how my daughter is very grateful to you to take care of her mother. Now, don't say anything about him. A little shady too – but – he cleans some things with a brush! Ain't that stupid?!"

I wanted to collapse. She went on this way for several more minutes. Again, I didn't know what to say or do. Would it even matter?

Tina knew the end was coming and that's why she announced she was changing doctors. She wanted another opinion, hoping someone would tell her she was going to live.

"I told her not to bring any students in here when she's examining me, and don't whisper," Tina said referring to her oncologist.

Tina said her doctor was insulting. I asked for an example. On a recent visit, Tina asked the doctor a question. The doctor turned to an intern and said, "See, I told you she was smart." This was not a compliment. Tina did get a second opinion. It wasn't good news, so she returned to her oncologist.

Several days later, Tina insisted that her doctors were telling her she was fine.

I asked, "Why do you think the doctors aren't telling you the complete truth, Tina?"

Wide eyed, she said, "*They are lying to me.* I don't know. The psychiatrist said I didn't need any help. I was well."

Mother's Madness

"...live or die but don't poison everything..."
Herzog
by
Saul Bellow

Chapter Fifty-Four

Stepping Toward Death

It was early Sunday morning in late fall. I was finishing breakfast, while scanning the Sunday Times when the phone rang. It was Tina's best friend, Ruth. They had been colleagues and friends for as long as I could remember. It was too early for her to call long distance to chat. Something had to be wrong.

"Janis don't tell your mother I called. You know how she is."

I put down my cup of Earl Grey tea. "What's wrong?"

"I think she needs to go to the hospital," Ruth said.

"Why? *What's wrong?*"

"She's in a lot of pain. I've been trying to get her to go to the hospital, but she won't listen to me. You should call her."

"Has she called the doctor?"

"No, she won't call Gaynor or her oncologist, what's her name? Runowicz? You've got to call. You're the only one who can get her to do anything!"

"Okay," I said. "I'll call." I didn't want to.

"Well, don't call her right now. She'll know I called you."

"Okay. Ruth, I'll do that. I'll be in touch." I could feel her relax.

I dreaded the call. Again I had no idea which one of Tina's personas would surface. The latest one was the Martyred Daughter on death's doorstep. Maybe the Little Girl would show herself or Tina the Professional. I remembered one childhood weekend when I called the police. As usual, Harry was threatening to kill her. The police arrived, and I heard Tina tell them, *"I'm a professional woman. I work for the city."* In other words, don't disrespect her because she's Black. She's smarter than you are. Meanwhile, Harry had to be "subdued" and taken to jail. I locked myself in my bedroom.

I waited an hour or two and then called Tina. She sounded worse than usual. I couldn't figure out what was wrong, but I told her that if she didn't call the doctor, I would.

Later that day, she went to the hospital where they kept her in the emergency room for over twelve hours. It would be weeks before I found out the real story of her hospital admission, how she made two trips to the emergency room in twelve hours. The first time, she got up and left saying she had to go home and pack. The hospital sent an ambulance to pick her up the second time. The admitting doctor asked (by now) a familiar question when I spoke to any of her emergency room doctors. Cautiously, he inquired, "Does your mother drink?"

I told him her history of alcoholism, but as far as I knew, given her illness, she had stopped drinking. Stupid me! When Tina was readmitted, she was clinging onto a plastic bottle with a straw, the kind you see runners and bicyclists using. Tina was sipping constantly. The nurses had to pry it from her hand. The plastic bottle contained vodka. Tina was so incoherent the doctor couldn't take her medical history. That's why he asked.

She was near death, again. Her gall bladder had abscessed to the point of near rupturing. They suspected a tumor was behind the gall bladder, but surgery was ruled out. The surgeon on call felt she would not survive it. Her oncologist felt differently. A bleeding ulcer was also discovered with a host of other maladies compounded over time by her inability or unwillingness to eat properly. She was put on a morphine drip, two additional sedatives and antibiotics. Tina insisted on being given Percocet.

Her oncologist said at this point, it didn't matter. Murphy and I drove down to New York.

When I arrived at the hospital there were three women seated in the hall, not too far from Tina's room. They said they were her friends. I smiled and thanked them for being there. As I walked to the Nurse's Station, one of the nurses' aides passed me, and said, "You must be Mrs. Pryor's daughter?" Her face became somber. "I don't think your mother's going to make it..."

What was I supposed to say?! I stopped at the Nurses' Station, introduced myself. One nurse located the doctor on call. The gist of the conversation with the doctor was Tina's dying. She had subjected herself to intolerable amounts of chemotherapy and they wanted to know who her Medical Proxy was. Had a DNR or a do not resuscitate order been signed? You could tell they wanted Tina to be free of her misery. All those stories about doctors not wanting to let go of patients, not being able to accept death, etc., not these doctors. I knew nothing about Tina's wishes for end-of-life care. She believed she was going to live forever! The doctor and nurses suggested I talk with her and let them know her wishes. I wanted nothing to do with this but that wasn't possible.

They gave me some papers for her to sign and pointed me in the direction of her room. I walked in and found Ruth. She almost burst into tears of relief. I asked her if she could give me a moment with Tina. She nodded her head, made a small noise, and left. This time, Tina had a private room. She looked a couple of pounds short of being a ghost. Lying in bed she reminded me of a mummified skeleton I had seen in the British Museum. She was conscious...sort of.

"Hi", she said. Propped up on pillows, her eyes were pale yellow. Her ashen skin continued to sink making her look more bird like. Every feature was more pointed, more sunken. She was hooked up to an IV drip. There were some machines making regular beeps. I assumed that was good.

"Tina, you know you're very sick, yes?"

"I am?"

"Yes, you are. You have to make a decision. The doctors need some information from you."

"What is it? Personnel…" Her eyes widened. Her mouth opened slightly.

"They need to know if you want extraordinary measures taken to save your life in the event of a…medical emergency, or if your heart should stop beating." My resentment ballooned every minute I was there. All I wanted to do was walk out and leave her, but I didn't, because that's not how Mama and Papa raised me. Good home training comes in many guises.

"My heart?"

"Yes," I replied.

"What would they do?" she asked. Her face was a clash of expressions: suspicious, skeptical, bitter, and what Black people call "evil".

"I'm not sure, but one option is to use a machine to help you breathe or resuscitate you with electric paddles. You've seen that on TV."

"I don't want anybody jumping in my heart. No." Her eyes widened.

"So, you want them to let you go? You don't want to be resuscitated? They call that a DNR, do not resuscitate."

"Oh no. I want to live! I don't want to die. But if they jump in my heart, they'll kill me!"

"No, no…that's not how it works." So, I explained it twice and realized that whomever her Medical Proxy was, he or she would have to make the decision. They needed to be notified. I had no idea who Tina cursed with this monstrous task. Maybe it was the assistant.

I was holding papers for her signature knowing she would have no understanding of what she was signing. I sighed and walked back to the Nurse's Station to let them know I needed to contact her lawyer. They looked relieved. Somebody was doing something!

Next was the waiting room where Ruth and these other women were. They all looked up as I entered. I told them Tina's condition was grave and her chances of surviving were slim. They gasped. Ruth looked stricken. One of the women said, "She's *that* sick?! I didn't think she was that sick!"

"*Then you're a fool,*" is what I wanted to say. Instead, I told her, "She's on a morphine drip. Her gallbladder almost ruptured. That's very serious."

"They should do something," the other woman said!

"Look, ladies…" I had to stop myself so I wouldn't snap at them. "You need to understand, Tina could die, soon. This is no joke."

"Oh no", one of them said!

Murphy and I drove back to Cambridge later that evening. I left a message on the lawyer's answering machine. The next morning my call was promptly returned. The lawyer told me I was named as her health proxy. The last thing I wanted was the responsibility for making that decision.

The proxy was faxed over to the hospital. But Tina rallied! The minute that proxy was sent, I knew she'd rise from the ashes of cancer, alcoholism, kidney failure, pneumonia, ulcers, and a long list of maladies only doctors can pronounce! In less than a week, she returned to Riverdale like a genetically flawed Phoenix, cursed to suffer.

She stayed alive for weeks on cocktails of painkillers including time-released pain patches. The attending physician described her to me as, "tough, but without any resources now. Her body can't take much more." The doctor told me she'd be back to the hospital. It was a matter of when, not if.

Cynically, I thought, *"Promises, promises. This woman was going to live forever and kill all of us in the process! So, what if her body had more chemicals than a toxic waste site! What if the drugs, including alcohol, had damaged her mind that was already suspect from the time I was five or six years old? This woman was going back to Riverdale, to a house that had acquired the air of a sealed tomb."*

A Word About Tina's Imaginary Family

Carl, the driver, Pam, the angel, and Fred, the coat hanger

On more than one occasion, the social worker assigned to Tina, (and there was a different one each time she went in the hospital) called me when Tina dodged death yet again and was sent back to Riverdale.

The social worker tracked me down regardless of where I happened to be. This one sounded upbeat, middle-aged, her voice drenched with a New York accent. After she uttered a few sympathetic sentences, she assured me that she and Tina had worked on a homecare plan. The social worker's voice was bouncing along when she began to tell me Tina had hired, "Biff", who was like a brother to me! According to Tina, Biff and I had grown up together. I told the social worker I had never laid eyes on Biff! Never seen or heard of him in my life! Silence hit like a mushroom cloud after the A Bomb dropped.

I eventually met Biff. He was in the music room, sprawled in a chair. I introduced myself. He knew who I was. Biff was the pot-bellied, beer guzzling alcoholic with no medical training who managed to take some jewelry and cash with him when he departed from Riverdale! Another former employee at Tina's school. Doing what, I didn't want to know.

The next time Tina dodged death, they sent her back to Riverdale where a man who resembled a coat hanger was waiting for her. Murphy and I drove down while "Mr. Coat Hanger" was on duty. Along with Biff, Mr. Coat Hanger was also a former employee at Tina's school. Tina had to let him go due to his affection for heroin and cocaine! But Tina spoke fondly of Mr. Coat Hanger. She hoodwinked the doctors and the social worker again. Ironically, it was because of him I found the first piece of evidence that evil had become Tina's active companion... and partner.

Mr. Coat Hanger had a name, "Sam". When we met, Murphy barked at him. That was enough for me. I looked at Sam and saw every mother's nightmare, every father's shame, every single woman's fear on a street late at night, every drug counselor's failure, every dealer's joy, and every cop's frustration. Tall, light brown skin, thin to the point of scrawny, bald, and bewildered with several very large teeth, there was something sad about Sam. He was what certain Southern women of my grandmother's generation would call "mannerable." He had a genteel politeness. At some point in his life, he had received some good home training. As I introduced myself to Sam, he was scratching his arms, but stopped long enough to extend his soft-skinned, bony hand, drop his head slightly and simply respond with, "Miss Janis." His voice weaved down the highway of his throat like a car barely pushing twenty or thirty miles per hour in the wee hours of the morning, the radio playing some woeful, sweet, song.

What was his value to Tina, because he had no medical training, unless shooting up with heroin counts? *He did whatever she wanted.* This particular evening, she wanted to cook chicken necks. He went to the store to buy some along with collard greens. It was then that I discovered what he received in exchange for his "care", unlimited beer. He came back from the store with nothing but beer! Eying the beer, I asked if he found what Tina wanted. His black trench coat loosely hung from his hanger like shoulders, while a large fedora hid half of his face.

Only his slightly opened mouth was visible. He sauntered into the kitchen, sat down, and pushed back his fedora hat.

He looked at me and said, "They didn't have no chicken necks, no greens."

I said, "Sam, this is *Riverdale*, not Harlem! You're not going to find any chicken necks and greens here."

With complete sincerity, he asked me, "Don't they know about Black cuisine up here?! I mean, people got to eat!"

This is when the angel and the driver appeared to fill out this odd constellation. Pam, the angel, was truly God-sent. She was straightforward, sane, and centered, also clean, sober, and honest. Why Tina warmed up to her, especially during these last weeks of her life was beyond me. Without Pam, I would've snapped weeks before Tina died.

The afternoon of Tina's last return home, the angel called from work to see how things were going. Sam answered the phone.

Pam asked, "How's Mrs. Pryor?"

"Fine. Fine."

"Well, I'm going to come up there after work. I'm going to bring some ice cream with me. The doctor said Mrs. Pryor could have some."

"I like vanilla ice cream. I like *all kinds* of ice cream."

"What do you mean, *you* like all kinds of ice cream? This is for Mrs. Pryor! Sam, are you listening to me?"

With a puzzled tone, he responded with, *"Who is this? Do you know where I am?"*

"Sam! You're at Mrs. Pryor's house."

"I'm at Mrs. Pryor's house?! You know, I knew these surroundings didn't look familiar."

Sam was now Tina's primary caretaker. For the short while he was there, he saw to it that Tina took her medicine. He got up in the middle of the night to attend her *if* he heard her cry out, helped her to the bathroom, helped her change clothes and even attempted to bathe her. I was horrified but not horrified enough to step in and take his place.

The angel told me that one of the few white people Tina considered to be in her corner then was former Senator Trent Lott of Mississippi, a very white man. Why? Aunt Ophelia was one of his supporters. Tina didn't go to Washington to see him. She had gone to Pascagoula, which is the Senator's hometown, and where Aunt Ophelia lived also. (Terry's youngest brother, Gerald, said, "Trent ain't so bad. Put him back in there," referring to an upcoming election.)

Given that home is Mississippi, Tina probably thought of herself as the Senator's constituent for as long as it served her. She used that grain of truth and stretched it to her convenience. I found a draft of a letter to the Senator, dated September 23, 1999. It said:

"*My Honorable Senator*

I come from Mississippi to Washington to New York to get the attention of my New York City Mayor. I know when you hear this story you will be more than happy to assist me because you have stood by us from the Lawrence, Cook family on Davis Avenue at Moss Point, Miss to the Veteran administrator and your office was more than helpful to my 93 year-old Aunt Ophelia who rose to both teacher and principal and was funeralized last year."

I asked Pam if she knew what happened? She said that Lott gave Tina some support by writing a letter saying she was a fine citizen. Pam said, "She was great at writing grants, proposals… I'm sorry I didn't learn from her before she passed over, because she had a great mind for that. She said she would pick up the phone at any time and call Senator Lott and get whatever she needed to help her. I don't know if that was the lucid truth…" Tina lied, so who knew the truth regarding Senator Lott's assistance?

Carl, the driver, who eventually married Pam, the angel, who kept an eye on Sam, the coat hanger, were Tina's caretakers during her last weeks on earth.

Chapter Fifty-Five

"Please allow me to introduce myself. I'm a man of wealth and taste..." *

I was sitting in what Tina called, the family room, part of an addition she had built shortly after Mama died that included a long hall, another bedroom, and a powder room. Nothing met building code(s). Tina bragged to me that she paid for the addition in cash. It was over a hundred thousand dollars. I asked her, "Whose cash, Tina?" She never answered me.

I got up to get something to drink. Murphy followed.

As I approach the dining room, I hear Tina mumbling. I turn around. Dragging the I.V. stand over the carpet in fits and starts, and holding a cigarette with the other hand, she stumbles towards the kitchen, her eyes darting about again, panic stricken. What hair she still had was pulled severely back from her face. Her feet? Swollen. They looked like slightly yellowed little pound cakes or tiny doll feet, stuffed in tinier satin slippers. The nylon knee highs were rolled down around her ankles. Her quilted robe came close to swallowing her. Your rational mind tells you she barely has the strength to walk, but you can sense the absolute determination that lifts those little legs up and down and propels her along. She's barely in control.

Sam is at the kitchen sink. I lean against the dining room wall to watch.

"Sam!" His name exploded from Tina's mouth.

"Yes ma'am..." Sam jumps slightly.

"I want the freezer cleaned out. I know there're some chicken necks in there. Clean it out! We gon' find them chicken necks!"

She takes a drag on her cigarette and forcefully blows the smoke through her nostrils.

I think to myself, *"This ought to be rich."*

Sam, somewhat wobbly, opens the freezer. It's packed. He carefully examines it, shelf by shelf, starting at the top. He takes out one item at a time for Tina to see. She orders him to put it back. Nothing is thrown out, including a half-eaten piece of frozen toast carefully wrapped in plastic. At the very bottom, he finds a small, black, velvet or felt square package tied with thread.

"What's this?" He holds the package so Tina can see it.

She yells, "Put that back! Who the hell told you to take that out?"

Stunned and confused, Sam starts to blither apologies. He puts the little black package back and shuts the freezer door.

I sigh and think to myself, *"God, she's started to hide money in the freezer. Maybe it's jewelry."* I discovered on a previous visit that she hid all her credit cards in a coffee can in the kitchen pantry. There were forty credit cards in a range of colors, silver, gold, black, and every store on Fifth Avenue. So why not hide money or jewels in the freezer?" I ask her, "What's in there?"

She turns around and snaps, "That ain't none of yo' business!" She takes another drag on her cigarette. The search for chicken necks and greens was officially over.

After everyone was asleep, I took the mysterious black package. I half expected her to be standing there to catch me, but she wasn't. I ran back to my room and threw it in my suitcase. It wasn't more than five inches by five inches. I was so preoccupied with hiding it, I didn't pay attention to what it felt like.

When I got back to Cambridge, I put it on the raised hearth of the living room fireplace. Something said, "You better open that." Reluctantly, I picked it up and then noticed it felt lumpy, too soft to be jewelry. I tried to rip the thread in two with my hands, and nothing. It was impossible. I looked at the package and said, *"What the hell is this?!"* Annoyed, I found some scissors and cut the thread. I opened it carefully, looked at the contents and muttered, *"Oh my God..."* My breathing became shallow. I didn't know what to do at first. As I focused on the contents it felt like something had wrapped itself around me and Murphy who was also on the couch. Slowly, I picked up the contents to examine what were five, small, hand sewn, Voodoo dolls, three or four inches in length. Each one had sewn faces with different colored hand-made outfits. They weren't purchased in any tourist shop. At the left end of the row, was a red doll, red face, red hands, and arms. I looked at it and knew that doll represented me. Each doll was tightly bound with thread, as if to restrict their movements.

I was transfixed by the detail. I started to shake with rage and fell back on the couch. I called a friend.

"You gotta come over here," I said.

"What's wrong?"

I can feel his puzzled look. "You need to come over here. There's something I want you to see."

"Where are you?" he asked.

"Cambridge. I'm back. You've got to come over here."

In less than twenty minutes, he arrived. He walked over to the coffee table, and I showed him the dolls. I don't remember what he said at that moment, but I do remember how he looked. His face became slack. His eyes widened, and then he frowned. The frown transformed from a worried look to one of fear. I confirmed his fears and then he said something I never anticipated. "You know, this kind of thing is usually handed down from generation to generation." I couldn't tell if he was being thoughtful, terrified, or both.

"My grandmother didn't do all this! Nobody handed anything down to me!" I thought he was crazy and then I remembered.

"Maybe they were afraid. Maybe your mother was afraid…of you. You told me she said you were born with a veil over your face. And what does that mean really? The significance of that… You came into the world with special powers." Powers he dismissed. If he only knew.

I remembered seeing Uncle George. I remembered all the accommodations I make daily to live with these "abilities" while faking normalcy. I thought about what it takes for me to get through an average day.

He left saying, "You be careful." All these people who say they don't believe in "these kinds of things" until they're confronted with something concrete yet unexplainable. They want to run! Murphy and I were left with the dolls. Voodoo. Tina was a practitioner. What else was she doing?

"What the hell am I supposed to do with this? How do I get rid of them?" They would stay on the fireplace hearth for almost a year collecting very little dust.

I called Carrie to let her know what I had found and if she had any idea Tina was involved with this.

"Oh yes," Carrie said. "She would go into the bedroom, close the door, and tell me not to bother her. I knew she was doing something. We would drive over to this store where they'd fix a package for her… I'd go in and pick it up."

I called Cousin Mary Frances (Mae). She knew. Apparently, Tina had paid Mae a visit in Indianapolis. Mae told me Tina left five tiny coffins with her. She told Mae that these caskets could help her control Fred, her husband. I asked Mae what she did with them, and she told me, "I threw 'em in the garbage. I didn't want that mess in my house." Mae explained that afterwards she anointed her house in the name of Jesus. It seemed like everybody knew about Tina's sideline activities, but me. It made me wonder, what else was Tina doing and for how long? But everybody made it clear. *Get rid of those dolls.*

*Sympathy for The Devil - Mick Jagger and Keith Richards

A Word About Tina's Bedroom

Cleaning out Tina's bedroom was like managing an archeological dig for an ancient site. It made my stomach turn and my head hurt. The room, like the rest of the house, was airless. Tina saved and hid everything! Terry had flown up and I told him we had to start cleaning things out.

The king-sized bed dominated the room. The furniture, the lamps, the ashtrays, all gold trimmed! The bedspread was chocolate brown. Her half bath was black and pink, and the bedroom carpet was a mix of orange and gold tweed. She had faux, antique lampshades atop bases of steel silver and black.

Terry looked around the room and said, "Where do you want to start?"

"Underneath the bed," I suggest.

"Underneath the bed!"

"I'll bet you she's got a ton of stuff under there."

We start at opposite ends of the bed. I kneel, lift the spread and pull out a large cardboard box. Clothes. I pull out another cardboard box. 15 handbags. I look through them wondering which ones I might keep, if any. The smell of loose cigarette tobacco permeated the interior of every bag and killed any interest I had in them. I find a marker and label the boxes.

"Dragon's blood," Terry says, bewildered.

I look up and ask, "What are you talking about?!"

Terry has a rectangular, plastic container, the kind you use to transport lasagna. He holds up a small, ornate glass bottle with dark red liquid and a label identifying it as Dragon's Blood. Standing next to Terry, I look at the glass bottle and then investigate the plastic container. There are over twenty tiny

Mother's Madness

bottles along with small containers of powder. "*What the hell is this?*" I mutter. Terry's standing. I had the feeling he was afraid to move.

"What is this stuff?" Terry asks.

"Yeah, Dragon's Blood... You know, I'm not really sure what this is used for, but I think it's for spells."

"Spells!" Terry's eyes grow wider. "What kinda spells?"

I was afraid of the answer. But I knew we would find out. We were in the bedroom of revelations. A rush of questions and thoughts were prompted by this discovery. I wondered how long she's been doing *this*, and what *is* this? How many people know? Terry and I are in the dark! He lived with her for years and never knew. If he has no clue, those dolls she kept in the freezer were the tip of the iceberg. I wasn't ready to examine the other vials.

We pull out paper bags Tina had pushed way back in one of her closets. The closet we looked in had one door that opened in her bedroom and another that opened in the hall. The closet is a tunnel! It's packed with clothing, boxes, and more paper bags filled with files, envelopes, and loose papers. I find several old books that I hesitate to open fearing the pages will crumble. I remember what my friend said, "These things are usually passed down from one generation to another."

We drag out bags and sit on the floor going through the contents. There's a small paperback with a pink cover and black letters titled, *Legends of Incense, Herb and Old Magic*, by Louis Claremont. *A Spell Book of Rituals for Good and Evil*, there's no author on the orange-colored paper cover, but Tina has a yellow post-it-note on the cover with names written and a partial grocery list itemizing margarine and lettuce. She had noted a date, 4/24, and page 25. A piece of scotch tape is attached to three separate pages in the book. I find a list of nine names, one that I recognize, a teacher at her school. Three names have the number four after them. Written around the edge is the name of the Assistant District Attorney, who led the prosecution against Tina.

I find illustrations of candles, a black skull, a *seven-knob* candle for wishing along with "image or figure candles" showing a man and a woman. There's a page explaining the significance of certain colors. Page twelve is devoted to the "Devil or Satan." Tina had underlined many passages on this page: "…for exorcism rites, write the name of the person you believe to be possessed and place it beneath a devil candle… A spell for winning a loved one is done with a Satan candle…"

The passage marked with a star and partially highlighted in yellow says, "A black magic use of the devil candle is done by writing the name of the one you wish to harm on the candle… The most extensive use of Devil or Satan candles is to clear one's home of dark forces…" The 28th Psalm is quoted, "Blessed be the Lord, because he hath heard the voice of my supplicants…"

There are instructions on how to use skull candles of different colors. "Black skulls are for more serious matters. They should be used with care and only when someone has intentionally caused you real suffering and pain." We found several black skull candles.

The instructions continued, "Those who use curses lightly and without cause are apt to have them come home with great force. The foe's name is written on parchment with Dragon's Blood ink." Terry and I now knew how she used Dragon's Blood. The bottle was half full.

There is a witch candle used for a, "potent love spell. Write your own name and that of the one you are for on parchment."

Beside this passage Tina had written several names, all were teachers at her school. A candle is lit, and a chant is said.

The spell book is comprehensive. There are 125 candle rituals, a section on Novenas, and the nine-day ritual used in the Catholic Church to obtain special graces. There is mention of the Jewish tradition that holds the number seven as sacred. A six-page list of prayers to the saints is followed by several pages of instructions on how to use psalms and candles in prayer for specific purposes. Tina marked with a red pen, the following prayers: "*...bend others to your will, compel others to come to one's assistance, confound those who have done harm, prevail over rejection and disappointments, receive kindness and mercy from all persons, restore lost hope, victory in a lawsuit or court case*" and with a big check mark, "*when you want revenge.*"

Two copies of *Voodoo and Hoodoo*, by Jim Haskins were also found. One copy is very worn. Tina's notations are in the margins. There's a handwritten list of the twelve disciples, with the notation of St. Matthew, chapter 20:2-4. On page 208 there are instructions to break up a couple. Underneath Tina wrote, "Giuliani + Vandor." There was a loose page with a checkmark next to instructions titled, "To Regain Money Stolen."

There are listings for books on African spirituality, magic with oils, magic with candles, witchcraft, Satanism, ancient magic, and the tarot. We find more black skull candles, candles of seven knobs in red, green, and white, diagrams on small pieces of paper neatly folded and placed in her wallets. Diagrams specifically for receiving money, obtaining money in a court case, receiving money from others.

Tina had several bibles. The twenty-third, ninety, and ninety-first psalms were marked. Chapter Eighteen, verses eighteen and nineteen were heavily marked by Tina. Verse eighteen: *Verily I say unto you, Whatsoever ye shall bind on earth shall be bound in heaven: and whatsoever ye shall loose on earth shall be loosed in heaven.*

Voodoo is a legitimate religion with deep roots originating in Africa, and later spreading to Haiti and New Orleans where Tina cruised around during her twenties. A contemporary priestess, Miriam Chamani, said "Voodoo is about finding ways to survive conflict and trouble." * That's what Tina was trying to do.

The November 30th, 2003 edition of the New York Times* devoted a half page on the resurgences of Voodoo and its Queen Leveau. Modern historians describe Leveau as a free woman of African, American Indian, and European blood. These are our bloodlines, also.

Terry and I were speechless. I suggested that we "take a break"! I'd need that because when we returned, I would find numerous documents where Tina forged my name regarding the sale of property that Mama and Papa had left in our joint names. There were trust fund accounts that Tina closed. Large amounts of money seemed to drift down some invisible hole. I tried to figure out how much of my money had vanished. It was dizzy making trying to follow this money trail. She kept receipts, statements, withdrawal slips, and it became easy to trace *some* of the money. But there were gaps, sixty thousand in one account gone, forty thousand in another that appeared to be siphoned off for who knows what. At this point, I was too tired to care, too tired to be mad. What's done is done. I ordered pizza for Terry and me. Terry would fly back to Gulfport, Mississippi, and along with Murphy, I'd drive back to Cambridge, Massachusetts.

Chapter Fifty-Six

Countdown

The next few weeks were spent in tight expectation. I was tense and tired. I stumbled through Thanksgiving, saying the right things, acting the right way, smiling appropriately. One friend asked, "How's your mother?"

All I could say was, "Still alive."

I didn't have to say anymore. As Christmas sneaked in, Tina was not getting any better. I called often to check in, but it felt like an absurd exercise. I continued to be amazed by her staying power. She wasn't really eating. She wasn't taking in enough fluids. In mid-December, she went back in the hospital. Would this be the final trip?

Tina took three thousand dollars in cash with her, just in case… She stuffed the money in a sock and pinned it to her bra. She also had five hundred dollars in her handbag. It was "spending change for odds and ends" according to Tina. One of her "ladies in waiting" probably relieved her of the three-grand. I spoke with the Chief of Hospital Security and filed formal charges. He was quite friendly, but then so was Detective DeGatano! Having talked with Tina, he referred to her as a "good ol' gal from Mississippi." I thought if Tina was telling people she was from Mississippi now, she's really sick. The money was never recovered.

One of the ladies in waiting called me regarding the Mercedes. She wanted to know, "Who will have it? Perhaps I should take care of it while Tina's in the hospital."

"*Perhaps you should go fly a kite!*" I didn't say that, but I wanted to. The car remained in the garage.

Tina was admitted to the hospital critically dehydrated. According to the doctor, she was malnourished and during her last office visit, almost catatonic. After that exam, the doctor ordered she be readmitted. Tina weighed eighty-one pounds.

I called Terry and told him if he wanted to see Tina before she died, he needed to get up here fast. We decided he would fly into Boston, and we would drive down to New York. It was a lot easier to get to Logan Airport in Boston from Cambridge than driving to LaGuardia or JFK from Riverdale. I needed Terry to keep me awake while driving and help keep me sane. We decided he would go first to see her while I stayed at Riverdale opening windows!

"Terry, you need to be prepared for what Tina looks like," I said.

"What… how she look?"

"Not like what you remember. She's lost a lot of weight. Most of her hair is gone. *You need to brace yourself.* If you want to call me, call. I just want you to be prepared."

After we unloaded the car and I walked Murphy, Terry took a cab to the hospital. The house was sealed tightly as usual. The air stagnant and the presence of plastic was overwhelming. Plastic seat covers, plastic place mats, plastic slipcovers, plastic runners, and several plastic plants. There were plastic lampshade covers and plastic covered windows to seal out the cold air.

I looked at Terry when he returned and said, "I tried to warn you."

"I know. I know. But I didn't think she would really look that bad. I walked in and had to walk right back out. You know, I had to compose myself." We stood in the dining room paralyzed for a few seconds.

Mother's Madness

"We should start cleaning out the house, Terry. We've got to start somewhere, but not tonight." The bedroom was just the beginning.

I woke up the next morning knowing I couldn't avoid going to the hospital. I took a cab. It was gray, damp, and cold outside. Unfamiliar streets flew by. I thought about how much I disliked most of the city. This was a section of New York that rarely made it into the movies much less my world. My privilege was showing itself. Like fog clearing, I remembered it was Christmas Eve.

I paid the driver and walked into the hospital. Hospitals today remind me of bus stations, crowded with a veneer of grime, the feeling that things aren't quite as they should be, an atmosphere that often breeds fatal mistakes. Albert Einstein, a teaching hospital, was a far cry from my childhood memories of Columbia Presbyterian where Papa had surgery, where I was born, and where I worked on the children's psychiatric ward for a Bennington non-resident work term, reporting to Dr. Charles Cassatt. Columbia Presbyterian, a stone's throw from the Audubon Ballroom where Malcolm X was assassinated, had a pristine, starched white, silent quality that inspired confidence and respect for the medical profession. Doctors were courteous, nurses efficient, and lives were saved. Hospitals were a refuge from illness. That was then. Now I associate hospitals with hostility, bureaucratic nightmares, indifference, haste, and making horrific mistakes, like removing the wrong limb or automatically assuming all patients are idiots.

Tina's room was on the tenth floor, directly across from the Nurses' Station. There was a lot of gray and blue with the walls painted a forgettable color.

Tina is now nothing more than flesh on the bone. It isn't her baldness that's transformed her, nor the loss of familiar features, not even the gauntness that's completely altered her face. It was her skin, smooth, not a wrinkle anywhere.

She's in the twilight stage between life and death. There's a darkness around her that you cannot see but feel. She's unable to talk, too weak to even sip juice through a straw, but not too weak to fight dying.

Two aides who each worked twelve-hour shifts were assigned to watch Tina. I walked into her room and one of the aides and I exchange weak smiles. I took off my coat and sat down. Then it hits me. There was a presence in the room generating a fear I had never known. Whatever it was, it was sharing Tina's bed. My breathing became shallow.

Her head turns and droops slightly. She stares right at me, but she makes no sign that she sees me. I wave my hand in front of her face. There's no reaction. I feel the aide stare at me. I look up and the aide has an incredulous look on her face. She gives me a peculiar, yet knowing smile and says, "Spooky, isn't it? She sleeps with her eyes open." I tried to gently close her eyelids. Only one would shut.

"How long has she been doing this?" I ask.

"Ever since she got here."

I lean back in the chair. I know something unusual is taking place, something more than a simple death. All my senses sharpen. I expect something or someone to appear out of thin air. Whatever it was, the room was saturated with it. If I were on the Presidential Detail of the Secret Service, I would be reaching for my gun.

When Tina wakes up, her eyes change. They become clearer but change from her normal color of pale hazel to jet black. She's lost her eyelashes, and her eyebrows are faint as mist. No more make-up. No more wigs, only an unopened tube of pink lipstick, resting on her bed stand that she tries to apply. Two days before when I spoke to her on the phone, she said, "I don't have much time." Today, she can barely get sounds out. When she does, they're incomprehensible.

    I spend three hours with her on Christmas Day, resenting every moment of it but fascinated by her decline. That same uneasy feeling takes over as I walk into her room. I speak to the aide seated by the door. Tina is propped up on pillows. Her skin looks better, and she's alert enough to know she's in pain and not getting her way. She wanted to go back to Riverdale. Every now and then a word or phrase crawls from her mouth. Sometimes she tries to pound her right hand up and down on the bed, but she doesn't have enough strength to do it more than once or twice. She's still not eating nor drinking, and now she's having trouble swallowing the painkillers. She tries to chew them or hold them in her mouth. I suggest to the aide that Tina might be better able to swallow the pills with some applesauce. The aide gets some and gives her a spoonful of applesauce with the pill. Tina swallows it.
    Moments later, she thrashes back and forth, turns her head from side to side and tries to pound her right fist on the hospital bed. Her voice, weak, angry, and bitter spits out orders. "C'mon, c'mon. Let's go home. I want to go home! C'mon!" Abruptly, she becomes silent, but tries to continue pounding her right fist. Then, that too stops.
    Watching this, I remembered the lines from Rilke's letter to a young poet, "Blood-Remembering", and what one must do "for the sake of a writing a single verse. ...one must...have been

beside the dying, must have sat beside the dead in the room with the open window and the fitful noises." Tina's breathing becomes increasingly labored. There are gurgling sounds that make me wonder if this is what's known as the death rattle or are these simply the fitful noises preceding that. Her head drops from one side to the other as she goes in and out of consciousness, her eyes never shutting but changing from that funny hazel color to jet black. I didn't know what to make of that.

Suddenly, she looks at me and says, "Pen." She motions to her black leather calendar. I give it to her. She flips through the pages searching, but she doesn't have the strength to continue. The look of frustration and desperation on her face is heartbreaking. Every few minutes she makes another attempt, but she can't do it. She gives up and turns her head away.

I had developed a habit of knitting my way through stressful times. Thankfully, I had something to work on. When Tina becomes motionless with sleep, I start to knit. Once, I look up from my knitting to find those black eyes glaring at me. It's chilling. For a second, I feel danger. I also feel silly. What could she do?

Tina has an astonishing cough. The phlegm is alternately clear and black. It turns my stomach, and I am thankful for the knitting. It keeps my mind focused and pushes out ridiculous thoughts, like the devil is in the vicinity. Tina is wide awake. There is only one other patient in the room. She walks to the bathroom, and I know Tina is summoning up her strength. Eyeing her roommate, Tina blurts out, "Where are you going?" The force of her voice startles us. Her voice seems to manifest from some other world.

There's silence for a few seconds. Tina looks at me and states, "I need money!" She makes a feeble fist out of her left hand and tries to smooth out her spread and blanket. In the clearest voice yet she says, "Let's go home with Mama and Papa." The feeling of being endangered comes back. I'm tired, worn down, annoyed and pissed off!

"Why am I doing this?" I ask myself. The view from Tina's room doesn't do much to engender the holiday spirit. There's a wide vista of apartment buildings, bridges, streets, and billboards, all in various shades of gray, black, and dull brick red. You'd never know it's Christmas, 1999. There are a few trees scattered along the sidewalks. I'm mystified by their ability to survive urban chaos. I think about the magnificent, ancient trees I saw in some of the forests and state parks of Ireland and how comforted I felt by them. It was as if I had met old friends. The lush green of Ireland and the haunting sense of peacefulness with this undercurrent of perpetual mourning had an aching pull on my heart right now. I hate New York!

I want to go back to the Cambridge I know, a place that doesn't reject people, where there's a sense of order, where I understand the people, the history, the energy of an academic urban village. Right now, there's a precarious sense of madness that makes me feel I'm on the edge of ruin or obliteration. Tina had become a cesspool of bitterness and rage. It was poisonous. I couldn't go back to Cambridge or Ireland at that moment, but I could leave the hospital and did.

Chapter Fifty-Seven

Tick Tock

Every visit I made to see Tina required a day's recovery. That's why Terry and I rotated. All I wanted to do was go to bed and pull the covers over my head. Pam, the angel, provided us with some semblance of Christmas dinner.

But the smartest thing I did the day after Christmas was visit the Gaynors. No one ever walked in the front door if you knew them. You walked up the driveway, turned right, up the steps to the deck, and knocked on the first of two back doors, the one that opened into the dining room. I saw the yard that Evelyn was so proud of and the mini-pond and waterfall that was installed all those years ago. It was Evelyn who introduced me to crocuses. I knocked on the door, didn't wait for an answer, and walked in. The dining room was the same. My paintings were still on the wall. It looked like nothing had changed, but everything had changed. The children were adults and Doctor Gaynor had remarried. But this household still kept me sane. Everybody was there except for Jenny. Although Mama and Papa loved me, the Gaynor household offered me contemporary comfort, affection, and safety. I always underestimated how much I needed those "things," comfort, affection, and safety. But not this time.

Maybe all the therapy had made a difference. After all, I was still alive. The therapists and mental health professionals I had over the decades had characterized Tina as a sociopath, someone with a severe personality disorder. For some Black folks the idea, never mind the reality, of "dissing" your mother was intolerable, no matter what she did. They couldn't understand why I had such a "low opinion" of my mother. Why did I insist on describing her as mad?

- She did not protect me; she continually put me in harm's way.
- She stole from me, forged my signature, destroyed documents, and controlled what she couldn't steal or hide from me.
- She used me; she betrayed my trust and faith.
- She had no regard for who or what I was, only for who and what she wanted me to be.
- She feigned a state of deliberate ignorance as a protective shield, her ultimate excuse was always, "I didn't know."
- She led a life sustained by denial.
- She was deceitful, manipulative, and lied with great ease proving the world of Blackness had become as corrupt as the world of whiteness.
- She had multiple personalities with matching voices and laughs.
- She endangered her parents' lives and those few people who tried to remain loyal to her.
- She drove Carrie, our housekeeper, to the brink of suicide.
- She had an addictive, hostile personality. Her weapon of choice was money. Her drugs were alcohol and tobacco.

Are those reasons enough?

She turned her back on me using a credit card or a cashier's check to stand in for her. Can you imagine what it feels like to be a child or adult and have your "mother" give you a hateful stare and scream, "Get outta my life!"

Do you still doubt Tina's madness? The original question being one more indication of what's wrong with our hearts.

How long will we be held hostage by our phobia of making that introspective journey where the answers reside next to the monsters plotting and scheming? The inability or refusal to recognize or understand the significance and consequences of emotional damage we've incurred terrifies us. That terror allows us to walk through life pretending until we can't.

I agree with Lama Surya Das who says, "*...the purpose of life is to know oneself, because without that internal self-realization, all other goals will be thwarted. When we fully know ourselves, we will know others. We will be able to comprehend reality and recognize our own inner wisdom, our own divine light... This realization will change our lives, our behavior, and our world. Seeing differently is believing differently and leads to different ways of living. Remember ... one definition of insanity is doing what we have always done and expecting different results.*" Tina wanted nothing to do with this. She wasn't alone.

Perhaps many of us who are not white are unable or unwilling to recognize Tina's madness because we as a people have accommodated and born the weight of suffering and oppression for so long, traded in our natural desires for healthy happiness in exchange for being allowed to *survive*, to keep breathing from one minute to the next, for conforming to cultural expectations of obedience, for being allowed to reach for those things that will always be slightly beyond our grasp, high-priced trinkets that bewitch us, leaving us wanting more, while giving us malevolent hearts, empty hands, and poor credit ratings to show for our efforts. This Tina did understand.

Chapter Fifty-Eight

Roughly 24 Hours

On December 28th, we returned to Cambridge. Tina could hang on forever. The hospital was ready to discharge her, and she was insisting on going back to Riverdale. Who would watch her? Who would administer the medication? Sam, the coat hanger? The only way she could return to Riverdale was with professional nursing care. But she didn't want any strangers in the house, much less any white nurses. Although Tina was barely audible, you felt her resistance and stubbornness in every word.

The social worker called, pressuring me to let Tina go home. I asked the social worker, "Have you talked to her?"

"Oh yes," she said. "And I can't really find a reason for her to stay here. We've done all we can. Your mother doesn't want to go to a hospice, so…"

"You really think my mother's competent enough to make that decision?" I asked incredulously.

The social worker was quiet. "Are you implying that she's not competent?"

"I'm not implying anything. I'm *telling* you she's incompetent."

"Well, it would take a day or two to arrange for some doctors…"

I cut her off. "Listen to me. My mother does not leave this hospital. Do you understand? You're telling me I don't have the authority to place her under hospice care?"

"Well…yes. As long as a doctor determines your mother is considered competent…"

"I suggest that you find whomever you need to find to make a judgment as to her competency. Until then, she stays in Albert Einstein Hospital, and if you or anyone else tries to discharge her, there will be hell to pay, all kinds of lawsuits not to mention a ton of really bad publicity. Am I making myself clear? I'd get on it right away if I were you."

Within the next two hours a small group of psychiatrists saw Tina. One asked her how she viewed her illness. She told them that she really wasn't sick and was getting well and would continue to get well if only they would let her go home. They thanked her, left the room, and judged her incompetent. Decisions regarding her care were now left to me. I checked once more with her attorney before arranging for her transferal to the hospice facility across the street from the hospital.

When I arrived at the hospital the social worker had left for the day. It took the supervisor two hours before he showed up. During that time, I sat and watched Tina. She was fitful. She kept talking and asking questions. Turning her head from side to side, she was crying out, weak but determined. I got up and stood at the foot of her bed.

"Oh Lordy, Jesus... Mama! Let me go where Mama is!" Tina repeats that several times, and then she abruptly stops. She looks at me and says, "I need money! Gimme fifty dollars quick, or I'll pee! I don't want to embarrass myself." She turns her head away from me and tries to pound both her fists on the bed. "Janis, take me home." The air becomes heavy, still, like the calm before a storm. Several long seconds go by. Suddenly, she sits straight up in bed, looks directly at me and states, "Janis, I'm dying now. I'm dying."

I look at her and say quietly, "I know, Tina." The torment on her face, her desperation and fear can be cut with a knife. Her features are becoming more extreme, more disturbing. Tina's chin was bobbing up and down. Her eyes? Almost colorless. Her skin, what's left of it, hangs from her bones and her legs are bloated. The suffering was palpable. Watching her, I thought, *"No one should die like this. No one."*

Calvary is a nationally known hospice facility directly opposite from Albert Einstein Hospital. The sky was overcast with heavy blue-gray clouds. It might snow. I throw on my coat, tell the aide I'll be back. Getting to Calvary requires dodging an arrangement of median strips and lanes of traffic with drivers who would just as soon run over you than stop. This was not Harvard Square in Cambridge where pedestrians stare down drivers forcing them to stop. In New York City the drivers will hit you! All I wanted to do was cross the street. Is this how those poor chickens felt when they wanted to "cross the road"? I was getting a little punchy!

I didn't know what to expect when I walked into Calvary. What I found was a gentle, soothing atmosphere with attentive staff. The doctor handling Tina's case put me at ease. He explained that they have a way for patients to see their pets. I took care of the paperwork and returned to Albert Einstein. I was growing more concerned about driving back to Cambridge. It was getting dark, and I hated driving at night. I walked into Tina's room and the social work supervisor was there. Smiling, yet nervous, he was relieved when I told him Tina was being transferred to the hospice. The aide says quietly, "That's good." Now I had to tell Tina.

Chapter Fifty-Nine

Soon

I've never seen anything like the transformation of Tina's face. One moment its twisted, the next moment blank, no expression(s), then her eyes fly around the room looking for something I don't see, but feel, and whatever it is, it's horrifying.

"Are we going home now?"

"No," I say. She looks shattered. "There's nobody to take care of you." How many times had I said this to her? Looking at her, I hear bits and pieces of her past conversations on God playing in my head like an endless loop. "...always God is there. ...I don't get out of bed without praying... I learned about God in Sunday School." Standing at the foot of her bed, I thought, *"You're learning about God right now."*

Straining to be heard, Tina says in a barely audible voice, "I'll get somebody. I'm gon' get well..."

"No. You're going to Calvary later this afternoon. They have the capacity to take care of you, to keep you comfortable."

She makes a rough noise and turns her head from side to side. More noise comes from a deeper spot in her throat. I get the sensation there's nothing and no one in the room but us. Tina begins to flail about. I am pulled back from her bed as her thrashing becomes more intense. Who or what pulled me back? I don't know. The noise coming from her is inhuman. The features on her face sharpen, way beyond angular. I heard myself think, *"Her face is becoming demonic."*

A dense but translucent white shield slowly drops in front of me. I knew I couldn't get through it. There was some force protecting me. I can't move. My breathing is slow, slight. White light, with a strength and force that shocks me, shoots out from beneath Tina's bed. She is moaning. At first, I think it's from the pain. But this struggle is something else. It's as if she's fighting with something or someone. Her face continues to transform. That face she carefully preserved with creams, eye tucks and who knows what else, is no longer human. My stomach turns to a lead weight.

Tina's fighting a war for her legacy, spirit, and soul, for how she will be remembered, and for how she will leave this earthly dimension. I realize Tina is embroiled in a spiritual negotiation between good and evil, the light versus the dark. Everything eternal is at stake. I'm transfixed, conflicted, wanting to run because I feel she wants to take me with her. I am not going but I am fascinated and terrified by what's going on. Questions fly through my head. What if evil wins? Will I know, and what will it mean? How does that feel? And who or what is protecting me from what's going on in this room right now and why?

I feel someone or something pull me back from the bed again. The suddenness and strength of it is chilling. Pouring like a waterfall over my right shoulder and engulfing me is a magnificent warm white and gold light, like what I saw surrounding Uncle George when I was three. I know I'm not alone. I hear myself whisper, "*God's mercy is great.*" Where that came from, I don't know. The words marched out of my mouth.

Tina slipped into a semi-conscious state, but she was still alive. As quickly as everything happened, it ended, even though I felt this battle went on for hours. The light was gone. The shield protecting me was gone. I exhaled and looked at the aide. She tells me, "I see a lot of strange things doing this work."

I get back to Riverdale. Terry, Murphy, and I hastily pack the car and drive back to Cambridge. I didn't tell Terry what happened.

Chapter Sixty

4:46 AM

Murphy settled in the back seat. During the drive, Terry and I devise a plan for cleaning out the house.

"Tina's got clothes with the tags still on them," Terry said.

"I know. What about her furs?" (I would find out a month or so later, she had seven fur coats.)

"She probably still got 'em in storage. Now, I told you about what she wants," Terry said cautiously.

"Are you about to say something that's going to make me drive off the road?"

He laughs. "You know how Tina is, now!" Terry became quiet. Romeo, Terry's father, and Tina are first cousins, and although the last few years had been awful for Terry given Tina's accusations, she was also a mother figure to him. His mother, Ethel, died from a heart attack while he was in New York. I went down home, for the funeral. Funny how funerals can end up being reunions for some families.

"Well," he continued, "she's got definite plans for her funeral now. I'm tellin' you!"

"What kind of plans?"

"Well, she's got a separate account for her funeral. The last time I saw it, she had $20,000 set aside for it."

"What? That's a lot of money for a funeral," I exclaimed.

"Oh yeah! But she wants a fleet of white limousines, a sit-down dinner with a live band, and she has a special white pantsuit that she wants to be buried in."

"Are you serious?"

"Oh yeah! A fleet of white limousines! And she's got that place for her to be buried."

"What place?" I vaguely remember her telling me this. The more Terry talked the more I remembered. I ignored him and then I heard him say something about limousines.

"She sho' wants them limousines though. White!"

"Let me tell ya' something. There will be no fleet of white limousines. And no sit-down dinner with a live band!"

"She gave Harry a big send off, had a band, sit-down dinner," Terry said with amusement.

"Oh please…"

"Oh yeah! I was there. I saw it. Big send off. All his friends came."

"Well, this is going to be a little different."

By 7:00 PM we were back in Cambridge. We were tired, including Murphy, but glad to be back. There's nothing like sleeping in your own bed. Terry was flying home the next day. He told me, he would take some vacation time after the holidays and come back to help clean out the house. We talked about this cautiously because deep down, we both knew that Tina could rise again and make it into the 21st century. The lights went out early on Bond Street that night.

The phone rang at 5:00 AM. Automatically, I pick it up and say, "Hello?" as if I'd been up for hours!

"Is this Janis Pryor?"

"Yes, it is. Who's calling, please?"

The doctor gives his name and simply says, "I'm sorry to inform you of this, but your mother passed away this morning at 4:46 AM." He then tells me her doctor would be available to answer any questions later that morning.

I thank him and go back to sleep with unusual ease. There was no point in waking Terry. What could you do at 5:00 AM? She was dead, but I knew it wasn't over. I knew her influence would linger and show itself in hundreds of ways, until I died. I sensed her presence was really gone. No visitations, nothing, just gone.

But Pam got up in the middle of the night and started praying for Tina.

A Few Words About The Funeral

I wish I could paint this for you instead of using words. It would be easier... for me. The holidays made scheduling problematic. I waited. No funerals on or near New Year's Eve nor New Year's Day. I couldn't do that to people.

What stands out after all these years? Being shown a room full of caskets. Being told she needed a special sealed casket because she'd be placed in a mausoleum and not a grave. Buying a "bed" of white roses for a ridiculous amount of money. Murphy and I being driven to the funeral home in a limousine. Watching Ruth not be able to finish her eulogy. Watching J.W. not being able to finish his eulogy. He'd finish a sentence and exhale or blow. It was troubling. Watching some woman whose name I've forgotten give a eulogy about a version of Tina I never knew. Tina the mentor, the friend, the supporter. The minister from that church Tina never attended insert himself in the program to announce that Tina was "saved" ...

I made sure I had no speaking role. What was I going to say? What a kind, loving mother she was? I let the absence of the Assistant hang in the air the way my absence hung in the air at Harry's funeral. The Assistant expected me to send her a ticket so she could fly in from one of the Carolina's for the funeral. I sent her nothing. She asked for some gold earrings she gave Tina. I never found them because I never looked for them! My objective was to plan a program that wouldn't be full of lies and still dignified.

I stared at the blank computer screen dreading the task of writing Tina's biography after planning the order of service. I still wasn't sure where Tina was born! I closed my eyes, took a deep breath, and said to myself, "*Just write, Janis. Just write. Something will come out.*" And it did.

"*Leontine Lawrence Pryor was born in Gulfport, Mississippi on August 7, 1920. She was the youngest of two children and the only daughter of Josephine and William Lawrence. To her friends she was known as Tina, and to her elders, her aunts, and uncles, she was known as 'Teene'.*

Tina attended grade school in Gulfport and went on to graduate from Spelman College in Atlanta, Georgia. After teaching briefly in New Orleans, she was admitted as a graduate student to Columbia University, where she studied early childhood education. She concluded her studies at Columbia with a Masters' Degree. In 1952, she was appointed Executive Director of Parkchester Bronxdale Day Care Center.

She devoted over forty years of her life to this field. In honor of her commitment, the Leontine L. Pryor Day Care Center was built during the seventies to serve young children, including those with disabilities. Mainstreaming disabled children in a day care facility at that time was considered a groundbreaking advancement. During her pioneering tenure in this field, she won many awards for leadership, community service, and dedication to advancing the quality of early childhood development for all children, but especially those in low income and minority communities.

In 1993, she was diagnosed with ovarian cancer and given six months to live. Instead of dying, she defied the odds and fought the disease for almost six years. On December 28, 1999, she yielded to the disease.

Leontine Lawrence Pryor, daughter of the late Josephine and William Lawrence, sister of George (deceased), "grandmother" of Prince (a buff cocker spaniel now deceased), and wife of the late Harry Pryor is survived by her only child, Janis Augusta Pryor of Cambridge,

Massachusetts, several cousins, a host of friends and colleagues and her 'grandchild', Murphy, a parti-colored cocker spaniel."

I remembered that well known quote from Dylan Thomas, "Do not go gentle into that good night/old age should burn and rave at close of day/Rage, rage against the dying of the light." She did that. I placed it on the cover of the program underneath her name, date of birth, and date of death.

But I was left with the empty back page. I looked through my cluttered desk, and there was a copy of one of my favorite books, *Anam Cara*, by John O'Donohue. I flipped through it, seeing passages I had high-lighted or underlined. I found "*A Blessing for Death*." That's what I put on the back cover.

I pray that you will have the blessing of being consoled and sure about your own death.
May you know in your soul that there is no need to be afraid.
When your time comes, may you be given every blessing and shelter that you need.
May there be a beautiful welcome for you in the home that you are going to.
You are not going somewhere strange.
You are going back to the home that you never left.
May you have a wonderful urgency to live your life to the full.
May you live compassionately and creatively
And transfigure everything that is negative within you and about you.
When you come to die may it be after a long life.
May you be peaceful and happy in the presence of those who really care for you.
May your going be sheltered and your welcome assured.
May your soul smile.

Mae dreamt of being visited by an Angel the early morning Tina died. Mae saw her seated at a table with Mama and Papa. Tina had a glass of water, drank it, held it up to Mae, and said, "All gone."

A Reflection

"Be kind for everyone you meet is fighting a great battle." – Philo, early Jewish philosopher, 30 B.C.E – 40 C.E.

Somewhere I read the connection that exists between mother and daughter is perhaps the most complex and primal relationship there is between two women. Even the best ones experience tension and can be strained to surprising limits. With so much pain between Tina and me, I never expected to find forgiveness. And I never thought it would look or feel like a pool of calm discovered after surviving a life-threatening battle.

My journey to forgiveness starts with understanding. I can't forgive what I don't understand. I tried to find out who and what Tina was, grasp her reality, know her story, understand why she did what she did. After all, her life didn't begin with my birth! I've accepted that this journey to understanding, for me, will be lifelong.

Forgiveness is tricky and complicated. I don't forgive easily, and I've got a long memory. But (sustained) anger can kill. It's a seductive problem for most Black people. We have a complicated relationship with it because anger, along with God, are often the only things we have from which to draw strength.

"One must be divine to forgive," they say. I am far from divine! I have inflicted pain and committed acts of vengeance and betrayal, knowingly or unknowingly like everybody else. I seek the same absolution that so many have urged me to give Tina.

I approach forgiveness with great caution and trepidation. It's slow work for me and it is *work*. Forgiving, according to Lewis B. Smedes, *"is a miracle...that few of us have the magic to perform easily. Nobody seems to be born with much talent for forgiving... We talk a good forgiving line if somebody else needs to do it, but few of us have the heart for it while dangling from one end of a bond broken by somebody else's cruelty. Yet people do forgive..."* I was guilty of simplistic thinking regarding forgiveness. A hug, a kiss, a warm and fuzzy moment and shazam! Everything's okay! I abandoned that notion. I let go of needing to wrench some form of restitution from Tina.

The impact and consequences of Tina's crimes of parenting have become my obligation to transform into a meaningful life with as few sacrifices as possible. All we, the children, need is to understand the dividing line between accountability and responsibility, theirs, and ours.

My life will always be framed by ongoing efforts to recover from having Tina in my life. As Anne Lamott said of her mother in *Plan B, Further Thoughts on Faith*, *"...she was like someone who had broken my leg, and my leg had healed badly, and I would limp forever."* That limp represents our sacrifice of emotional security, joy, hope, our ability to function comfortably, not to mention our overall mental health. Too often children are collateral damage of deeply dysfunctional homes. Our sacrifices are unimaginable and too often, indescribable.

Every day I get through is testament to the raw gracefulness of surviving. Making it through a day, a week, a season, finishing a year, being able to give and receive love, to stand my ground with dignity, to accept my mistakes and face my flaws, constitute the miracle of surviving the toxic wells of harmful parents who never should have had a child.

But it's important for me to remember the pain and never succumb to forgetfulness or numbness least I find myself repeating a pattern. For me, strength is continuing to function in the absence of hope and the presence of despair. Living and struggling not to hurt myself is how I measure success daily. Can I get out of bed this morning? Will I be able to open the mail? How often will I laugh while haunted by the early lesson of, "never cry." Can I carry the weight of being a caul bearer and manage the perceptive abilities that leave almost everyone I encounter, emotionally naked to me, an open book before our meeting is over? Staying sane under these conditions is hard work. I sacrificed young womanhood. I sacrificed having children, fearing I would do to them what Tina did to me. By the time I understood what went wrong it was too late. I live a very careful life that often looks eccentric to most people. I try to breathe and live a useful life that's described in Marge Piercy's poem, *To Be Of Use*.

> "I love people who harness themselves, an ox to a heavy cart,
> who pull like water buffalo, with massive patience,
> who strain in the mud and the muck to move things forward,
> who do what has to be done, again and again."

Living a conscious, useful life is my form of recovery, my communion, and salvation. With all of this, and what I went through, if I'm honest, I have to say my life has been very privileged, very painful, and very blessed. I try awfully hard to remember that every day.

This Is The End of My Report

...treat your children well...

Everybody likes a happy ending. **Daughter Survives Mother's Lunacy**. What a story! No. *That's not my story.* Writing *Mother's Madness...* was not a cathartic exercise. I didn't write this to feel better. For me, this story is a cautionary tale. For me, who lived this, the story is about parenting, responsibility, compassion, betrayal, and the *price of survival*. It doesn't come cheaply.

Don't underestimate your power and influence as a parent. There's nothing harder than raising someone to become a healthy, compassionate, adult, free from crippling, paralyzing dysfunction. If you can't do that, your child's survival is jeopardized because their *instinct* to survive is damaged. Not every child heals.

Is the price of survival ever too high? My truth says, yes. Some parents aren't interested in *helping their children thrive*. What it took for me to thrive threatened Tina, so she had to kill it or die trying. Thriving is joyful and full of light. Surviving is dark and exhausting. Surviving isn't a passive activity. It's like living in a field with land mines. You never relax.

There's not enough therapy in the world to help me carry that dysfunctional load of her narcissism, jealousy, fear, and manipulation without confronting the damage. And then what? You keep going until you can't.

This book could've gone on for another hundred plus pages, given what a friend found out about the lineage of my maternal great grandparents, Tina's paternal grandparents. What they owned, how they were classified by others, and some unusual circumstances made me wonder how all this impacted Tina. The only clues I had were the lies she told.

Tina's been dead a little over twenty years as I write this in 2023. The ripple effects of having her in my life still touch me in concrete and abstract ways. Pockets of money she left in various accounts spread throughout New York City kept popping up for eight years after she died. She made bad investment decisions and then she made worse decisions. Remember, no one could tell her anything because she knew it all. That "knowledge" sent hundreds of thousands of dollars out the window of the estate straight to the government. Signing all those checks to settle her estate is something I don't need to ever experience again. It made me dizzy and enraged. She undermined my ability to believe in good and believe in myself. But I've had two years of bliss since then, and I treasure that time. My gratitude for that is inexpressible. It's a miracle it happened at all.

Not every child survives a violent household of radical dysfunction. There are many ways to be damaged by another person's madness. We don't even have the language to describe it yet. And if you're the target, you can die in a thousand ways and keep going, no one the wiser.

"But you got through it," people say.

Did I? My body is still here. I've found a way to keep going…sort of. Children who survive an attempted soul murder, who witness and/or become a target for domestic violence, who are taught or choose isolation, who trust no one completely *for their own protection* – all of this and more creates that "limp" Anne Lamott was referring to earlier. It's what Kelly McDaniel calls *Mother Hunger* in her book of the same name. It's an injury, she says, that hurts all the time, an unacknowledged, invisible burden we carry all by ourselves. *

Remember each one of us must research normalcy on an ongoing basis to see if we can convincingly imitate it and get through the day. Otherwise, that mask we wear falls off, our truth is revealed, and we're pushed to the edge led by our companion(s).

After Tina's funeral, I saw my psychopharmacologist. I remember saying to him, "You know, it's odd. I don't miss her at all." I thought maybe I would. I didn't know.

He looked at me and said, "What's to miss?"

Forgive and Forget, Healing the Hurts We Don't Deserve, by Lewis Smedes

Mother Hunger, How Adult Daughters Can Understand and Heal from Lost Nurturance, Protection, and Guidance, by Kelly McDaniel, LPC, NCC, CSAT

To Be of Use
By MARGE PIERCY

The people I love the best
jump into work head first
without dallying in the shallows
and swim off with sure strokes almost out of sight.
They seem to become natives of that element,
the black sleek heads of seals
bouncing like half-submerged balls.

I love people who harness themselves, an ox to a heavy cart,
who pull like water buffalo, with massive patience,
who strain in the mud and the muck to move things forward,
who do what has to be done, again and again.

I want to be with people who submerge
in the task, who go into the fields to harvest
and work in a row and pass the bags along,
who are not parlor generals and field deserters
but move in a common rhythm
when the food must come in or the fire be put out.

The work of the world is common as mud.
Botched, it smears the hands, crumbles to dust.
But the thing worth doing well done
has a shape that satisfies, clean and evident.
Greek amphoras for wine or oil,
Hopi vases that held corn, are put in museums
but you know they were made to be used.
The pitcher cries for water to carry
 and a person for work that is real.

Marge Piercy, "To Be of Use" from *Circles on the Water*. Copyright © 1982 by Marge Piercy. Used by permission of Alfred A. Knopf, an imprint of the Knopf Doubleday Publishing Group, a division of Random House LLC. All rights reserved.

Mother's Madness

Teach Your Children
Song by Crosby, Nash, and Young

You, who are on the road
Must have a code
That you can live by
And so become yourself
Because the past is just a goodbye

Teach your children well
Their father's hell
Did slowly go by
And feed them on your dreams
The one they pick's the one you'll know by

Don't you ever ask them, "Why?"
If they told you, you would cry
So, just look at them and sigh
And know they love you

And you, of tender years (can you hear and do you care)
Can't know the fears (and can't you see)
That your elders grew by (we must be free)
And, so, please help them with your youth (to teach your children what you believe in)

They seek the truth (make a world that we can live in)
Before they can die
Teach your parents well
Their children's hell
Will slowly go by

And feed them on your dreams
The one they pick's the one you'll know by
Don't you ever ask them, "Why?"
If they told you, you would cry
So, just look at them and sigh
And know they love you

Acknowledgments

Writing a book is a very solitary pursuit. It can make you a little crazy. And if you're writing about a "crazy person" you're fanning the flames of your own sanity wondering if you should "sprinkle" some gasoline around and see what happens!

Writers need community and support to keep them grounded. I want to acknowledge those people because without them, I think the drafts of this book would still be in a box.

First, the late Mary (Mae) Frances Oakley, who stood by me, stood up for me, held me up when no one else would, whose wisdom, comfort and love continue to sustain me. And to her daughter, Janice, who seems to be picking up where her mother left off.

To the late John Mack, M.D., my neighbor, and friend who became my anchor and safe harbor in the absence of my grandfather.

To the late Fee Hun Soo Hoo and Braunwyne Miller, whose friendship continues to heal so many of my wounds incurred from this life.

To the late Cathy Paradis, who served as witness and comfort to the reality of "crazy Tina."

To the late Sue Cantril, whose homemade Florentine cookies she sent from Washington, D.C., whose encouragement, reasonable conversations about politics, and back issues of POLITICO shipped from D.C. to Cambridge, MA kept me grounded and hopeful.

To the late Susan Martin, therapist, LISW, who clarified just who in my life was crazy and in what way.

To Emily Hiestand, who encouraged me to start this book.

To Dr. John Purcell, whose dry humor and stoic presence, did more for me than any prescription he ever wrote.

To Pam Barnwell, whom I'll never be able to repay for her kindness and doing what I could never do for Tina during those last months.

To the late Joanne Johnson, who helped sustain me during our fifty-plus years of friendship, through our language of laughter, and somewhat twisted view of the world! She was there when no one else was.

To all those "down home" and *from* down home, who represent part of my true north, thank you.

To Lyn May, a unique friend of forty some years, who read and re-read parts of this book, and survived! Thank you.

To Wendy MacPhedran, sister from another mother and another time, who read this manuscript and researched some of the ancestry of my grandfather's family, a heart-felt thank you.

To Lisa Boyd, a second sister from another mother, who generously gave her time reading and re-reading *Mother's Madness*... and giving her honest, precise feedback! Thank you.

To David Rosenbaum, a fellow New Yorker, who said decades ago while reading an earlier version, "I believe in you, Jan." A heart felt thank you.

To Lydia Spitzer, another friend I'll never be able to repay for her kindness, compassion, generosity, and detailed reading of this manuscript, but most of all for her friendship. Lydia, you are a treasure. I'm not sure this book would've been *finished* without you. Thank you.

And last, but not least, Judith Moose, my agent who has managed to embrace the wide range of my work and extraordinary experiences of my life. Thank you.

About the Author

There are people who have known me for decades and will be shocked when they read this because the last place where most of me was known was Bennington College. They knew I was an artist, a writer, an activist, a thinker. I was allowed to simply be all of who I am. When I graduated from Bennington roughly thirty years of compartmentalization started.

So there are those who only know me as the award winning media professional, the editorial broadcast journalist, the radio talk show host, the documentary producer, the veteran political operative, the strategist, the communicator, the "Special Assistant" to local, state and national politicians. They know I've had some impressive bosses over the years, the late Senator Edward Brooke and the late Senator Edward Kennedy, U.S. Secretary of State John Kerry during his maiden run for the Senate. I've worked with and for Jesse Jackson, Anna Deveare Smith, and Boston's Ten Point Coalition to name a few. George Miles, a former boss at Boston's NBC affiliate said, "The idea of Janis having a boss is absurd!"

Then there are people who only know me as a writer, beginning with my first published piece in Essence Magazine shortly after I graduated from college. I've written freelance pieces for several publications in metropolitan Boston, written numerous speeches, briefing papers, and co-authored a column in the Cambridge Chronicle for two years. I spent twenty-three days writing the two hundred and fifty page first draft of White Roses... and a year re-writing it. How I came to write White Roses... is a separate, stunning story that deserves to be told at another time. Three years were spent writing a memoir about my mother. It's been sitting in a manuscript box for over a decade waiting for me to rewrite it. I must do it before I die.

The poetry of Anne Sexton, Audre Lorde, Adrienne Rich, Marge Piercy, Nikki Giovanni, and the wisdom of Caroline Myss, Matthew Fox, Black Elk, Oriah Mountain Dreamer, James Baldwin, John O'Donohue and Vine Deloria have sustained me through many versions of hell on earth.

In New York City, a small group knows I performed in an off-Broadway repertory company for young people before I graduated from high-school. They know about my penchant for acting and comedy, and that I've always loved the theatre, movies and ballet. I've been told I don't suffer fools easily if at all. Over the years, I've had many nicknames, Red, The Little General, and Little Bits are a few. Sometimes they just call me, Pryor. My role models? Katherine Hepburn, Jackie Kennedy, Tina Turner, Jane Goodall, Georgia O'keefe, Anna Wintour, Ella J. Baker, Twyla Tharp, Hannah Arendt, Caroline Myss, Fannie Lou Hamer and Miss Piggy. There are men who impress and inspire me for a variety of reasons: Liam Nesson, Bishop Desmond Tutu, Albert Camus, Vaclav Havel, my friend the late Dr. John Mack, Anthony Goldwyn, Matthew Fox, and the Kennedy brothers, John, Bobby and Ted. All of these people have taught me a great deal about the complexity of life and survival, and the courage it takes to simply live in these difficult times.

Very few know of my lifelong interest and curiosity about God, or the Divine, or the Source. Naming It doesn't concern me so much as knowing It and It knowing me. Still fewer know that I have an interesting array of "gifts" that have served me very well over the years. I was born a Caulbearer. One person's death forced me to embrace and acknowledge these gifts and seek the peace of remote places.

There are scores of people who know me as the woman with cocker spaniels, who loves beautifully made clothes, expensive shoes, Lillet Blonde, peonies, hydrangeas, tulips. Two people know the significance of white roses in my life.

For me, justice transcends fairness, and the frailty of loyalty can be easily shattered by a thoughtless remark or the tone of one's voice. I buy books before paying bills. All forms of incoming mail are viewed suspiciously and with contempt, unless it's a magazine or a book. I hate getting dressed up, and I've been told that I think really differently than most people.

Three very different parts of the United States, the Gulf Coast of Mississippi, New York City (Manhattan specifically) and New England have shaped me along with some very progressive schools.

People ask me where is home and I tell them, "I haven't gotten there yet." I am a contradiction for whom linear thinking is simply one option.

Other Books by Janis A. Pryor:

White Roses
Dinner with Trixie
Victoria's Family

www.ingramcontent.com/pod-product-compliance
Lightning Source LLC
Chambersburg PA
CBHW070124080526
44586CB00015B/1547